*Europe and Islam*

## THE MAKING OF EUROPE

*Series Editor: Jacques Le Goff*

The *Making of Europe* series is the result of a unique collaboration between five European publishers – Beck in Germany, Blackwell in Great Britain and the United States, Critica in Spain, Laterza in Italy and le Seuil in France. Each book will be published in all five languages. The scope of the series is broad, encompassing the history of ideas as well as of societies, nations and states to produce informative, readable and provocative treatments of central themes in the history of the European peoples and their cultures.

# Europe and Islam

Franco Cardini

Translated by Caroline Beamish

BLACKWELL
*Publishers*

Copyright © Franco Cardini 1999

English translation copyright © Caroline Beamish 2001

First published in Italian as *Europa e Islam* by Ginus. Laterza & Figli in 1999. First published in English by Blackwell Publishers Ltd 2001, and by four other publishers: © 2000 Beck, Munich (German); © 2000 Critica, Barcelona (Spanish); © 2000 Editions du Seuil, Paris (French).

2 4 6 8 10 9 7 5 3 1

Blackwell Publishers Ltd
108 Cowley Road
Oxford OX4 1JF
UK

Blackwell Publishers Inc.
350 Main Street
Malden, Massachusetts 02148
USA

*British Library Cataloguing in Publication Data*

A CIP catalogue record for this book is available from the British Library.

*Library of Congress Cataloging-in-Publication Data*

Cardini, Franco.
 [Europa e islam. English]
 Europe and Islam / Franco Cardini; translated by Caroline Beamish.
  p. cm. – (The making of Europe)
Includes bibliographical references and index.
 ISBN 0-631-19732-X (hardcover: alk. paper) – ISBN 0-631-22637-0 (pbk.: alk. paper)
I. Islamic Empire–Relations–Europe. 2. Europe–Relations–Islamic Empire. 3. Islamic Empire–History, Military. 4. Islamic Empire–History–750–1258. 5. Crusades. 6. Civilization, Islamic. 7. Civilization, Medieval. 8. Europe–History–476–1492. I. Title. II. Series.
 DS38.3 .C3713 2001
 909'.09767101–dc21
                                                    00-011576

Typeset in 10.5 on 12pt Sabon
by Kolam Information Services Private Ltd, Pondicherry, India
Printed in Great Britain by MPG Books Ltd, Bodmin, Cornwall

This book is printed on acid-free paper

# Contents

# Series Editor's Preface

Europe is in the making. This is both a great challenge and one that can be met only by taking the past into account – a Europe without history would be orphaned and unhappy. Yesterday conditions today; today's actions will be felt tomorrow. The memory of the past should not paralyse the present: when based on understanding it can help us to forge new friendships, and guide us towards progress.

Europe is bordered by the Atlantic, Asia and Africa, its history and geography inextricably entwined, and its past comprehensible only within the context of the world at large. The territory retains the name given it by the ancient Greeks, and the roots of its heritage may be traced far into prehistory. It is on this foundation – rich and creative, united yet diverse – that Europe's future will be built.

*The Making of Europe* is the joint initiative of five publishers of different languages and nationalities: Beck in Munich; Blackwell in Oxford; Critica in Barcelona; Laterza in Rome; and le Seuil in Paris. Its aim is to describe the evolution of Europe, presenting the triumphs but not concealing the difficulties. In their efforts to achieve accord and unity the nations of Europe have faced discord, division and conflict. It is no purpose of this series to conceal these problems: those committed to the European enterprise will not succeed if their view of the future is unencumbered by an understanding of the past.

The title of the series is thus an active one: the time is yet to come when a synthetic history of Europe will be possible. The books we shall publish will be the work of leading historians, by no means all European. They will address crucial aspects of European history in every field – political, economic, social, religious and cultural. They will draw on that long historiographical tradition which stretches back to Herodotus, as well as on those conceptions and ideas which have transformed historical enquiry in the recent decades of the twentieth and twenty-first centuries. They will write readably for a wide public.

Our aim is to consider the key questions confronting those involved in Europe's making, and at the same time to satisfy the curiosity of the world at large: in short, who are the Europeans? where have they come from? whither are they bound?

Jacques Le Goff

# Preface

The purpose of this book is to trace the development of the contact between Europe and Islam and to examine how and why it occurred. We shall look at the historical process of its development from a variety of points of view, and at the ideas, prejudices, disinformation and anti-information that have formed and coloured Europe's attitude towards Islam. Deliberately omitted from the book (although the reader will come across many references to it: it would have been inconceivable to ignore such a point of view) is the reciprocal perspective. An examination of this can be found in works such as Bernard Lewis, *The Muslim Discovery of Europe* (New York, 1982).

The Islam under consideration within these pages is primarily the Islam of the Mediterranean. Given the realities of the historical process under scrutiny here, this focus is legitimate and, to an extent, obligatory. This is the version of Islam with which Europeans came into contact over a long period. The fact that Islam is in no way homogeneous should be borne in mind: there are many varieties of Islam – as there are many varieties of Christianity – and although all respect the profound unity that links the *umma* of all believers, all have developed along different lines and produced different characteristics over the years. The traditions and historical/philological culture of Southern Europe have been affected solely, or almost solely, by the Islam of Turkey, the Middle East and North Africa, whose versions of the religion are closely related to one another. Anyone identifying with this tradition and culture should look carefully at other European environments in which history and politics have developed in different ways: in the German-speaking world, for example, and also in Poland and Russia (and to some extent in the Baltic and Central Europe), from the eighteenth to nineteenth centuries onwards, attention was focused mainly on the Middle East and

Central Asia, whereas in England, Portugal and Holland awareness developed towards India and the Far East, parts of the world that did not generally fall within the intellectual range of the countries of Southern Europe. I am referring to an intermediate state of consciousness, conditioned by education and the media. With regard to this point, I should stress that I have consistently adhered to the distinction between Near East, Middle East and Far East, avoiding the Italian habit of referring to the area between the Eastern Mediterranean, the Euphrates and the Arabian Peninsula as the 'Middle East'. This of course raises the question of whether such expressions are not 'Eurocentric'; in fact, the terms 'Western Asia', 'Central Asia' and 'Eastern Asia' are equally Eurocentric, for the simple reason that the notion of a continent stems from the cultural traditions of the West. Attempts at political correctness are more misleading on this subject than on any other; this is inevitable when a language is used to highlight ethnocentricity, since the terms are deeply rooted in the lexical and structural fabric of the language itself. On this subject, see the opinions (which I share) of G. Vercellin, 'Fine della storia, storia orientale e orientalistica', in *Studi storici*, 32, 1 (1991), pp. 97–110.

# 1

# A Prophet and Three Continents

## Europe and Asia, Christianity and Islam: Comparisons and Ambiguities

Any comparison, from whatever point of view, between Europe and Islam soon encounters a sense of conflict: this may be because the relationship between Europe and Islam continues to be thought of (or at least implicitly perceived) as a kind of continuation or renewal of the (historical) clashes between Christianity and Islam. It should, nevertheless, by this stage be difficult to think of the juxtaposition in terms of the *Christenheit oder Islam* proposed by Novalis; this is merely a rhetorical device. The process of secularization which is endemic in the Western world today makes it impossible to consider Europe any longer as synonymous with Christendom: Europe is only *one* Christendom. Nevertheless, so long as the Western world (which is itself no longer synonymous with Europe) anxiously follows the spread of the Islamic movements incorrectly termed 'fundamentalist' (Islam, with all its different faces, cannot be blanketed under the single term 'fundamentalist'), there exists in Europe a widespread tendency to view Islam as a potential adversary. Although this tendency could be regarded as of recent origin, many Europeans experience it as a revival, the replay of a *déjà vu*, the return of an ancient conflict which, some might say, is linked to certain historical and political facts and is therefore ineradicable.

It is worth considering, therefore, whether the confrontation between Europe and Islam (if it is definable or comprehensible as a confrontation) is not frequently viewed as being roughly synonymous with the

West and Islam (or modernity and Islam: this would introduce a further complication deriving from our tendency to consider modernity and the West as inextricably linked). Or, on the other hand, should it be seen as the logical continuation of the ancient and classical conflict between Europe and Asia as perceived by Aeschylus in his *Persae* and reiterated in full by Hippocrates in his *De aeribus*? Hippocrates perceives the conflict in climatic/environmental terms: their mild climate and government by monarchy make the Asians unwarlike, their harsher climate and political freedom make the Europeans much more active and bellicose. In Aristotle's *Politics* the conflict is viewed as the result of a 'natural' difference of temperament. Indeed, however unacceptable the identification of Christendom with Europe may be, the reduction of Asia to Islam or vice versa is even more so: the whole of Asia is not Muslim, as we know, and furthermore the *dar al-Islam*, the 'land of faith', extends well beyond the borders of the continent of Asia.

Added to this there is the evident asymmetry between the terms 'Europe' and 'Islam': one refers to a continent, the other to a religion. But, and here we come to the first conceptual key to help us out of our dilemma, Bernard Lewis observes on this subject:

> The asymmetry is more apparent than real. 'Europe' is a European concept, as is the whole geographical system of continents, amongst which Europe was the first to emerge. Europe conceived and created Europe: Europe discovered America, gave it its name and in some respects created it. Centuries earlier, Europe had invented both Asia and Africa whose inhabitants, until the nineteenth century – the period of European world supremacy – were totally ignorant of the names, the identity and most of all the system of classification invented by the Europeans for their own consumption and use.
>
> Islam is not a location; it is a religion. But for the Muslims the word 'religion' does not have the same connotations as it has for Christians, or as it had for Christians in the Middle Ages [...]. For Muslims, Islam is not simply a system of faith and worship [...]. Religion concerns the whole complex fabric of life, and its tenets comprehend elements of civil and penal law, and even elements of what we would think of as constitutional law.[1]

Like the conflict between the West and the East, the conflict between Europe and Asia has a geographical, historical and political status far older than that of the tension between Europe and Islam. Some people claim, nevertheless, that at certain periods – for example at the time of

---

[1]   B. Lewis, *L'Europe e l'Islam* (Rome-Bari, 1995), pp. 5–6 *passim*. (Originally published as *Islam and the West*, New York and Oxford, 1993.)

the crusades, or during Ottoman Turkish rule over the Eastern Mediterranean and the Balkans – the conflict between Europe and Asia and the East/West conflict took on the aspect of what is frequently, if inaccurately (at a symbolical level), referred to as the 'duel between the crescent and the cross'. If we delve beyond the descriptions given by the ancient geographers, however, and ask ourselves how and when the modern notion of Europe and the European identity was born, we realize the extent to which Islam was a factor (albeit a negative one) in its creation. Repeated Muslim aggression against Europe between the seventh to eighth and the tenth centuries, then between the fourteenth and the eighteenth centuries, whether it was successful or was simply viewed as successful by the Europeans, was a 'violent midwife' to Europe. And although a few historians have (paradoxically?) hailed the Prophet as the 'founding father' of Europe, a similar role could later be attributed to the Turkish Sultan Mohammed II and Suleiman the Magnificent who, by forcing the continent to defend itself and to find ways and means of concerted action, encouraged it towards a stronger sense of self – and a strong sense of 'the Other'.

## The Muslims beyond the *Maghreb al-Aqsa*

Medieval authors were unanimous (although wrong) in their opinion that Europe was the main seat of Christianity, if not its only one. They also believed that anyone living in Europe who was not a Christian was either an outsider or an invader. It was the anonymous cleric of Toledo who, in the mid-eighth century, in his *Continuatio Hispanica*, the continuation of the *Historiae* begun by Isidore of Seville, hailed the victorious Austrasians as *Europenses* after the battle of Poitiers fought in 732 (or, according to some, 733). Did he himself feel *Europensis* because he felt like a Christian, or because the Iberian Peninsula was attached to Europe by Roman geographers? Or was he no longer able to present himself as such since the Berber Arabs, by invading the Iberian Peninsula, had forced it into the *dar al-Islam*? If so, this would suggest the existence of mobile borders and a firm division between Europe and the *dar al-Islam*; it would also rule out the possibility of talking about 'Muslim Europe' when referring to parts of the continent of Europe conquered by Islam and colonized by the Muslims, or to the new faith of recent converts.

The debate about whether Poitiers halted the Muslim invasion of Europe is by now both outdated and otiose. Perhaps it was simply a symptom of the battle fatigue of invaders who lacked the energy to proceed any further. By this stage the importance of that armed conflict looks very limited, and in any case it is incorrect to describe the expansion of Islam in the seventh to tenth centuries as an invasion. The Arabs could never have produced enough soldiers from their own ranks to overrun in a few decades a territory which extended from the Pillars of Hercules in the south to the Indus and the Syr Darya in the north, and from the Caucasus in the east to Nubia in the west. After the campaigns waged by the caliphs who immediately succeeded the Prophet, that is, from the 630s onwards, the expansion of Islam never resembled an inexorable military conquest, much less a *Völkerwanderung*. It was in fact a continuous, not always consistent process of conversion, imposed although seldom provoked, of groups belonging to exhausted or crisis-ridden societies – for example the Monophysite Christians of Syria and Egypt, harshly treated by the *basileus* of Byzantium, or the subjects of the Sassanian emperor; these people were eager to shake off aged, ossified forms of authority and to find a new identity with a new catalysing agent, in this case submission to the Word of God, as propagated by His *rasúl*, Mohammed. Many nevertheless preferred to remain loyal to their own faith, accepting payment of the capitation tax (*jizya*) and of the surtax imposed on the land of non-Muslims (*kharadj*), and to be considered as *dhimmi* – 'protected' as well as 'subject'. They thereby demonstrated, incidentally, their opinion of government by the infidel as being preferable to government by their co-religionists.

The myth of Poitiers, nevertheless, propagated by a colourful page in Edward Gibbon, has certainly contributed to the view of the history of Europe as a history of the conflict with Islam: it has been claimed that, without Poitiers and the heroism of Charles Martel, the name of Allah would be called by the muezzin over the dreaming spires of Oxford, the Koran would be studied in that famous university and the history of the world would have been quite different.

Further scrutiny of the importance and the role of the battle is superfluous. Although prudence needs to be exercised in minimizing or 'demythologizing' the significance of the event, it is no longer thought by anyone to have been crucial. The 'myth' of that particular military engagement survives today as a media cliché, than which nothing is harder to eradicate. It is well known how the propaganda put about by the Franks and the papacy glorified the victory that took place on the road between Tours and Poitiers, a few kilometres north-east of the confluence of the rivers Vienne and Creuse, for the purpose of confirming France as the 'firstborn of the Church of Rome'. The intention may at the same time have been to eclipse the fame of *basileus* Leo III the Isaurian who, in 718, forced the Muslims to abandon the siege of Constantinople which they had begun the year before, and who appears successfully to have thwarted their control of the high seas by retaining possession of the Black Sea, the Aegean and the Central Mediterranean, and to have discouraged them for many years from making further attempts at penetrating the Anatolian Peninsula. The Latin Church's flock was certainly not in a position to pay homage to the iconoclast Leo III. Fault would later be found with his membership of the civilization of Byzantium, viewed for years by Western prejudice as vile, decadent and degenerate. In fact, what the myth of Poitiers has helped to conceal from the modern world is the inadequacy and inaccuracy of contemporary sources dealing with Islam. It is also known that the period corresponding to the great explosion of the Muslim conquest coincided with a long period of economic depression in the Western world: silence and lack of information are due primarily to deliberate disinformation and ignorance. It is possible also that, in the climate of the day, it was difficult and possibly fruitless to distinguish Muslims from other invaders or other hostile raiders: there would have been no point in attributing to them any particular importance or significance. The fall of the Roman Empire in the West, in the second half of the fifth century, has been described as a 'noiseless fall'. The advance of Islam into eight-century Europe was probably just as noiseless. Or, more probably, the noise was confused with other noises. Muslim sources say more about Poitiers than their Christian counterparts: the episode is known as 'Balàt al-Shuadà', the 'Way of the Martyrs', and scant importance is attributed to it.

What took place in depressed and underdeveloped Europe should come as no surprise, given that the much better-informed Byzantine sources only realized that the Muslims were not *barbaroi* relatively late. They also took some time to recognize the importance of the new faith, Islam.

In the early Middle Ages Europe received an unexpected gift from Byzantium: the magic word Sarracens, later corrected to Saracens and interpreted, using a clumsy form of *lectio facilior*, as 'sons of Sarah'. The term was incorrect in that it had originally served to denote a people whose origins were claimed to be in *Arabia felix*, linking them with the progeny of the union of Abraham and the Egyptian slave Hagar (rather than with his legitimate wife Sarah) according to the Book of Genesis. By long-standing tradition, the peoples of the desert are descendants of the Patriarch and the Slave – and thus bastard brothers of the people of Israel through their son Ishmael (hence the name Ishmaelites); a more appropriate name for them, and one which is generally recognized, would be Hagarenes. The derivation of the word Saracens from Sarah is probably a piece of *a posteriori* pseudo-etymology, based on the first half of the word and the misinterpretation of a form from Arabic or

Syriac. The word has been compared with various Arabic words: its derivation from *sharq*, 'orient', is unlikely, particularly as the first wave of Muslims to enfeoff Syria came from the south (unless the term is Egyptian in origin). Another compelling theory is that the word is linked with the desert wind *Sharuq* (not to be confused with *Sharquiyya*, the sirocco). Others have borne in mind the aspect of the marauding desert hordes and their tendency to congregate in tribes when carrying out raids: this has led to consideration of the concept of *shark*, 'a gathering of people', or *sharika*, 'society', 'company'. It has also been suggested that the Saracens were so named by their non-nomadic opponents (and occasional victims), and that the name related to the concept of *sarq* ('plunder', 'theft') and the verb *saraq* ('to steal'), from which are derived the analogous concepts of *sâriq*, 'thief', and *sarrâq*, 'plunderer', 'pick-pocket'.

Those defined in the texts as Ishmaelites, Hagarenes or Sarracens soon begin to occupy the limelight in our sources. Unfortunately we know little about the accusation levelled against Pope Martin I (649–53) that he had sought contact with the Saracens to oppose *basileus* Constant II and his Monotheletism. The early Islamic attempts at conquest of the Mediterranean were the cause of great anxiety to the Byzantines at this time. We know that, at the end of the seventh century and the beginning of the eighth, this collection of peoples, heirs to the traditions of the *Pars occidentis* of the Roman Empire, which had arisen at the end of the fourth century from the Theodosian Settlement and had absorbed 'barbarian' input and the monarchies that stemmed therefrom – basically, the 'Western Europeans' as we now call them – did not possess the wherewithal, either at this period or within the next few decades, to withstand Saracen aggression along their coasts and on the seas along their coastlines.

By this time the Islamic conquest of the Mediterranean had begun. After the invasion of Syria and Palestine by the Arabs between 633 and 640, and of Egypt between 639 and 646, Syrian and Egyptian mariners embraced the new faith or submitted, presumably willingly (they were mainly Monophysite Christians who were persecuted and discriminated against by the administration of the Byzantine Empire), to the service of the followers of the Prophet. In 649 a leader destined for the caliphate, Muhawyya ibn Abu Sufyan, governor of Syria, cousin of Caliph Othman and future founder of the Umayyad dynasty of the caliphate, attacked Cyprus; in 652 some modest incursions were made into Sicily, which still belonged to the area dominated by Byzantium; three years later a big naval battle off the coast of Licia signalled a crisis in Romano-oriental thalassocracy. The same Constant II, heading a fleet of five hundred ships, was defeated.

The peoples of poverty-stricken Western Europe would have known nothing and understood even less of these events. They were still predominantly Mediterranean, their eastern borders extending only as far as the Rhine and their northern borders to the Upper Danube. But, in order to explain the silence and absence of information provided by Western sources in a little more detail, we should attribute these deficiencies to an overriding lack of interest in matters Islamic rather than to ignorance. In fact, the Frankish chronicler known as Fredegarius, writing in about 658, made reference to astrological predictions circulating in the empire at the time of *basileus* Heraclius which described the defeat and conquest of the Byzantine forces by a circumcised horde; it contained evidence of knowledge about various aspects of the first spread of Islam in Asia Minor. Still in the world of the Franks, in the early eighth century a monk named Peter, who may have been Syrian, translated from Greek into Latin a text whose Syrian original came from northern Mesopotamia: the text was the *Revelationes* of the so-called Pseudo-Methodius, used several times subsequently in eschatological propaganda of a political nature. According to this text, Ishmaelites from the desert of 'Ethribum' (or Jathrib, the Prophet's chosen city of Medina) conquered the Orient, invaded Sicily and reached as far as Rome; their exploits threw the woods, mountains and cities into confusion. This attack by the Ishmaelites was supposed to herald the immediate arrival of the Antichrist: but a Christian emperor is alleged finally to have subjugated the vanguard of the Enemy. In short, some facts were known, but they were recorded in absent-minded fashion.

The Muslim occupation of the Iberian Peninsula and Septimania (Languedoc) during the 720s must have brought about changes. In Visigoth Spain, still troubled by the lingering remains of the Arian heresy and squabbles amongst its own aristocracy, anxiety had long been felt over reports of an Arab advance along the coasts of North Africa. During the Council of Toledo in 694, King Egica sounded the alarm. A rumour was spreading that the Hebrews, infuriated by repressive measures taken against them, were getting ready to assist the new barbarian hordes advancing from the East. Meanwhile, a civil war was raging amongst pretenders to the Visigoth throne of Toledo: one of the pretenders, rather than surrender, sought the help of the *Mauri*, the Arab conquerors and the Arabized Berbers who had converted to Islam and who lived alongside them. These were the people known then, as now, as the Moors, the ferocious yet fascinating enemies-cum-companions of the Spanish Christians. It has been suggested, in fact, that in Spain and Septimania, as had occurred in the majority of the former Byzantine territories conquered by the Muslims, the new arrivals were well received by at least a proportion of the population, and their rule preferred – because it was less oppressive – to the rule of the despotic Christian princes.

The former Roman province of Africa, called Ifriqiya by the Arabs (comprising modern Tripolitania, Tunisia and Algeria), was invaded by the Muslims in 647; it was not until about fifteen years later, however, that Byzantine and particularly Berber resistance began to give way. The Arabs identified three ethno-social groupings in the territory they were in the process of conquering: the *rum*, a term referring principally to the Byzantines, subjects of the Roman Empire (from the Greek *Romàioi*), but used on the African coast north of Sirte to designate people of Latin origin or who spoke Latin; the *afriki*, autochthonous peoples who had by now converted to Christianity; and finally, the *berbers*, from the Latin *barbarus*, who had remained outside the civilization brought by Rome and who had only (recently) sporadically been converted to Christianity. The Berbers eventually accepted Islam, but were never assimilated by the Arabs. Although Berbers and Africans were unused to life at sea, the supply of Syrian and Egyptian sailors soon persuaded the Muslims to look towards the Mediterranean. By 665 they were already using the naval base of Jaloula, which they had seized from the Byzantines. In 670 the city of Qayrawan (Kairouan) was founded, its name being derived from the Arabic term for a military encampment. In the year 700 a viable port was organized in Tunisia and about one hundred Egyptian families, all specialists in boat-building, were brought in. About five years later the whole of North Africa, as far as the area known to the Arabs as 'the Far West' (*al-Maghreb al-Aqsa*), Morocco, was in the hands of the conquerors, and the laborious process of Islamicizing and Arabizing the Berbers was under way. Probably at the end of July 711 a large Muslim fleet commanded by the Berber Tariq ibn Ziyád landed in the Bay of Algeciras, which had been raided only the previous year. The Arab–Berber forces numbered about ten thousand men. Having vanquished the troops of the Visigoth King Rodrigo, the invaders aimed for Seville without delay, then occupied Córdoba and in 713 seized Toledo. Aragon was conquered the following year. By 720 the Muslims had occupied Catalonia and Septimania, in other words, all the Visigoth territories to the south and north of the Pyrenees. So rapid was the conquest of the land called by Arabs al-Andalus (they had learned to call it thus in Africa, where it was still 'the land of the Vandals') that, in order to explain it, the complicity of the Hebrews, the Heretics and the Visigoth factions that were opposed to Rodrigo was used as an alibi.

Having occupied Narbonne in 718, the Arabs marched on Toulouse in 721 and captured Nîmes and Carcassonne in 725. By this time their theatre of operations was the whole of Provence and the Rhône basin. Autun was burnt down in 725 (or, according to some, 731).

From Spain and Septimania it was but a short step to the south of Gaul, dominated by the Franks since the beginning of the sixth century, but where institutions were fragile and social structures unstable. The Bishop of Rome, Gregory II, who closely followed events involving the Frankish people, the 'firstborn' of his church, encouraged Odo, Duke of Aquitaine, to resist the Muslim invasion of Toulouse in 721. As eulogia he sent some fabrics which had been used as altar cloths at St Peter's in Rome. These were torn to fragments and swallowed by the Christian soldiers as part of the sacrament.

The Saracen conquest of the Iberian Peninsula was not total, however: in rocky, inaccessible parts of the Pyrenees and the Cantabrian mountains there were pockets of Christian resistance. In the Asturias, in 720, Pelagius the Goth set up a principality which twenty years later had become a kingdom, with its capital in a new city, Oviedo, founded in 760. The Basque-Navarrese people – who had managed to withstand the Visigoths – remained independent; in similar fashion, in the 830s and 840s, the Galicians, Cantabrians and Asturians, with the support of a handful of refugee Visigoth warriors, set up the small principality of Navarre, and this seems to have become a kingdom about a hundred years later. Shortly afterwards, the movement known as the *Reconquista* seems to have begun in the Asturias, Navarre and northern Aragon.

The battle of Poitiers was less important, therefore, than the myth to which it gave birth. To give some idea of the context in which the battle took place, other episodes, possibly more influential than Poitiers, should be considered. Among these were the Berber leader Murnuz or Musura, who installed himself as leader of an area of the Eastern Pyrenees, in Cerdagne, and married one of the daughters of Duke Odo of Aquitaine before being expelled for leading a revolt against the Emir of Córdoba in 729; or Moronte, Duke of Provence, who opened the gates of Avignon to the Muslims in 734.

Poitiers did not stop the progress of the infidel: in 734 Avignon was occupied, Arles was looted and the whole of Provence was overrun. In 737 the raiders reached Burgundy, where they captured a large quantity of slaves to take back to Spain. Charles Martel responded with continuous campaigns against the Muslims in the south of Gaul between 736 and 739; but betrayal and duplicity were the order of the day, and none of these actions was really successful. The Berber Arabs, with their raids, were part of a complex political struggle to which religious motives were ascribed only tens of years later, when collective memory, fuelled by epic poetry, had worked its transformation.

Events such as these help to explain the note of alarm that was beginning to creep into Western writing, from the Latin translation of the Pseudo-Methodius produced in the Benedictine monastery of Saint-Germain to the notes written in 735 by the Venerable Bede in the revised version of his *Historia ecclesiastica gentis Anglorum* just before his death. He refers anxiously to the progress of the Saracens and mentions the armed encounter in Poitiers. Anglo-Saxon sources provide a discreet key to exactly how much knowledge about Islam there was, although it was lacking in continuity. For example, from the two synods held in Britain in 786 we know that, probably through information gleaned from papal legates or from the Benedictine monks scattered over the island, the tradition of Ramadan was familiar to those taking part.

Islam, as we know, has enjoyed only the briefest periods of effective unity over the centuries. This runs contrary to what was believed in the Middle Ages, when the tendency was to think of Islam as even more of a unified whole than was Christianity (although propaganda insisted that this was how Christianity ought to be). For us, enabled by distance to adopt a global perspective, the view taken by the Europeans in the Middle Ages appears almost justified – even if only because of a coincidence: by the first half of the eighth century, Islam had expanded from the *Maghreb al-Aqsa* to the borders of China and from Anatolia to the Horn of Africa. In 717 the Arabs found themselves under the walls of Constantinople again, as they had been nearly forty years earlier. Their leader this time was Maslamah, brother of the Umayyad caliph; *basileus* Leo III drove them off with difficulty, assisted by the power of 'Greek fire'. Meanwhile, in the first fifteen years of the eighth century, the governor of Mesopotamia al-Haggiag subdued the Khwarazm, crossed the Oxus (now the Amu Darya), occupied Bukhara and Samarkand and got as far as Baluchistan: the powerful Persian Empire, which had held the Romans and Byzantines at bay, melted away like snow in sunshine. By dividing the Altaic areas, the battle of the Talas in 751 marked out the borders between Muslim expansion and the expansion of Tang-dynasty China.

Nevertheless by the middle of the century the expansionist rush seems to have slowed down everywhere. The Byzantines, thanks to the tireless efforts of Leo III, seem to have gained the upper hand over the Muslims in Asia Minor; the thrust to the east stopped at the border of the Chinese Empire; the Berber Arabs, conquerors of the Iberian Peninsula (with their numbers swollen by many local Christian converts), lost their impetus. In 732 or 733, on the road between Poitiers and Tours, all that the Muslim commander Abd ar-Rahman wanted (and it was no small thing) was to plunder Saint-Martin, the national sanctuary of the Franks. It was probably never his intention to proceed any further, and he did not have the military might to do so. In any case, as we have seen, he was stopped in his tracks. A few years later, in 759, the Franks under the leadership of Pepin the Short – son of the victor of Poitiers – expelled the infidels from Narbonne and pursued them as far as the Pyrenees. The echoes of these wars between the Franks and the Muslims at this period, as well as the celebrated battle of Roncesvalles and the events immediately following it, provided material for a spate of epic poems and *chansons de geste*, although these were not written down (nor did they acquire fame) until about three centuries later. However, after Poitiers, the Austrasian Franks were attracted towards Aquitaine: this may have been the culmination of a lengthy process whereby the territory of Aquitaine achieved the status of a 'cushion' between the Franks and the Muslims.

It is difficult to estimate just how much the bloody and violent change in the caliphate in 750, from the Umayyads to the Abbasids, influenced the crisis and the succeeding lull in this first wave of Islamic expansion. The party that remained loyal to the deposed caliphs in Damascus fared better in the Iberian Peninsula, in spite of harsh confrontation with supporters of the new dynasty. Nor did the emirate of Córdoba, which was perfectly legitimate, have an easy time. In addition, the subdivision of Islam, the rise of the new caliphates, the appearance of the Shiite and the Ismaili sects and fierce repression by the Abbasid dynasty were all crucial factors in the disintegration of Muslim unity and the crisis that led to a temporary halt in Muslim expansion.

### Charlemagne, between al-Andalus and Baghdad

In 777 the king of the Franks, Charles, son of Pepin, was in Paderborn, in Saxony, taking part in a military campaign. He received a visitor: Suleiman ben al-Arabi, the Muslim *wali* of Barcelona, Gerona and Saragossa, who had traversed the whole of France in order to request the assistance of his powerful Christian neighbour in opposing the tyranny of the Emir of Córdoba. We do not know by what route the *wali* reached Paderborn, nor what hardships he encountered on the way. He promised the king the allegiance of many centres south of the Pyrenees, beginning with his own flourishing cities. Muslim Spain, Suleiman assured Charles, was irremediably divided, and little effort would be required to conquer it. Despite the later political and epic gloss lent to all these events, which seems to have invested them with a thick overlay of religious significance, there was apparently no prejudice between the two contracting parties that could be ascribed to their differences of faith, or to the fact that the Muslim enemies of the Emir of Córdoba would be fighting their co-religionists in the company of Christian militia.

At Easter 778 the Frankish expeditionary force, with the blessing of Pope Adrian I, set off for Spain. Everything seems to have gone according to plan and the Muslim adversaries of the Emir of Córdoba proved true to their word: the *wali* defeated the emir's troops with the assistance of various supporters. But when the Franks decided to make Saragossa their headquarters in readiness for a further campaign along the Ebro, the city seems to have rebelled against them and their leader: it may be that the Franks, anxious about the repeated successes of the infidels and unsure about whether their own people would continue to support their prolonged campaign against the emir, made a sudden change of plan. The circumstances of this turnaround are far from clear: we know that when the rebellion against the emir started again, Charles had to lead his troops home – having first ordered the walls of Saragossa to be almost completely razed to the ground by way of revenge. During the retreat, on 15 August (according to tradition) the Frankish rearguard was attacked and massacred by wild Basque mountain-dwellers in the valley of Roncesvalles. In the epic poem that made this minor skirmish famous, and transformed it into a major episode in Christian literature, the Basques are changed into Moors.

For the time being, Emir Abd ar-Rahman I made no retaliation against the invader from beyond the Pyrenees. In 793, however, his son Hisham (788–96) waged a bitter offensive against Frankish Septimania, whose governor at the time was the king's cousin, Duke William. The Muslim raiders again attacked Narbonne, but did not manage to conquer the city; from there they moved on to Carcassonne. In spite of their early losses the expedition, led by al-Hakam, the emir's son, was a success. With the booty from their raids it appears that they were able to finance part of the construction of the great mosque in Córdoba. It was a fine investment. Meanwhile, from the coasts of al-Andalus and the Maghreb the first Saracen naval expeditionary forces took off for the Balearic Islands, whose inhabitants turned for assistance to the emperor of the Franks.

Following these events, Charlemagne began the campaign that led eventually to the formation of the Spanish March. Duke William was the leader of this new undertaking, which culminated in 801 in the conquest of Barcelona by the Christians; the Christian conquerors did not, however, manage to reach the Ebro, nor to install themselves firmly in the town at the mouth of the Ebro, Tortosa. Thus between Barcelona and Tortosa a kind of 'no man's land' was established which was not to be shifted until the twelfth century, when the Aragonese advanced southwards again. Meanwhile, the new Christian emperor – whose diplomatic contacts with the *wali* of Barcelona and the Empress of Byzantium, *basilissa* Irene, must have taught him much more about the scale and complexity of the world than he could have leaned from learned discussions with Alcuin of York or Paolino of Aquilea – was looking around for new interlocutors who could help him, directly or indirectly, to regulate his relations with Spain. He was lucky to find some excellent support.

In fact there had been many before him. Although the Carolingian monarchy – heirs to the Merovingians and allies of the papacy, and thereby linked to the outlook and cultural aspirations of both – had a fairly restricted view of the forces at work in the Eastern Mediterranean in the eighth century, where a quite different set of allegiances was in play. For example, both Constantinople and Baghdad were well used to keeping an eye on events and selecting, from the chessboard of forces at work, either possible allies or potential 'friends of enemies' who were, in fact, adversaries. The court of the caliphs had recently been established in the new capital of Mesopotamia, a few miles from the ancient capital Ctesiphon; the city was founded in 762 and at first was given the name of *Medinat as-Salam*, 'City of Peace'. Here the seeds of that lack of interest in civilizations other than Islamic that was so much a feature of the culture born of Mohammed's religious revolution may already have taken root; with distant hindsight, it could be identified as a possible component of today's crisis. In addition, a close watch was kept on Byzantium, India and China, whilst much less attention (quite justified at this period) was paid to the barbarous inhabitants of the extreme north-west who appeared hardly worthy of consideration at the time. Nevertheless, it must quite soon have become evident that problems could be encountered from the Umayyads in Córdoba, who were continuing to refuse to recognize the new authority embodied in the caliph, or the empire of *Rum*, known to us as Byzantium.

Between 765 and 768 there had already been an exchange of ambassadors between the Abbasid Caliph Jafar al-Mansur (754–5) and Pepin. Pepin's son had two sound reasons for resuming contact with the new caliph, the great Harun ar-Rashid (768–809), the sovereign in the *Thousand and one Nights*. In the Iberian Peninsula the conflict continued between the Emirs of Córdoba, still nostalgic for the old Umayyad dynasty (or using this as a pretext for adopting a political stance that maintained their religious prestige), and the *walis*, who preferred to set their sights on the 'Prince of the Believers' residing in distant Mesopotamia (or who considered their loyalty as a useful pretext for their refusal to submit to the rule of the Umayyad dynasty that had been imported into al-Andalus). In 799 the Saracen governor of Huesca sent costly gifts to Charlemagne in Aix-la-Chapelle, with the promise that the city would be his if he undertook a new campaign south of the Pyrenees. The second reason concerned the city of Jerusalem, ruled by the Abbasid caliphs but visited by a growing number of pilgrims from the West: the Frankish ruler was keen to join the debate between the clerics, the sanctuaries of the Holy City, and Christendom – a debate he did not intend to leave to the exclusive participation of the *basileus*. He had been host to a mission from the Patriarch of Jerusalem and had returned the compliment, having received blessings and relics from the envoys. The *Annales regni Francorum* mentions the 'handing over of the keys' of the Basilica of the Resurrection and the chapels of the Calvary and the Holy Sepulchre; the diplomatic expressions of courtesy may in fact be slightly exaggerated.

Charlemagne, meanwhile, in 797 – only four years after the al-Hakam incursion, and while he was organizing the Spanish March – also sent a diplomatic mission to the caliph. The mission consisted of two lay members, Lantfrid and Sigismund, and Isaac the Hebrew, plus (according to a document from the monastery of Reichenau, the *Miracula sancti Genesii*) two ecclesiastical members sent by Gebhard, Count of Treviso, to procure relics of Saints Genesius and Eugenius from the Holy Land.

In June 801 the emperor, who was resident in Pavia at the time and who had dismissed the messengers of the Patriarch of Jerusalem only two months earlier, received the news that the ambassadors of the caliph were at anchor in Pisa. This was the response to his mission of four years earlier. On board were a representative of the caliph and an envoy from the Emir of al-Abbasiya (now Fostat in Tunisia), who announced that the one survivor of the three ambassadors sent to the court of Baghdad in 797, Isaac the Hebrew, had returned to Europe with gifts from the Prince of the Believers. Isaac had had to disembark on the coast of Africa because one of the gifts was proving too cumbersome for him to continue his journey.

A Frankish naval battalion was sent forthwith to relieve Isaac. The battalion returned to Portovenere the following October bringing with it, among other things, the gift so anxiously awaited by the emperor: the elephant Abul Abbas. There was no question, however, of subjecting the huge animal to an Alpine crossing in winter, Charlemagne having by this time returned to his home in Aix-la-Chapelle. He was obliged to wait until July 802 before coming face to face with this animal, mentioned so frequently in Roman history but not seen in the West for hundreds of years. Sadly, Abul Abbas did not survive the Rhineland climate for very long: it was too different from the hot climate of his native India (whence domestic elephants were imported into Persia). He died in June 810, to the intense sorrow of the Frankish ruler who had grown very attached to him. His body was watched with curiosity by all as they waited to witness his bones turning into ivory – as legend said would happen.

It is probable that, apart from the elephant, Harun offered Charlemagne certain privileges (albeit only honorary ones) connected with the Holy Sepulchre in Jerusalem, an obvious manoeuvre aimed at reducing the *auctoritas* of the *basileus* over the Christian Holy Places. Although Arab sources make no mention of it, the real subject of their meeting may have been the Spanish question. Less likely is that they discussed economic matters: the *pallia fresonica*, a high-quality woollen fabric, sent by Charlemagne as a gift to Harun, would hardly have impressed the court of Baghdad with its splendour. The many Muslim commodities and coins mentioned in 812 by the chronicler Theodulf of Orleans as being in circulation in southern Gaul, where the busy port of Marseille was situated, do not testify to any particularly close ties with the Orient: apart from the pearls, the Muslim items to be found there were all from Spain or North Africa. However, in 807, Charles received a further diplomatic mission from the caliph, as well as (in the same year) a legation from the patriarch of Jerusalem.

Made anxious by the diplomatic relations being forged between Aix-la-Chapelle and Baghdad, and by the continual internal rebellions in his own country – these had even reached Córdoba and Toledo – the Umayyad Emir al-Hakam (796–822) resigned himself to the fact that the border with the Franks extended as far as the Ebro. There followed a series of treaties between him and Charles, in the years 810–12. But the insurrections in Muslim Spain continued unabated: the rebellion in Córdoba in 814 was quelled only by violent repression by the emir's troops, the soldier-slaves known as Mamelukes (from the Arabic *mamluk*, 'property', 'slave'). Things were no better under the next emir, Abd ar-Rahman II (822–52), who had to cope with rebellions in Mérida and Toledo and who tried in vain to win back Barcelona – a clumsy move which had the effect (thanks partly to the timely response of Duke Bernard of Septimania) of strengthening the nascent Catalan identity.

New clouds were gathering meanwhile on the Mediterranean horizon, and over Southern Europe. The Norman invasions that laid waste to the coast of Europe in the ninth century and early years of the tenth are regarded (along with maritime attacks by the Saracens and land attacks by the Hungarians) as determining factors in the deepening crisis affecting Europe at the time. The period is also characterized by the destruction of power in the areas involved in the Carolingian experience, by internecine struggles between the kingdoms of the so-called Heptarchy in England and by economic depression. One should bear in mind as well the fact that, while Europe was in a state of recession, Islam was also going through a difficult phase. The vast structure that was the caliphate of Baghdad was progressively losing control over the rich territories on its outer borders, to the west of Saina and to the north-east of Persia. The Aghlabites became independent in Tunisia in the early ninth century and in 827 began a campaign against Sicily which, seventy-five years later, gave them possession of the island. The Tulunids gained control of Egypt in 869. An immense area between Transoxiana, the Khwarazm and Seistan – bordered by the Syr Darya, the Aral Sea and the Indian Ocean – was successively controlled by the Tahirids, the Safawids and the Samaruds, whilst at the end of the ninth century a revolt of the Quarmatian 'heretics' in Bahrein, on the Arabian coast of the Persian Gulf, put an end to commerce from and to Basra and thereby disrupted the capital's economy; the flow of commodities being transported from the Far East to Egypt, the Mediterranean and Byzantium shifted towards the Horn of Africa and the Red Sea.

Meanwhile the Normans, after repeated savage incursions into Europe via the coast, were directing their energies towards al-Andalus. In 844 a fleet of about fifty powerful ships, having attacked Nantes and then sailed round the Atlantic coast to Lisbon, which they attempted to ransack, arrived at the mouth of the Guadalquivir; from there a group of ships set out for Cádiz whilst the majority of the fleet sailed on to Seville, conquered the city and subjected it to wholesale looting and plunder. Pressure from the Muslim population, who were capable of reacting with sufficient strength, forced the Normans to withdraw and to take to their ships again in a great hurry. The large number of prisoners taken on this occasion appears to have increased the already impressive number of blond-haired, blue-eyed Spanish Muslims, heirs to the Vandals and the Visigoths. Over the years many slaves were taken from the Slavonic world as well (the word 'slave' is itself evidence of their provenance).

The Norman onslaught of 844–5 persuaded the Umayyad emir of the need to build the *ribats*, a chain of small fortresses not unlike the old 'Saracen towers' which were scattered all over the coast of Europe as far as the Aegean. The *ribats* were manned by volunteers, the *murabitún*, who established themselves therein as part of the *jihad*, leading a life of prayer and contemplation. Thanks to them, the Normans were thenceforward forced to keep their distance from al-Andalus. However, in 859, they succeeded in burning down the mosque in Algeciras and, more than a century later, in 966, the Danes under the leadership of no less a personage than Harald Blatand ('Bluetooth') inflicted a resounding defeat on the Spanish Muslims near Lisbon.

The Muslims were not, therefore, the sole perpetrators of the continual raids carried out along the coasts of Southern Europe and the

Mediterranean islands during the final two centuries of the early medi-eval period – some of the toughest, most troubled times in the history of Europe: as has been described, they were occasionally also the victims of raids. Nevertheless, the Western Europeans considered the Hagarenes to be largely and most directly to blame. As time passed, memories of the Mediterranean raids and the wars in the Iberian Peninsula seem to have become exaggerated out of proportion, partly through repetition and partly thanks to the epic tradition: rightly or wrongly, this is viewed as constituting the challenge to which the crusades were expected to pro-vide a response.

# 2

# Between Two Millennia

## The Struggle for Possession of the Sea, the Islands and the Coastline

Henri Pirenne's celebrated contention that the collapse of European unity was due to the rapid rise of Islam is still the subject of debate. According to Pirenne, Western Europe retreated into itself and became ruralized as a result of the Muslim threat, and this heralded the beginning of the Middle Ages; the medieval period, therefore, dates from the second half of the seventh century and not from the fall of the Roman Empire in the West. It seems clear, in fact, that economic recession was already well established before the seventh century, and that trade and standards of living were in sharp decline between the sixth and the seventh centuries and the ninth and the tenth centuries, particularly in the Western Mediterranean. The process of decline was a gradual one and there were many contributory causes: it is not acceptable, therefore, to attribute the decline solely to the pressure exercised by the Saracen navy. Pirenne's main thesis has been accepted, but the supporting detail rejected. The consequences of Muslim piracy were important factors in the crisis, indeed sometimes decisive, producing social and economic as well as psychological and cultural distress: there was a drastic decline in navigation in general, a reduction in the number of Christian ports and coastal towns, widespread impoverishment, a contraction in the monetary economy and, finally, general fear and anxiety.

The raids on islands and on the Christian coastline of the Western Mediterranean originated from the coasts of Spain and North Africa. The incursions affected the Greek islands, Sicily and Sardinia from the eighth century onwards, and resulted in the ruin of numerous coastal settlements, whose people fled to the more inaccessible central areas of the islands. Usually the raiders' objective was a rapid foray, the kidnapping of young people for the slave trade and the occasional imposition of taxes or ransom. Occasionally they would establish a 'nest' of corsairs, who would form a small commercial and military colony.

We know that the Balearic Islands were invaded in 798, although permanent conquest by a Muslim leader from Spain did not take place until 902. The arrival of the occupying forces of the Aghlabite Emir Ziyahad Allah I in Sicily in 827 marked the beginning of almost two centuries of Saracen rule in the whole vast maritime area that lay between the Iberian Peninsula, the peninsula of Italy and the Maghreb. The Byzantines withstood the Muslim advance into Sicily with great courage, particularly in the eastern part of the island, and the invasion was not in fact completed until the early tenth century. The capture of Crete in 827 and of Malta in 870 stripped Byzantium of the bases that allowed it to participate so effectively in action in the Western Mediterranean: Sicily and Sardinia were henceforward abandoned to their fate.

The incursions made by the Muslims and their attempts at establishing themselves have been too often interpreted as the outcome of expansionist ambitions fired by deliberate choices. This was not always the case. On the contrary, the Saracens frequently became involved in local disputes by taking sides with one or other of the contenders at the outset: it was not unusual for their assistance to be requested by those whose side they were on. For example, the Saracens who were in the process of conquering Sicily and who had recently captured Palermo were on several occasions invited by the rulers of the city of Naples to help them in their struggle against the Longobardi and the Byzantines. They were exceptionally skilled at exploiting the confusion and weakness of the different powers that were at variance all over Southern Italy, and had no scruples about serving first one side, then the other, lording it the while over those they served.

The cities of Campania realized far too late that using the services of the Berber Arab troops was a mistake. They joined forces with the Longobard princes in once again requesting the assistance of Lothair (840–55), the Holy Roman Emperor: the emperor would probably not have reacted if the Saracens occupying the peninsula had not felt secure enough to press on as far as Ostia in 846, sailing up the Tiber and devoting their energies to sacking the basilica of St Peter in Rome.

This was going too far. Louis, son of the Emperor Lothair, descended into the peninsula with an army composed of Frankish, Burgundian and Provençal soldiers. Pope Sergius II (844–7), the Doge of Venice and the Dukes of Spoleto and Naples joined him. Meanwhile, however, the Prince of Benevento had enlisted the services of Muslim mercenaries, who were by this time completely out of control. They carried out a

series of indiscriminate raids, looting and plundering everything that
stood in their way, until they arrived finally at the lands surrounding
the monastery of Montecassino.

In spite of this, Adelchi of Benevento did not refrain from using these
ill-disciplined mercenary armies. He forced the inhabitants of Bari, who
had remained loyal to him, to accept the protection of the Berber leader
Khalfun, thought to have come from Sicily via Taranto. By way of
payment, the Berber Arabs were permitted to loot and burn religious
buildings; in fact, their leader went so far as to raze the city of Capua
practically to the ground – it was later rebuilt. By 848, Khalfun was
finally in control of the handsome capital of Apulia. Prince Louis, who
arrived in Southern Italy at about this time, was only able to liberate
Benevento from the mercenaries, in whose possession it was, and procure peace amongst the warring Longobard princes by acting as a
guarantor for the subdivision of the territory of Benevento into two
principalities, Benevento and Salerno, and the country of Capua.

It was not an honourable solution, neither satisfying nor comforting
Pope Leo IV (847–55), who was now occupied in surrounding the area
of St Peter's with walls, transforming it into a citadel in order to prevent
a repetition of the desecration of 846. It was under his patronage that a
fleet assembled by the people of Campania vanquished the Saracens off
the coast of Ostia. Louis advanced on Bari again; he had been crowned
emperor in the interim (as co-regent) and was encouraged in this undertaking by the supplications of the abbots of Montecassino and of San
Vincenzo al Volturno. The support provided by the Longobard princes
was so dilatory and so hypocritical that he retreated in indignation
without matters having reached a satisfactory conclusion. Bari continued to be governed by an emir who imposed a heavy tax on the
income of the abbeys of Montecassino and San Vincenzo and who
handled the local powers with great skill and dexterity. He issued safe-
conduct passes with apparent benevolence (but for a fee) to European
pilgrims passing through Bari to board boats bound for the Holy Land,
and treated the prosperous and scholarly Jewish community in Oria with
great cordiality.

In fact, Emperor Louis II had not got over what had taken place in
Apulia. Once he became sole ruler, he attempted conquest again, urged
on by the abbot of Montecassino and the Longobard lords of Benevento
and Capua – but not the lord of Salerno, who was currently in disagreement with the others. Plans for the new attack were written into the
*Constitutio* of 865 and still survive. There was to be a gathering of
troops in Lucera the following March. Another year was to pass, however, before the emperor could overcome the general indifference of his
Longobard and Campanian subjects, and thwart their double-dealing

and treachery. The campaign that began in 867 concluded, after a complex series of events, four years later, in 871. Louis benefited from the assistance of Frankish troops sent by his brother Lothair II (although unfortunately, many of the soldiers were affected by an outbreak of plague), and the support of a Byzantine fleet and a fleet from Venice, the latter including Croatian and Dalmatian reinforcements. With the allegiance of Adelchi, Prince of Benevento, and the people of Gaeta (although not the people of Naples, who offered the hospitality of their harbour to the Saracen ships), he was finally able to get the better of the most recent Emir of Bari, Sadwan, who fought him off like a lion – managing during a sortie to loot the sanctuary of the Archangel Michael on Monte Gargano. In spite of this, Sadwan was permitted to withdraw to comfortable captivity in Benevento with his quasi-friend, Prince Adelchi.

Was the emperor's generous treatment of the emir a mistake? He had reconquered Bari and had certainly acquired great glory in the process. But the Byzantine Empire, meanwhile, had also emerged from a long period of economic depression and was regathering its strength thanks to the energetic and unscrupulous efforts of Basil I (867–86), founder of the Macedonian dynasty. Basil's fleet had been of great assistance in gaining victory for Louis, 'King of the Germans' (whose imperial status, in Basil's opinion, was no match for his own), but the Byzantine emperor had no intention of allowing Louis to impose his authority on Southern Italy which, ever since Justinian had reconquered the peninsula, the *basileus* of Constantinople considered to be his personal fiefdom. Greek culture was deeply rooted in the area and the Byzantines were able to control access to the Adriatic through their domination of the big ports. The machinations of Basil I and Sadwan had the desired effect: a revolt amongst the Longobardi of Benevento resulted in the emperor's imprisonment for nearly two months, between August and September 871, whilst the Emir of Kairouan sent a new expeditionary force to Apulia, this time numbering about 20,000 men. Calabria and Campania were subjected to ferocious attack. Louis II managed to gather the strength to return to Southern Italy, where he conquered the Muslims in Capua in 873. He died two years later.

Meanwhile, the Saracens continued to operate from their one remaining stronghold, Taranto, the centre of the slave trade. From there they could threaten the territory of Apulia and Campania as far as Volturno. The inhabitants of Bari no longer had any reason to maintain their links with the Holy Roman Empire; in 876 they returned to the authority of the Byzantines in Otranto and were successful in making their city the capital of the *theme* of Longobardia. The Byzantines managed to win back Taranto in 880, but they were not powerful enough to stop the

Muslims making continual incursions along the Adriatic coast, as far north as Comacchio and Grado.

The Berber Arabs were a long way from defeat. As they completed their occupation of Sicily with the conquest of Syracuse in 878 and Taormina in 902, they were also making inroads into Campania and forming alliances with Capua and Salerno. They again reached the lands controlled by the Bishop of Rome and forced him to pay them tribute money; they destroyed the abbeys of San Vincenzo al Volturno and Montecassino. In 882 they established a base at the mouth of the Garigliano from which they could keep the city of Rome within their sights. This nightmare for the Romans was removed only in 915.

Once the Kalbite emirs were securely established in Sicily under the formal authority of the Fatimid caliphs of Cairo, they were able to concentrate in the tenth century on systematically attacking the coast of Southern Italy, particularly the coasts of Apulia and Calabria. Scattered bridgeheads, such as Agropoli in Campania and Santa Severina in Calabria, resisted for years. The attempt made by the Saxon Emperor Otto II, who embarked on a vigorous new campaign similar to the one launched by his predecessor Louis II a century earlier, was thwarted in 982 near Capo Colonna. Thenceforward the Saracen offensive in Southern Italy continued more or less unchecked until the death in 1036 of Emir al-Akhal, whose reign was followed by the irreversible destruction of Islam in Sicily. The ports of Sardinia and Corsica were all under the control of the Saracens until the early eleventh century and the islands remained a no-man's land.

The coastal bases of North Africa, vital footholds of the Muslim thalassocracy in the Eastern Mediterranean, were meanwhile being reinforced. The fortress-city of al-Mahdiyah was established between 915 and 920 on the coast of the Sahel, at about the same latitude as the island of Pantelleria. In 960 the Berber leader Buluggin ibn Ziri founded Algiers. Later, in 1060, the city of Bujjiah was established on the coast between Algiers and Bône (Annaba).

The Saracens' privateering war continued to rage in the Northwestern Mediterranean too, with the aggressors using the Spanish ports and island as their base. In about 890, at approximately the same time as the Saracens were establishing their base on the Garigliano, Muslim forces arrived on the coast of Provence. A group of them succeeded in setting up a stronghold in Fraxinetum (now La Garde-Freinet), not far from Saint-Tropez, from where they harassed the coastline and adjacent countryside as far as Marseille, Toulon and Nice, and also organized expeditions to places further afield. They even got as far as the Western Alps, where they attacked parties of pilgrims and merchants as they crossed the mountains. In 906 they destroyed the monastery of La Novalaise.

The area between the Gulf of Lions and the Tyrrhenian Sea was also scoured by corsairs from Ifriqiya, for example the raiders from al-Mahdiyah who, between 934 and 935, attacked Genoa. The corsairs of Fraxinetum, who had managed to enter into agreements with various local rulers, including Hugh of Provence, finally went too far: in 972–3 they captured a Cluniac monk – perhaps unwittingly, perhaps by mistake – with the intention of kidnapping him and demanding a ransom for his return. The monk was none other than St Mayeul, the great Abbot of Cluny: such effrontery persuaded the aristocracy of Provence to take steps towards eliminating, once and for all, the colony in Fraxinetum.

Were the people who created and gave life to these Saracen coastal townships, and who often also gained control over extensive tracts of the adjoining territory, merely corsairs or pirates? The economic and commercial activity of the townships was not very different from that of the cities on the Italian coast: in fact, the resemblances between the two were very strong, although the initiative belonged to the Muslims, who were undoubtedly the first to arrive. The rebirth (or simply birth) of the coastal cities of Christian Western Europe appears, therefore, to have been partly the outcome of Islamic expansion. Not surprisingly, relations at sea between the Christian and Islamic powers, whatever their relative size and importance, were characterized by surprise attacks and naval skirmishes, but these did not seem in any way to jeopardize the fairly good commercial relations that existed between the two communities. Somewhere around the beginning of the eleventh century, however, the initiative changed sides: during the earlier period the Saracens were consistently more active and dynamic, always the first to attack. Later, however, their position became a defensive one, whilst Christian strength and power showed a steady increase.

One of the principle factors in the development of these small 'republics' of Muslim sailors, pirates and merchants (*bahriyun*) was the capture and sale of slaves. Almeria is typical in this respect: the town's growth during the tenth century was mainly due to a flourishing slave trade. The *saqaliba* or white slaves were a particularly desirable commodity: the Jews in nearby Pechina specialized in castrating them.

The situation developed along different lines in the Eastern Mediterranean. Thanks to a sustained counter-offensive by the *basileus* of the Macedonian dynasty, during the second half of the tenth century, the islands of Cyprus and Crete again came under Byzantine control. Even commerce, after the most critical phase of Muslim maritime expansion between the second half of the seventh century and the beginning of the eighth, began gradually to pick up. The Western Europeans were neither its strongest protagonists nor its best clients, however. About half-way through the ninth century, in his *Book of Routes and Kingdoms*, Ibn Khurdhadhbah speaks of merchants coming from Western Europe who were certainly resident there, but who could not strictly be defined as Western Europeans: the Jews known as Radanites (established perhaps at the mouth of the Rhône?) brought Western merchandise, including slaves, weapons and furs, to the East. They would unload the goods at the ports of the Nile Delta, whence they would proceed by land on camelback to the Red Sea, and then re-embark in the Arabian ports of al-Jar and Jedda for the journey to India or China. From those distant countries they imported musk, aloes wood, camphor and cardamom, not only to Egypt but to Constantinople and also to the (relatively) unrefined courts of Western Europe. Between the ninth and tenth centuries, commerce (and consequently Arab-Muslim geographical knowledge) seems to have had almost no interest in the Tyrrhenian Sea north of Amalfi or Gaeta, nor in the world of Western Europe. The tendency to ignore anyone of a different culture, so characteristic of traditional Muslim culture, was manifest from the earliest days of Islam.

Opportunities for contact – apart from in military or commercial circumstances – were in ample supply, nevertheless. One of these opportunities might have been captivity or slavery, even if only temporary. This may have been what happened at the end of the ninth century to someone like Harun ibn Yahya – his name gives no clue as to whether he was Christian or Muslim – against his will. His travels took him to the two Romes, the New and the Old, one after the other. He was captured on the shores of Palestine, possibly during a pirate raid. It is not clear, however, whether he was captured by Byzantine pirates or whether he himself belonged to a team of Arab pirates (which could have included some Christians) who, whilst attacking a Greek ship, were themselves set upon and beaten. He was taken as a slave to Constantinople. From there, we do not know how or why (he may have been sent on a Byzantine diplomatic mission), he made his way back to the Balkan Peninsula and reached Italy via the Veneto, eventually reaching Rome. His wanderings and his experiences have come down to us through the writings of the tenth-century geographer Ibn Rusta, who recounts the narrative in the form of a legend, as did the authors of *Mirabilia* or Books of Wonders (which were passed on from Byzantium to the world of Islam). During the description of Harun ibn Yahya's wanderings we read of the bronze-coloured embankments through which the Tiber flows, and of the amazing automaton-bird on top of a column in front of St Peter's; also described are the riches and huge population of a city which in fact, between the ninth and tenth centuries, is supposed to have been sparsely populated and economically depressed.

Of the few items exported by the Frankish world to the world of Islam at this time, iron was the most in demand, particularly in the shape of 'Frankish swords', whose only comparison was the Yemeni *qauhar*, a weapon made of white steel as beautiful as a costly fabric. Another much sought-after commodity that could reach the *dar al-Islam* either from the 'land of the Franks' or from Byzantium, via the great rivers of Russia and the Black Sea, was timber. It is unsurprising to learn, therefore, that in 813 Pope Leo III informed Charlemagne that certain ambassadors from Saracen lands had chosen to make the journey to Sicily in Venetian boats (*in navigiis Beneticorum*). This information confirms the severe shortage of wood in the Islamic world and the consequent problems faced by North African navies, and is also an indication of the frequency with which the Venetians went to the Muslim countries. Like the Byzantines, the Venetians for years imposed laws against trading with Alexandria and Egypt, both Muslim conquests, and in general with any country occupied by the *nefandissima gens Sarracenorum*. Sometime during the second third of the ninth century, however, Venetian merchants stole the relics of St Mark from Alexandria in an episode designed to dignify, or possibly destroy a regulation which in any case does not seem to have been much observed. In 960 the prohibition against trading in slaves and carrying foreign passengers on Venetian ships was endorsed, but in 971 another document lets slip that the Venetians were in the regular habit of bringing timber, metal and arms to sell in the markets of Alexandria. Shortly after this time, it is true, the Venetians' economic and commercial scope was dramatically enlarged under the leadership of Doge Pietro II Orseolo (991–1008), the conqueror of Istria and Dalmatia; he was also responsible for the radical redefinition of trade relations with Constantinople (as we know from the celebrated gold seal of 992) and with the Fatimid Caliph of Cairo. There is no evidence of agreements being made with Egypt, but the friendship between Venice and Egypt dates from this period and seems to have survived for several centuries, withstanding the impact of the crusading movement, the collapse of the Fatimid caliphate in the twelfth century and the Mameluke *coup de main* in the thirteenth century.

The almost complete absence of written evidence relating to trade between the Muslim and 'Frankish' worlds in the ninth and tenth centuries (when the Gezirah of Cairo was in fact extremely wealthy) has been amply compensated for by the discoveries made by submarine archaeologists, whose finds consist mainly of the remains of ships and ceramics. These artefacts provide proof of considerable circulation of merchandise in the Northern Mediterranean at that period.

The scale of Arab commerce in the Mediterranean can also be judged by the spread of Muslim coinage, which soon matched, and in many areas virtually replaced, the predominance of the Byzantine *denarius*, the celebrated *hyperper* or gold *solidus*, and the *bezant*. Like the *denarius*, the Arab *dinar* – the Arabic coins of Sicily are well known – was made of gold and weighed 4.25 grammes. Much more widespread was the quarter *dinar*, the *ruba'i*, which spread rapidly, not only throughout Sicily but also throughout mainland Southern Italy, where it was known as *tarì* ('fresh', or newly minted money), a name that remained traditional in the monetary system of the region until quite recently. Silver coinage consisted mainly of the *dirham* (the name, having passed through Persian, derives from the word *drachma*), weighing 2.9 grammes, and the small *kharruba*, weighing 2 decigrammes. The *tarì* was so ubiquitous and so much in demand that in the tenth century imitations were produced in Amalfi and Salerno; these are easy to recognize because of the pseudo-Kufic script on them, which bears a passing resemblance to the Arabic alphabet but which is in fact meaningless. Arab coinage was also in circulation in Rus': little gold has emerged (it was probably hoarded very carefully, further evidence of the chronic lack of precious metals in the region), but there is a great deal of silver: 'the old Russian coin *nogata* corresponded to the Arab *dirham* and took its name from the Arabic *naqd*, "genuine coin"'.[1]

## Islam: Crisis and Transformation. The East

Throughout the history of the Mediterranean, from the eighth to the eleventh centuries, trading and raiding went hand in hand – to such an extent that it is not always easy to distinguish one activity from the other. What is clear, however, is that the conditions created by the irruption of Islam into the Mediterranean countries in the seventh century changed quite abruptly, although patchily and with some repeated reversals of the prevailing trend, particularly after the second half of the tenth century. With apparent (and sometimes real) symmetry, probably fortuitous although a series of striking coincidences might suggest otherwise (institutional and structural crises within the different Islamic groups also helped to bring about the changes), the Muslim offensive gradually slowed to a halt all over the Western Mediterranean and the

---

[1]	F. Kämpfer, *Russi e slavi occidentali*, in *Storia d'Europa*, Vol. 3, *Il medioevo*, edited by G. Ortalli (Turin, 1995), p. 620.

adjoining territories. For a variety of different and independent reasons, it ceased completely between the end of the tenth century and the first thirty years of the eleventh.

The authority of the Abbasid caliphate of Baghdad was undermined by the birth of two competing caliphates: the Sunni Umayyads of Córdoba in 929 and the Shiite–Ismaili Fatimids, who emerged from the Berbers of Eastern Algeria in 910 and established themselves in the new Egyptian city of Cairo, founded in 969. Cairo was destined for a great future as the trading post on the Nile to which merchandise came from Yemen, Zanzibar and Ethiopia (in addition to the valuable spices from India and China); goods would be transported by sea to Aydhab on the Red Sea and then, after a short journey across the desert on the back of a camel, they would be shipped up the Nile to the delta ports. Gold also poured into Egypt from the mines of Nubia (nearly exhausted by this time), and also from Sudan: it was brought by emissaries of the King of Ghana, who also brought white gold (ivory) and black gold (African slaves). The birth of the new power base in Egypt, independent from the Abbasid caliphate by this time and in competition (if not conflict) with it, was a symptom of the decadence of the Baghdad caliphate, its position now fatally undermined by continual rebellion by the Kharijite and Carmathian 'seven'. As a result, the caliphs began progressively to seek the protection of Turkic mercenaries from Central Asia, who had converted to Islam during the course of the century and had penetrated the heart of the empire with the complicity of the Samanid dynasty. The Samanids were responsible for the security of the northeastern area held by the Abbasids. At the end of the tenth century, the Turkish khan Alp Tegin took advantage of the weakness of the Samanids to occupy Ghaznah, in what is today Afghanistan, and founded a splendid court there; we know that the scientist al-Biruni and the poet Firdawsi were both received as guests there at one time or another. In 999, meanwhile, the Kara-Khanid Turks occupied the city of Bukhara and founded a new dynasty there. Persian princes and governors were superseded almost everywhere: the caliphs had to adjust to the new Turkish arrivals, recently converted Sunni Muslims and, as such, extremely intransigent. Before long, the members of a federation of tribes called the Oghuz had begun to make their mark; by the mid-tenth century they had settled in the pasturelands north of the Caspian Sea and Aral Sea and now, in deference to their semi-legendary founding father, Seljuk, they began to call themselves Seljuks.

Initially, the Seljuk Turks maintained good relations with the Samanid Persians; in about 1040, however, they drove them out and took their place, founding an 'empire' which extended from Khorasan to Central Persia. At this period the Caliph of Baghdad was heavily influenced (in fact, almost held hostage) by a dynasty of Shiite 'major-domos', the Buyids; this religious dominance served as a pretext for the Seljuk khan Tughrul Beg to march on the capital in 1055. The Turkish occupation was presented as a 'Sunni liberation' and the caliph was coerced into submission. The Seljuk leader was proclaimed sultan, and for the time being was more or less ruler of the caliphate. He solemnly announced his ambitious military programme intended to liberate the Abbasids from their current crisis and to allow Islam to resume the expansionist advance that had become exhausted in Asia three centuries earlier. As has already been discussed (and will be returned to shortly), their expansion slowed down in the Mediterranean just over a century earlier and in its place there was a tremendous recovery by the 'Frankish' peoples of the West.

The first adversaries to appear before the Seljuks, who were keen to continue with the westward expansion of the Sunni version of Islam, were the Byzantines and the Shiite caliphs of Egypt.

When faced with their Egyptian opponents, the Turks began a vicious campaign for control of Syria and Palestine: it took the arrival in the area in 1096–9 of that disconcerting armed pilgrimage which we now call the 'first crusade' to put an end to the enmity between the Abbasids and Seljuks and the Fatimids; the situation was further complicated by rivalry between the Turks and the Arabs. When the crusade reached the northern borders of Syria, the Fatimid Caliph of Cairo sent an embassy to find out whether he could join the 'Franks', or use them in some way against the Turks.

In 1071 the new sultan, Alp Arslan (1062–73), won an important victory at Manzikert – now Malazgirt – in the upper Euphrates not far from Lake Van. This paved the way, a few years later, for the founding of the 'sultanate of *Rum*', whose capital was Iconium (now Konya); this gave the Seljuks control over the centre of the Anatolian Peninsula. *Rum* ('Rome') was a term used in the Arab-speaking world (in Islam, therefore) to designate the area we mistakenly refer to as the Byzantine Empire, in its full geographical extent. Anatolia was therefore located in *Rum*. Henceforward only the Euxine Mountains in the north and the Taurus in the south separated the new Muslim conquerors from, respectively, the Black Sea coast and the Gulfs of Antalya and Alexandretta on the Mediterranean, all of them still under Byzantine control. Fear struck the capital on the Bosphorus as it had not done since the siege of 717–18. The new *basileus*, Alexis I Comnenius (1081–1118), who had recently ascended the throne, had to withstand three virtually simultaneous barbarian attacks. To the west, the Normans attacked the coast of Epirus under the leadership of Robert Guiscard who, with the support of the Pope, was in the process of consolidating his power over Southern

Italy, whilst his brother Roger waged a campaign against Sicily. To the north, the Ural-Altaic Pechenegs, later called the Comans (the *polovzi* of the Russian sources), carried out raids throughout the Balkans and by 1090 had almost reached the walls of Constantinople. They were driven off with difficulty. The Turks, to the east and south, had divided Central and Eastern Anatolia between them, but this division was now being fought over by two rival sultanates, the Seljuks of Iconium and the Danishmends of Melitene, now Malatya.

New conversions of massive groups of Turkic and Mongol peoples in the ninth and tenth centuries, greatly extending the reach of the *dar al-Islam* in Central Asia, could have had quite a different effect on the macro-continent of Eurasia, and not only on its religious history, if all the opportunities for conversion of the restless Indo-European and Turkic-Mongol peoples had been taken. Possibly the particular structure of the Muslim *umma* may have contributed to this series of missed opportunities: like Judaism, Islam lacks proper ecclesiastical institutions or priestly functions. Other ethnic groups allied to the Seljuks and the Kara-Khanids may have been prepared to accept the Koranic faith. Muslim penetration of these areas was pursued again at a later date, during the second half of the thirteenth century, closely following the upheaval caused by the conquests made by Genghis Khan. It appears, in fact, that Islam arrived in a number of areas of Central Asia via mercantile trade routes from the beginning of the tenth century onwards. The Bulgarians of *magna Bulgaria*, that great loop in the Volga, embraced Islam in this way, as did the Hazars, whose ruling class had previously embraced Judaism. The Chronicle of the twelfth-century Russian monk Nestor states that in 986 the Bulgars, who were Muslims, introduced themselves to Vladimir, Prince of Kiev, a pagan, and suggested that he convert to Islam. The prince, it seems, would not countenance the suggestion because circumcision and abstinence from alcohol and pork were not to his liking. Two years later, Vladimir (later known as 'the Great') accepted the offer made to him by the Byzantines and joined the Greek Orthodox Church.

The motives for his choice may seem crude, or perhaps the chronicler was ingenuous to present them as he did. Leaving aside his horizons and the audience at whom the chronicle was aimed,

what consequences would the adherence of Russia to Islam have had for the course of history? Christian Europe would have been held in a stranglehold: the Slav fleets in the Mediterranean would have been fighting for the Greeks, not the Arabs. Islam would have erected a bulwark along the eastern flank of Europe and might have spread to Scandinavia before the Christian missionaries had time to get there!

This provides another proof, if one were needed, of the necessity of thinking of history in the conditional mood, with every possible 'if' and 'but'. Only in this way can the weight of events be appreciated for what it is, heavy with consequences, instead of possibilities being advanced that have already been rejected. Relationships between individuals and groups can be juggled with, the past and the environment can be interpreted in different ways, and many events simply cannot be accounted for.

### Islam: Crisis and Transformation. The West

In Spain, Emir Abd ar-Rahman III (912–16), who led the neo-Umayyad dynasty in Córdoba to its greatest glory and, in 929, conferred upon himself the high office of caliph, managed to extend his influence over part of the Western Maghreb. Córdoba at this time seems to have had about 300,000 inhabitants. The impressive ruins of the city and royal palace of Medina Azahara, the 'City of Flowers', survive to remind us of the splendours of this period. The city glittered with marble, crystal and mosaics, all fashioned by Byzantium's greatest artists; tales are also told of a fountain of 'living silver', meaning mercury, which astonished guests with its sparkling cascades of light in the centre of a reception room glinting with gold.

The Arabs and Berbers had never properly merged. The fiercely aristocratic temperament of those who considered themselves as the Prophet's only authentic heirs held the African *parvenus* in scorn. Nevertheless, slow but steady integration soon began to take place between the Arabs and Berbers on one hand, and the descendants of the Celtic Iberians, the Latin Iberians and the Suevian Goths on the other. The most important social distinction remained that between Muslims descended from the conquerors, local people who had converted to Islam at some point (the *muwalladun*), and Christians who had not renounced their faith but who were Arabized in language and customs – although in many cases, Latin or the vernacular tongue that had developed from it was still remembered (these were the *musta'riba*, better known in the West by the Spanish version of the name, the Mozarabs).

From the start, the Umayyads passed on to the Hispano-Muslim world the basic characteristics of the great Syriac culture that was their trademark. Nevertheless, as time went by, the attractions of the Abbasid way of life, enjoyed at the Islamic courts in North Africa, began to make themselves felt. Even the Christian *dhimmi* were fascinated by this authentic intellectual treasure trove. As early as the ninth century, Alvaro of Córdoba was complaining that Christian scholars were wasting their time imitating Arabic script, and neglecting the Scriptures and the writings of the Fathers of the Church.

Relations between the Caliphs of Córdoba and the 'Franks' north of the Pyrenees were complex but satisfactory. In 953 John, Abbot of Gorze, was received by the sovereign, having been sent by Otto, King of Germany, to request the assistance of the caliph in clearing out Saracen settlements in the Alps. The caliph responded by sending the king (now emperor) the Mozarabic Bishop Recemund of Elvira, well known as the dedicatee of the *Antapodosis* of Liutprand of Cremona.

After the death of Abd ar-Rahman, the caliphate of Córdoba had no incumbent of the same calibre. Hakam II (961–76), who enlarged and embellished the city of Córdoba, nevertheless enjoys a good reputation in retrospect. Hakam had the debatable good fortune (politically speaking) to enjoy the support of a minister and collaborator so energetic that he almost seemed to outshine his master: Mohammed Ibn Abi 'Amir implemented the caliph's plans and for his deeds was dubbed al-Mansur, 'the Victor' (he is the Almanzor of the Spanish chronicles and epic poetry). For thirty years, between 978 and 1008, the *wizir*, a pure Arab by origin, was the lord and master of Spain and Morocco. He made the Christian King of León acknowledge his status as vassal of the Caliph of Córdoba and in 997 he attacked the sanctuary of Santiago de Compostela. After his death, however, violent dynastic disputes broke out between surviving members of his family, with the result that Muslim Spain was divided into a dozen or more emirates often at loggerheads with one another; these emirates were known traditionally in Spain as *reinos de taifas*, or 'kingdoms of factions'. These princely courts continued to sponsor the arts as the caliphate had done, albeit at a more modest level.

Until the end of the twelfth century at least, the Western Europeans knew almost nothing about Islam east of Jerusalem: in 906, for instance, Bertha, Countess of Tuscany, wrote to the Caliph of Baghdad, al-Muktafi, because she had recently learnt (from prisoners taken from boats coming from Ifriqiya) of the existence of a Muslim dynast who was more powerful than the Aghlabite Emir of Kairouan, with whom she enjoyed good relations (although naturally this did not exclude sea battles between rival corsairs).

On the other hand, the importance of the *reyes de taifas* was increasing for the Western peoples. In the early eleventh century one of these rulers, Mujahid, the Emir of Denia, devised and almost succeeded in implementing a comprehensive and coherent political programme based on control of the Balearic Islands, Corsica and Sardinia – which in practice meant the entire North western Mediterranean from Valencia to the Tyrrhenian Sea. Since 1010 Mujahid had taken advantage of the crisis in the caliphate to acquire power and, with the support of a number of sea captains, had assumed leadership of the Balearics. His ultimate aim was control of a vast area, reaching as far as Sardinia and the Tyrrhenian Sea. Apparently at the behest of Pope Benedict VIII, the two maritime cities of Genoa and Pisa joined forces to oppose this threat; both cities in the past had sustained repeated Saracen attacks. Between 1015 and 1021, after a lengthy and difficult war, they succeeded in getting the better of their adversary. The battle of the Pisans and Genoese against Mujahid was the first of many notable exploits in which Christian forces were united against a common Muslim enemy. This was evidence of the fact that such warlike episodes possessed a religious component of some kind, whether implicit or explicit. The same feature of the eleventh century also appeared in the vigorous promotion of religious and ecclesiastical subjects carried out by centres such as the Abbey of Cluny.

Ever since the age of Constantine, Christendom had grown accustomed to supporting or justifying (some would even call it sanctifying) its warmongering by claiming religious motives for it. In Byzantium, the concepts of 'sacred armies' and 'holy war' were a commonplace, since everything relating to imperial authority was held to be sacred: fighting pagans and spreading the Christian faith were a part of military rhetoric and symbolism. The Byzantine Church, however, always remained detached from the sanctification of arms and warfare. The Latin Church behaved quite differently: it had no option but to accept, then neutralize or try to eradicate the ancient warrior traditions that were connected with myth and religion. The Germanic peoples proved extremely reluctant to give them up. After the Carolingian period the increasingly close connection between high-ranking clergy and the exercise of power resulted in a growing militarization of values and customs, well illustrated by the Romano-Germanic liturgy of the blessing of arms and the *novi milites*, one of the earliest manifestations of the ethics and practice of chivalry. In this kind of context, it was a simple step to transform the occasions for armed warfare against Muslims into evidence of religious strife, in which (with the cast of mind that already existed) the two faiths were engaged in a kind of contest to see which was the stronger and therefore the better. It is important to remember, however, that this cast of mind was implicit rather than explicit and was more often found among the laity than among the clergy. The latter tolerated it but only very rarely encouraged it.

The Church ritual of the blessing of banners and arms should be seen in its social context: every object at the time was a candidate for blessing, including work tools, and all human activity had its proper place in a universe pervaded by the Sacred. Since the seventh century, too, the tradition in confrontations with Muslim enemies had been to defend life and property first, but also to defend the Church and relics. The blessing of arms and the defence of the Church encouraged the idea that war against this new enemy could be considered 'just', or even 'holy'. In spite of this, the names 'Ishmaelites', 'Hagarenes' or 'Saracens' were based on terms that, although not referring to ethnic groupings, were none the less genealogical: they referred to the Biblical story of the progeny of the patriarch Abraham. In other words, the enemy was never called by any name that would emphasize in a negative way his religious status as a non-Christian, thereby giving the impression of wanting to justify making war against him in the name of this difference of faith. When a mid-eighth-century text, the *Life* of Saint Eucharius of Orleans, mentions the perversity of the 'ill-omened nation of the Ishmaelites, who have left their homeland in order to march into the Province of Aquitaine and to depopulate it', he is not alluding to the religious beliefs of the sons of Ishmael. His intention is to portray the ferocity of the invaders, as the Latin sources had done for centuries when discussing conflict with the various 'barbaric' races.

Nevertheless, something changed during the ninth century, when the Popes in Rome returned to their time-honoured attitudes towards imminent threat of attack by Muslim corsairs. Examples of this are Gregory II's gift of the old pontifical altar cloths to the Duke of Aquitaine, engaged in battle with the Arabs near Toulouse in 947, or Adrian I's encouragement of Charlemagne before his Spanish expedition in 778. It would be far-fetched to regard Pope Gregory's gesture as any kind of forewarning of a 'holy war': as for the Frankish soldiers who tore the fabric of the altar cloths into shreds and swallowed them, their gesture was devotional with perhaps some overtones of magic, but it certainly did not imply that making war against the infidel was spiritually meritorious. Things were different in the case of Leo IV: the day after the Saracen attack on Rome in 846, he promised eternal life to anyone willing to give up his life in defence of the faith and the Church; similar promises were made by Nicholas I (856–67) and John VIII (872–82).

During this period, the Christians of the West were shocked by news from another part of Islam, a part that was well known to them: Spain. The event that shocked them was the incident of the 'martyrdom of Córdoba', recounted by Eulogius who, in 848, travelled right through Christian Spain, becoming involved in controversial anti-Islamic propaganda. From Spain he travelled to other parts of Europe in search of members of his family who were scattered over the continent, apparently on business. The travels of St Eulogius serve as a useful reminder that trade between Europe and Islam was much more regular and frequent than is generally supposed, although it was never straightforward.

In Córdoba, in about 850, fifty or so men and women defied the ban on preaching against the laws of the Prophet and were put to death. It seems that they were motivated by a strong attraction towards the Last Trump rather than by a longing for martyrdom. Once the Gospel had been spread to the whole world, the end of the world and the Last Judgement would be at hand. In 858 two Benedictine monks from Saint-Germain were travelling through Spain in search of the relics of St Vincent; they reached Córdoba and were able to bring home the bodies of three of the martyrs. The episode made a deep impression on the West and seems to have been held as exemplary for a long time: nearly four hundred years later, the Franciscans used it as a model. Still under review is whether and to what extent the events surrounding papal pronouncements in the second half of the ninth century and the question of the 'Martyrs of Córdoba' were important to the genesis of the idea of the crusade or – an even more difficult question to answer – of the 'holy war'.

The Aghlabite Emirs of Tunisia, summoned to Sicily by all accounts by a Byzantine official who was having trouble with a rival faction, took more than seven years to take possession of the whole island: compared with the overwhelming surge that in a brief space of time had turned most of the Iberian Peninsula into an Islamicized subcontinent, this was a very slow process. After the surrender of Taormina in 902 the island remained an important region of the *dar al-Islam* for nearly two centuries. The Christians, reduced to the status of *dhimmi*, did not leave the island, but Sicily was nevertheless profoundly affected ethnically and linguistically by the Arab and Berber occupation. The ethnic composition of Sicily was already complex and very mixed: it included pre-Indo-European Pelasgian, Punic, Hellenic, Latin and Graeco-Byzantine peoples. Nevertheless, the linguistic contribution made by the Berber Arabs can still be detected in the Sicilian dialect, particularly in vocabulary connected with agriculture, irrigation and the tools and techniques of land cultivation. Travellers from Muslim areas where conditions were more arid gasped in admiration at the abundance of water and forests in Sicily, whence came timber for all the fleets of Islam. In the tenth century, Ibn Hawqal discussed the island with some disdain, considering it as marginal in comparison with the flourishing Islamic areas of the Maghreb. In fact, Palermo, which he saw in 973, was one of the largest cities in the Western Mediterranean and was well equipped with beautiful places of worship and palaces, fresh-flowing fountains and well-stocked markets. Little of this elegance remains: the baths of Cefalù still exist, in ruins. The cultural and artistic profile of Muslim Sicily was, however, perpetuated in the Norman twelfth century: the Zisa, the Cuba and the Cappella Palatina recall a quality of life and a *joie de vivre* of extraordinary sophistication, and this corresponds with what we know and what we can still see of the palaces, gardens, waterworks, mosques and madrassahs of Spain and the Maghreb.

Similarly, contemporary accounts from the Norman period give a picture of intense intellectual life. Sicily was a fertile ground for studies in theology, philology and grammar; it was home to a school of poetry, which produced works of heart-breaking beauty – as the (lost) anthology of Ibn al-Qattah and the verses of the reputedly exiled poet Ibn Hamdis seem indirectly to demonstrate. From exile in Andalusia, both poets lamented the loss of Sicily, just as the Andalusian refugees to the Maghreb were to do four hundred years later. Ibn Hamdis was said to have left Sicily on the arrival of the Normans, and then to have fled from Andalusia on the arrival of the Almoravids; he died, either in Majorca or in Bujjiah, in 1133. Sicilian Arab poetry was 'classical', and derived from the forms of the great tradition of al-Andalus; it may have been at the root of the vernacular poetry of Sicily which appeared, apparently from nowhere, during the Suevian period.

As had happened in Spain with the caliphate of Córdoba, when Emir al-Akhal (1019–36) died and the emirate that had united the island ended, power became fragmented: in time this opened the way for the Norman conquest. For years the small local courts, like the *reyes de taifas*, managed to sustain the traditions of magnificence and refinement that had characterized the court in Palermo.

# 3

# *Europe's Response: The* Reconquista *and Naval Exploits*

## The Road to Santiago

Although the Mozarabs of Spain had become Arabized and were long accustomed to Muslim domination, they were nevertheless none too fond of their rulers. Many escaped to the north of the Iberian Peninsula, either to the northern part of the Ebro or to the area around the cold, wet Cantabrian cordillera, near the Asturias and Navarre. They introduced Mozarabic culture to the area, with its horse-shoe arches (derived either from Islamic forms or from a development of Visigoth forms) and its illuminated commentaries on the Apocalypse. They continued to display the characteristic Mozarabic taste for bright colours and visionary images, made famous by the 'Beato of Liebana'.

In fact, the high-ranking clergy of Mozarabic Spain made living with the Muslims into an art. The choice of the doctrine of Adoptionism by Eliprando, Archbishop of Toledo, at the end of the eighth century was probably an unspoken concession to strict Islamic monotheism. Christ was God's chosen one, 'adopted' by him, but there remained only one Divine Persona. As a reaction to this doctrine, a strongly trinitarian version of Christianity was developing in the northern part of the peninsula, which had scarcely been penetrated by the rapid Islamic conquest. It seems reasonable to interpret this development as a powerful rejection of Islam.

The kingdom founded around Oviedo in 720 by Pelagius the Goth proclaimed and practised a type of Christian faith which in the future would become strongly identified with the Iberian character. It is in this context that we should view the *inventio* in the early ninth century, in the

Galician town of Compostela, of a body claimed (in spite of great initial opposition) to be that of James the Apostle, miraculously transported across the sea to the north-west coast of Spain. James was traditionally credited with the conversion of the Iberian Peninsula. The discovery of his relics gave a patriarchal status to the Church in the kingdom of the Asturias (because it was 'founded' by an Apostle), and a primal quality which allowed it to compete with other great Christian centres such as Rome, Alexandria, Antioch or Constantinople. The Venetians apparently requested that their Church be dignified in the same way after the *translatio* of the body of Mark the Evangelist from Alexandria. The cult of 'Santiago' (a neo-Latin contraction of *sanctus Jacopus*) was vigorously promoted by the Asturian ruling family in order to continue pressure for the return of the Visigoth crown, carried off during the Berber Arab invasion. The project also included a policy to repopulate the valley of the Douro, where a number of new settlements had recently been established, including the city of Burgos – surrounded in the mid-tenth century by its own county. A number of ancient, venerable settlements which had gradually lost their populations were revived. This was possible because climatic conditions had improved everywhere, and populations were increasing all over Europe. The surge in population reached its peak between the tenth and twelfth centuries, and was followed by a period of stagnation in the second half of the thirteenth century. When under Alfonso III, the Great (866–910), the capital of the Asturias was transferred from Oviedo to the Roman town of León (which gave the kingdom its new name), the policy of extending the boundaries southwards and enlarging the settled area towards the plateau of the *meseta* became explicit. It was impossible to lead a big offensive against the Saracens, however, but lightning raids (*aceifas*) were common.

Similar plans were being hatched in Navarre, which became a kingdom in 926 and was later joined to Castile; in Aragon, a kingdom since 1035 when, on the death of Sancho III of Navarre, the group comprising Castile, Aragon and Navarre split apart permanently; and finally in the Catalan county of Barcelona, which had by now emerged from the Carolingian Spanish March. At the end of the tenth century the fluid Iberian frontier between Christians and Muslims was fought over along the Douro: the Catalans, who had managed to repel a series of attacks made by the Moors on Barcelona between 985 and 1003, hoped from their northeastern corner to push the area they controlled at least as far as Tarragona, half-way between their capital and the Muslim city of Tortosa at the mouth of the Ebro.

Al-Mansur, the great minister of Hisham II, realized that as long as the caliphs supported one another these thrusts from the north could be contained. He responded with a violent counter-offensive, culminating in 996–7 in an attack on the city of Compostela, which was looted and damaged. Fortunately the relics of St James the Apostle were spared.

This was more than just a reasonably successful raid. It was an episode with enormous symbolic overtones, which in fact produced effects that were the opposite of those desired. The *wizir* sensed the importance of the new phenomenon that had taken progressive hold during these years. The tomb of the apostle in Compostela, made famous by a series of miracles, was visited by ever-increasing numbers of pilgrims from the lands beyond the Pyrenees. What he could not understand was how the cult had established itself throughout Europe: news of the desecration of the sanctuary, far from arousing fear and dismay, or causing disaffection, aroused extraordinary indignation and renewed fervour. The cause of James the Apostle became the cause of the whole of Christendom: what had been a pilgrimage now became associated with the defence of the sacred tomb threatened by the 'pagans'.

Very soon, with the assistance and under the protection of the powerful monastery of Cluny, a whole network of roads had been organized. These routes fanned out through Germany, Italy and France, converging on the north side of the Pyrenean passes and then proceeding to Galicia via a series of stopping places in Navarre, Castile, León and the Asturias until Santiago was reached. While making for the most celebrated sanctuary of them all, the road passed all sorts of minor places of worship (some of them important in their own right), each with its own relics and legends, its miracles, and its *feria* and fair. Bridges and pilgrims' hospices were built along the road to make the journey easier, and confraternities were formed to look after the travellers' needs, and to house them and take care of them if they were taken ill on the road. A new breath of spirituality surrounded this passion for pilgrimage: Church institutions were revived and the moral reforms carried through by the Church were strongly encouraged by the atmosphere of spirituality that surrounded the reforming Popes and the Cluniac congregations. Although the traditional pilgrim centres, Rome and Jerusalem, were still attracting the faithful, the pilgrimage to Santiago was fast becoming the cornerstone of the new European way of life, boosted by a rise in population and by economic and commercial revival. The energetic Abbot of Cluny, Odilon – known ironically as 'King Odilon' by his critics – was the butt of much criticism because of the passion with which he organized military expeditions against the Muslims. Evidently pilgrimages and the campaign against Islam in Spain were closely connected.

The pilgrimage to Santiago rapidly assumed a warlike aspect: early in its course, the route of the *Camino* circumnavigated an area that was in places quite close to the 'no-man's land' dividing Christians from Muslims. It was claimed that during the battle of Clavijo in 844 James the Apostle appeared in dazzling robes, on the back of a snow-white charger, and guided the Christians as they fought the enemy: he was thenceforward called the 'Moor Slayer', *Matamoros*, following the tradition that attached epithets to rulers in commemoration of their victories (Basil II, Emperor of Constantinople and conqueror of the Bulgars, was dubbed *Bulgaroctonos*).

In fact, we do not know for certain when the Apostle's warlike aspect took over from his image as a pilgrim and worker of miracles: surviving representations of St James are relatively recent and the military prowess attributed to him appeared no earlier than the twelfth century. The legend was certainly current in 1094, however, when some Christian warriors originating mainly from France were engaged in the siege of Coimbra, in Portugal. These soldiers had probably heard stories of a similar episode that had taken place just one year earlier during a battle between Normans and Saracens at Cerami in Sicily. On this occasion, St George appeared with a white ensign fixed to his lance and fought alongside the Normans.

Apparitions of this type seem to have occurred frequently during the Norman conquest of Sicily, as they did during the curious series of events that took place later, between 1096 and 1099, and which are now usually referred to as the 'first crusade'. The apparitions were a feature of the sacralization of the conflict against the Saracens, which might well be interpreted as propaganda put about by the reforming wing of the Church, but which was also rooted in the general atmosphere of religious enthusiasm, or collective excitement, and in the new mood in favour of combat and martyrdom.

After the collapse of the caliphate of Córdoba, Muslim Spain was divided between the various *reinos de taifas*, and was riven by conflicts between Arab and Berber families. This highly unstable situation had its counterpart amongst the Christian kingdoms in the north. The situation began to change in about 1055 when Ferdinand I – King of Castile and León since 1037 – felt sufficiently confident of his strength to launch an offensive which won him the lower valley of the Douro. Coimbra was conquered in 1064, after the sovereign had made the pilgrimage to Compostela to pray for the assistance of James the Apostle in his undertaking. As has been described, the military reputation of Santiago *Matamoros* was acquired at the battle of Clavijo. The Aragonese front was threatened with collapse after the death of the king, Ramiros I, during the siege of the Saracen stronghold of Graus. The Infante, Sancho, was still a minor, so it fell to Pope Alexander II to take over the reins; in the same year as the conquest of Coimbra, the fortress of Barbastro, not far

from Saragossa, was taken by an expeditionary force which included a
large number of French knights – and which provoked a tremendous
wave of military and religious fervour.

The loss of both Coimbra and Barbastro dealt a severe blow to al-
Andalus. The Moorish 'kings' of Saragossa, Badajoz, Toledo and Seville
were forced to pay a tribute to Ferdinand of Castile who, in a ceremonial
cavalcade specially laid on for the occasion, finally reached Valencia.
Ferdinand died in León in 1065, shortly after paying homage for the first
time to the relics of St Isidore of Seville, returned to him by the Moorish
kings, in his newly built cathedral.

The Barbastro campaign of 1063–4 was probably the critical episode
in relations between Christians and Muslims. The papal bull sanctioning
the campaign, issued by Pope Alexander II, became the model for the
subsequent pontifical documents which came to constitute the canon
law of the crusades: the bull granted as an indulgence remission of sins to
anyone participating in the enterprise, including William of Aquitaine
and knights from various parts of France. Alexander II was Anselmo da
Baggio, one of the leaders of the reformist wing of the Church; he
probably handed the Duke of Aquitaine the *vexillum sancti Petri*,
which placed those volunteering to fight in the campaign under the
protection of the Church of Rome, and which also foreshadowed an
important law promulgated by the Church relating to victories that
might arise as a result of this undertaking.

In Spain, on the Tyrrhenian Sea and in Sicily (as we shall see), an
atmosphere was being created which, between the end of the eleventh
and the end of the twelfth centuries, would lead to the complex series of
military expeditions and religious and spiritual acquisitions which has
since been given the generic (and misleading) title of 'crusade'. It is
important to recognize the various factors that contributed to the development of this atmosphere and these situations: the inevitability of the
struggle against the Muslims from the Iberian Peninsula to Sicily (and
later to Syria); the (erroneous but comprehensible) feeling that Islam
constituted a tight, homogeneous group from Central Asia in the East to
the Iberian Peninsula and the Maghreb in the West; and, finally, the
sentiment produced by Church reformers in the consciences of the civil
and military aristocracy of the day, who gleaned their response to the
situation from Church propaganda or from membership of the *pax Dei*
movement. *Pax Dei* imposed periods of truce on the feudal warfare that
was endemic in Western Christianity, but meanwhile held out the prospect of war against the infidel as a source of gain through looting and
territorial acquisitions, which would be ample compensation for the
loss of income suffered as a result of the inevitable interruptions caused
by the conflict between *milites* as well as for the taxes that merchants

and pilgrims were obliged to pay along the pilgrim routes. The 'export of warlike violence' beyond the borders of Christendom, the Church's sanctioning – almost amounting to sanctification through indulgences and the Pope's *vexillum* – of the benefits deriving from it, and the relationship now established between Christian conquests and the huge increase in the scope of economic opportunities they afforded, now became the stimulus to a new dynamic in which religious, political and economic justifications converged.

The use of the lay aristocracy to implement programmes for the reformed Church was particularly conspicuous under Gregory VII, who had no hesitation in enlisting the support of one of the Roman Church's staunchest allies, William, Duke of Aquitaine, against his arch-rival, the Holy Roman Emperor Henry IV. The Church's programme ranged from the fight against continuing lay influence over the appointments and possessions of the Church, to the war against the infidel. Although the Church and the lay aristocracy might be seen as being complementary to each other, in practice situations and events arose periodically which pitted one group against the other. In 1074 the Pope involved Duke William in his plan to send military assistance to the Eastern Christians, who were threatened by the Turkish advance. Significantly enough, this was twenty years after the beginning of the Schism in the Orient and three years after the battle of Manzikert, in which the *basileus* was routed by the Seljuks. The Pope's intention was to heal the Schism, or at least to mitigate its effects and to settle differences with Constantinople; he also hoped to extend the prestige (if not the power) of the Bishop of Rome in the East. Spain's morale was boosted by the popularity of the Road to Santiago and by the first successful Christian counter-offensives in the Iberian Peninsula, and this atmosphere of optimism was crucial to the events that followed in the Mediterranean area.

The death of Ferdinand I of Castile in December 1065 provoked a lull in the lengthy and unsteady process which has since been described as the *Reconquista*. One of Ferdinand's sons, Alfonso VI, finally succeeded in reuniting Castile and León and beating the Moors; he was assisted in this by a person who soon became a legendary figure – namely, Rodrigo Díaz de Bivar, known as El Cid Campeador (*campi ductor*; Cid is in fact derived from the Arabic word *said*, 'gentleman'). The foundation of two great new cathedrals, in Barcelona in 1058 (the earlier one was destroyed during al-Mansur's raids on the city, between 985 and 1003), and in Santiago in 1075, was an indication of the prevailing feeling that religious and military affairs were closely linked – and also a confirmation of the prosperity that follows victory.

On the other hand, the complicated story of El Cid, the unruly companion-at-arms of a ruler who himself was not always quite trustworthy, conveys a clear idea of what the *Reconquista* was really like: the war between the Moors and the Christians was characterized by moments of enormous religious fervour, sometimes quite violent, alternating with phases of unscrupulous *Realpolitik*. Rodrigo fell into disgrace with the king and was banished from the kingdom in 1081, for crimes which included failure to honour the guarantees given by Alfonso to the Moors. Rodrigo then offered his services to the *rey de taifa* of Saragossa, who was fighting his counterpart in Lerida, the latter supported in his efforts by King Sancho of Aragon and Raymond-Berengarius II, Count of Barcelona. This criss-cross of alliances between Moors and Christians, against equally mixed adversaries, was completely normal. Alfonso VI achieved his most glorious victory, the capture of Toledo on 6 May 1085, whilst supporting the Moorish *malik* of Badajoz against the *malik* of Toledo, al-Qadir. The assassination of al-Qadir provoked El Cid to lay siege to the city of Valencia, by way of revenge for his Saracen friend – Valencia had refused him hospitality. Of course he was eager to take part in the conquest on his own behalf as well. After a siege lasting twenty months, the town fell on 15 June 1094 and El Cid, now reconciled with Alfonso, ruled Valencia until his death in 1099.

The king survived his vassal by about ten years. His strong connection with the world on the far side of the Pyrenees is demonstrated by his marriages to three different Frenchwomen, and the marriages of his two daughters to a Burgundian and a man from Lorraine, both of whom had come to Spain to fight the Moors. From 904, his Burgundian son-in-law, Henry, married to the Infanta Teresa, was lord of a Castilian county established between the Minho and the Douro, the nucleus of the future Portugal.

Alfonso was much more straightforward with his Muslim neighbours than he was with his own subjects and allies. He forced the Christians of Toledo to hand back to the Saracens the city's mosque, captured during the occupation of 1085, and he intervened on several occasions to force his *fideles* to pay compensation to any Saracens under his authority against whom they had committed violent acts.

After the capture of Toledo, things were not easy for either Alfonso or El Cid. The king rode down to Tarifa on the far southern tip of the peninsula, opposite Africa: he spurred his horse on into the sea, as if to challenge the darkness rising from the waves in front of him – the Islam of the Maghreb. A futile gesture, as it turned out.

The Muslim ruler of Seville, the brilliant and cultivated al-Mutamid, a *qadi* who ran a kind of aristocratic republic of notable men, was beginning to sense that the fortunes of al-Andalus were declining. Beyond the Columns of Hercules the power of a very strict confraternity called the *murabitun*, 'men of the *ribats*', was becoming established. The *murabitun* were the inhabitants of the austere fortress-monasteries which had originally been built across the distant desert on the banks of the rivers Senegal and Niger; these tower-dwellers had by now taken possession of Morocco and Algeria and were called the Almoravids.

Al-Mutamid cannot have approved of these mysterious fanatics, nor did he appreciate having to deal with their leader, Yusuf ibn Tashfin. But if anyone asked him to explain why he had made this dismal choice, he would apparently reply: 'I would rather end life as a camel driver in Africa than as a swine-herd in Castile'. The *amir al-muslimin* therefore crossed the sea. When Alfonso requested an audience with him, he is said to have replied with the following martial couplet: 'I have no other cards to play than the sword and the spear, nor any other ambassador than my well-stocked armies'.[1]

The battle took place at Zallaqa (now Sagrajas), near La Guadiana, on 23 October 1086, and was one of the greatest Christian defeats of all time. King Alfonso just managed to escape with his life, with a few hundred knights, taking refuge in Soria. The severed heads of those killed were stacked in gruesome triumphal mounds. Henceforward the Christians and Muslims in Spain had to face Islam of another variety; the sparkling silver fountains of Medina Azahara must have seemed very far away.

The people of al-Andalus paid a high price for this victory. Yusuf obliged all the *reyes de taifas* to submit to his authority: anyone seeking to ally themselves with the Castilians and to offer resistance was ruthlessly subdued; the preferability of ending life as a camel driver under this prince was no longer nearly so self-evident. Toledo remained in Christian hands, but south of the Tagus none of the conquests made in recent years withstood the onslaught. In the Muslim cities the ordinary people, in an attack of religious fervour fuelled by their enthusiasm for military victory, supported the fierce, sanctimonious power of the Almoravids. The old emirs of al-Andalus were considered corrupt libertines by their new masters and were sent off into exile. Some, like the poet-*qadi* of Seville, al-Mutamid, died in chains (and certainly not as a camel driver) in Africa.

On the other hand, in spite of the acts of cruelty committed by the mysterious keepers of the *ribats*, the years of Almoravid rule – whose

---

[1] Al-Maggarî, *Anecdotes sur l'histoire et la littérature des arabes d'Espagne*, edited by R. Dozy, G. Dugat, I. Krehl and W. Wright, Vol. 2 (Leyden, 1861), pp. 674, 678.

power extended from the Tagus to the Sahara – were prosperous and serene. The few big battles were bloody, the initial repression severe, but the new masters respected the Koran to the letter and put very little fiscal pressure on the *muslimin* and the *dhimmi*. They promoted urban development, greatly enlarging another recently established capital city, Marrakesh (created by Yusuf ibn Tashfin in 1062), and laying the complex groundplan of Fez. They protected commerce and the manufacturing activity that was developing in centres like Tlemcen and Sijilmassa in Africa and in Almeria in Spain; at a later date, Almeria contained eight hundred silk-weaving workshops, nine hundred hostelries for travellers and warehouses for goods (*khans* and *funduks*), numerous metal workshops and a port used by all the ships of Mediterranean Islam. The gold coins produced in the Almoravid cities (called *marabottini* in the West) were valid and accepted everywhere. Nor had the mysticism of the *ribat* confraternity stifled intellectual life: on the contrary, theological and legal debate flourished. The madrassah and the library in Córdoba experienced an extraordinary phase of expansion surpassing the splendour of the period of the caliphate and producing a wave of cultural development which, from the following century on, was to benefit the whole of the Western world.

Meanwhile, the career of Rodrigo Díaz was drawing to a close. As the Castilian poem *Cantar de mío Cid* recounts, the great warrior died in Valencia on 10 July 1099, exactly five days before armed Frankish pilgrims, the *cruce signati*, entered Jerusalem on the other side of the Mediterranean. Legend has it that Rodrigo won his last battle as a corpse, emerging from the gates of the besieged city and galloping towards the Moors, who fled in fright at the sight of him. His faithful horse Babieca bore her master's embalmed body in the saddle, held upright in his stirrups by a wooden plank. Yusuf marched on the city without delay, but met with fierce resistance. The King of Castile did his utmost to hold the city, but his efforts were in vain: at the beginning of May 1102, he was forced to surrender. Rodrigo's wife Dona Jimena took her husband's remains to his native Burgos, where she buried them.

Having sought desperately to turn the tide after this defeat, Alfonso was beaten again at Uclés, between Toledo and Cuenca, where he lost his sole heir, Don Sancho. The prince, who was the son of a Saracen refugee, Zaida, daughter-in-law of the *qadi* of Seville, had been very dear to his father.

After the triumph of Seville, the conflict between Christians and Muslims in the Iberian Peninsula closed in anti-climax. Matters were developing very differently elsewhere, however, in the Mediterranean, Italy and Syria.

## Heroes and Martyrs

High the peaks, and gloomy the valleys
Dark the rocks and sinister the gorges
The French today passed through in great dismay
The noise is heard fifteen leagues away...

This is the beginning of the famous sixteenth *laisse* of the *Chanson de Roland*. The text is of uncertain date and there are many variants. Generations of Western Europeans have sung the lines – or others very like them – committing them to memory and experiencing the same *frisson* at each crossing of the rugged road between Ostabat and Puente la Reina in the Pyrenees. This is where the pilgrim routes from Tours, Vézelay and Le Puy meet to join the 'southern route' from Saint-Gilles, thence proceeding via Logrono, León and Burgos to the wondrous *Campus Stellae* in Compostela, where James the Apostle awaits pilgrims. If ever a route qualified for the designation 'European', this is it: the conscience and identity of Europe were forged along this route as along no other.

Roland is the protagonist of the most important, and possibly the first, of the epic *chansons* in the Northern French *matière de France*, attributed to the late eleventh century. We have almost no information on the historical person who, in the eleventh to twelfth centuries, became one of the leading heroes in the European epic tradition. The name, with a number of variants – *Hruodlandus, Rothlandus* – is known to have belonged to a member of Charlemagne's royal entourage; numismatic evidence exists, with the name to be found on coins minted in 781, plus documentary evidence in the lists of the names of people at court. The most important piece of indirect evidence, however, is to be found in the *Annales qui dicuntur Einhardi*, in which the ambush set in the pass of Roncesvalles in 778 is discussed; the rearguard of the Frankish army, reduced in numbers after an unsuccessful campaign in Navarre and Aragon, was ambushed by mountain-dwellers called *Wascones* (Basques or Gascons, certainly Christians). The *Annales* state only that, in this confused minor episode, several royal dignitaries appointed by the sovereign to command the column, surprised by the ambush, were killed. Eginhard's *Vita Karoli*, published between 829 and 836, takes up the story and amplifies it, adding the names of the most illustrious persons to have lost their lives in the fray: Seneschal Edgard, Count-Palatine Anselm and Hruolandus, *Brittannici limitis praefectus*, in other words, Roland, Count of the Marches of Brittany. The historical memory of the events of 778 may have survived without a break until the eleventh century, when it entered the epic tradition or, to be more precise, when as far as we know the epic tradition was first set down in writing. The distinction between written and unwritten material needs to be strongly emphasized: the debate continues between those who support the gradual uninterrupted development of the *chansons de geste* from the oral *cantilenae* of the Carolingian period (these are known to have existed, but there is no surviving evidence of the substance of their texts), and those who support a sudden flowering of the epic poetry of the *matière de France* on the pilgrim routes and from the battle fronts of the *Reconquista*.

The legend of Roland has its basis in a verifiable (if minor) historical event. A kind of 'embellishment of the loss' seems to have emerged almost at once, possibly at the express wish of Charlemagne. Military disgrace is elevated to martyrdom, the Christian (as they certainly were) aggressors are transformed into Muslims, and the fact that they were simply defending their lands from foreign intruders is conveniently forgotten. Thus the military failure is turned into a political and public relations success. The succeeding three centuries of conflict between Christians and Muslims in the Mediterranean basin, the Iberian Peninsula and Sicily, and finally in Anatolia and Syria-Palestine had the effect of elevating the defeat at Roncesvalles into a key moment in a centuries-long – indeed, in symbolic terms, eternal – conflict between Christianity and Islam. Roland became the lay patron saint and martyr, an exemplar for Christianity in as far as his death resembled a true Passion.

An episode must undoubtedly have taken place in which the 'long-term' conflict (which had become chronic, and was therefore generally, if not inevitably, lacking in 'critical' moments) must have found its normative fulcrum. Another such fulcrum may have been the battle of Barbastro, which provoked a reaction all over the Christian world. Contemporary and later battles in Italy and Syria may also have influenced the subject matter of the *chansons de geste*; Spain, on the other hand, used the deeds of Charlemagne, promoted by the reformed Church as the paradigm of the Christian emperor, to draw attention to the corruption of the rulers he was fighting. The doctrine, spirituality, aesthetic and rhetoric of what would eventually become the crusade was drawn up on the road that led to the *Reconquista*, and on the pilgrimage to Santiago de Compostela. The Carolingian legend was repeated, reinterpreted and often distorted. In various passages the *Roland* alludes, sometimes obscurely, to a text: an 'ancient Geste' or 'Gestes of the Franks', although no hint is given as to whether it is poetry or prose, or what its sources are; this may simply be a literary artifice added to give greater credibility and authority to the tale being told. Perhaps more information can be gleaned from references to real relics that could be viewed and venerated, in the same spirit and along routes that were not very different from those taken by pilgrims from France on their way to Santiago; the tomb of Roland (and, less certainly, the tombs of Oliver and Turpin) in the church of Saint-Romain in Blaye; Roland's horn, the oliphant in the church of Saint-Sévérin in Bordeaux, is the *tuba eburnea* mentioned in the celebrated twelfth-century manuscript known as the *Codex calixtinus*, now in the cathedral in Santiago. Unfortunately, the devastation caused by the Huguenot wars, then the French Revolution, has removed much of this evidence. The committal of the *Roland* material to written form is evidence of the existence of places of worship connected with the memory of his sacrifice: presumably, they are closely connected with the oral development of the epic which led to the version of the poem that we now know.

In his *Gesta regum Anglorum*, compiled in about 1125, William of Malmesbury informs us that, during the battle of Hastings in 1066, some of the Norman troops could be heard intoning a *cantilena Roll-andi*: it is impossible to know if this refers to the real *chanson* or to one of the many oral compositions that preceded it and provided models and material for it. The chronological distance between the events of 1066 and the appearance of the *Gesta* makes precise dating impossible. It is difficult to know whether to side with those who think the *Chanson de Roland* was written slightly before the first crusade, or with those who think it was written just after it; we know that it appeared at around that time. It can be stated with confidence, however, that the poem and the events of 1096–9 draw their life-blood from the same cultural and economic sources and are closely connected.

In many respects, the *Chanson de Roland* provides an interpretative criterion and a propaganda framework for the crusade, and for other military undertakings against the Saracens from the twelfth century onwards. During seven years of war, Charles has conquered the whole of Spain. Only the city of Saragossa remains. The King of Saragossa, Marsilio, sends his ambassador Biancardino on a mission to the King of the Franks. The manner of reacting to residual Saracen power in Spain provokes a conflict between supporters of the war, including first and foremost Roland, and supporters of peace, amongst whom is Roland's stepfather, Ganelon. The rivalry between the two results in Ganelon, Charles' ambassador to Saragossa, urging Marsilio to take up arms against the Paladin; together they plan the ambush at Roncesvalles in which Roland dies as the hero-martyr. Charles arrives too late to save his favourite nephew, but in time to pursue the fleeing Saracens. At this point the vanquished Marsilio receives in Saragossa the ambassadors of his sovereign Baligante, Emir of Babylon, who is planning to come to Spain to pit his strength against his arch enemy, the Emperor Charles (the scene inevitably recalls the appeal made by the *reyes de taifas* to the Almoravid emir). The battle between these two great rulers is the defining moment between Christendom and the pagan world. Charles is victorious, Saragossa is taken, Marsilio dies, Roland is buried at Blaye and Charles can return to Aix-la-Chapelle. Here Aude, Roland's betrothed, dies of a broken heart on receiving the news that her beloved is no more, and Ganelon receives appropriately gruesome punishment.

The *Chanson de Roland*, and the subsequent compositions claiming to be its continuation or completion, enjoyed extraordinary success between the twelfth and the sixteenth centuries. The name of Roland, the companionship between Roland and Oliver, and visual representations of Roland's person in illuminated Carolingian poetry and epics, Carolingian sculpture and stained glass survive as testimony to the subject's enormous appeal.

Iconographic evidence of the popularity of Roland and his deeds is particularly widespread and often early – although doubt has been cast on the authenticity of some examples. A number of images may have been too hastily identified as being of Roland, and others may have been subjected to traditional but philologically inaccurate interpretations. The two statues on the portal of Verona Cathedral were thought definitely to depict Roland and Oliver, an identification that seemed to be confirmed by the inscription *Durindarda* adorning the Paladin's sword. The interpretation of the other figure in the pair as Oliver seemed less convincing, and there were even doubts about Roland on account of the uncertain date of the inscription. In other words, it is not impossible that the two warriors keeping watch over the portal of the cathedral in Verona originally represented someone quite different; or that the increasing popularity of the epic Roland cycle led to the identification of the pair as Roland and Oliver and to the inscription of the knight's name on the blade of the sword held out by the figure who, ever since, has represented Roland in the public mind without a shadow of doubt. (Another interpretation identifies the two warriors as the heroes of another epic cycle, William of Orange and the Saracen Renoardo.) There used to be an impressive (and genuine) representation of the Roland epic on the mosaic floor of Brindisi Cathedral: a series of Biblical scenes in the centre of the mosaic was surrounded by a broad band two and a half metres wide which told the story of the defeat at Roncesvalles. Unfortunately, two devastating earthquakes in 1743 and 1858 completely destroyed the floor so that today the mosaic has to be interpreted from faded printed reproductions.

Events in the *matière de France* and the *matière de Bretagne* tended to become a little confused during the twelfth and thirteenth centuries. This was not due to contamination of the Arthurian cycle by the Charlemagne cycle: it happened because the older cycle, originally purely epic, gradually assumed characteristics and scenes that were typical of the later one – love scenes, voyages and vicissitudes set against a background of magic and romance.

Between the twelfth and the thirteenth centuries, the poet Bertrand de Bar-sur-Aube, author of *Girart de Vienne* and also probably of *Aymeri de Narbonne*, talks of three epic 'cycles' of *gestes*. The twenty-four cantos of the *Geste de Guillaume*, dedicated to Duke William of Aquitaine, Charlemagne's contemporary, can be recognized (although the lines may equally refer to the memory of the hero of Barbastro and the favourite of Gregory VII). The *Geste de Guillaume* reiterates the theme of the loyal servants of a weak and insecure ruler, threatened from inside as well as outside his kingdom. The epic tradition meets history head on and becomes inextricably interwoven with it.


### Sailors on the Tyrrhenian Sea and Norman Warriors

There are two conflicting theories about the extraordinary expansion of the West from the eleventh century onwards. According to the first theory, the growth was induced and dominated from outside. According to the second, however, the process occurred independently; its roots and its strength were to be found inside the continent of Europe.

Maurice Lombard, who subscribes to the first theory, emphasiszes that the Mediterranean world, from Córdoba to Cairo, from Kairouan to Damascus and from Palermo to Baghdad, and above all the Muslim world, was full of cities hungry for consumer goods and raw materials. The European West was forced to equip itself to process the products that it possessed or produced in abundance – timber, iron, tin, honey, weapons and (circumventing ecclesiastical disapproval) slaves. These vigorous trade relations helped re-establish contact between the various ports around the Mediterranean littoral. In spite of continuous naval dog-fights and acts of piracy, they brought wealth and vitality to the bloodstream of barbarian Europe, only now emerging from the winter of the early Middle Ages. Supporters of the second theory – including Marc Bloch, Lynn White Jnr, Georges Duby and others – have firmly laid the emphasis on a series of related causes, from climatic to demographic and technological. As has been obvious for some time, all these causes need to be kept in mind if the full picture is to be gained, each cause being given its appropriate weight. Although it is tempting to isolate single or primary causes, it is the complexity of the whole process that needs to be emphasized and explored. What is clear is that the Muslim gold circulating in abundance in the Christian coastal towns between the end of the tenth and the eleventh centuries had many different origins. In Barcelona, for example, it could have included the wages paid by the Spanish-Arab potentates to Catalan mercenaries. Most of it, however, came from the profits made by Western commerce (the export trade was becoming increasingly important and lucrative). Last but not least, it was the result of raiding.

In the late tenth and early eleventh centuries, Pisa and Genoa were still threatened by Muslim raids. Nevertheless, their economic and naval expansion is nowadays considered already to have begun. A short time later, in any case, they were to prove their strength in the difficult struggle against the *malik* of Denya and the Balearic Islands, Mujahid, whom they conquered in 1021. Henceforward the Pisan navy engaged in vigorous bellicose activity, in parallel with and complementary to the mercantile and diplomatic activity being pursued by the city's civil inhabitants. The Pisans sometimes set forth in the company of the Genoan navy, sometimes without them; the race for control of the Tyrrhenian Sea had begun. Documents in the State Archives in Pisa show that relations with Muslim principalities along the north coast of Africa were good from an early date. The monk Donizone, the scholarly biographer of Matilda, expressed his horror when in the mid-eleventh century the port of Pisa was visited by African *tetri*.

Fighting alternated with interludes of peace. In 1034 the Pisans attacked the Algerian city of Bône; in 1063–4 they attacked the port of Palermo. With the proceeds of this raid they began building their cathedral, whose shape and proportions, like those of the nearby baptistery of Bonanno, were based on accurate measurements taken from the church of the Holy Sepulchre in Jerusalem and the church of the Nativity in Bethlehem. The attack on the port of al-Mahdiyah took place in 1087; little importance was given to this attack by contemporary historians because of a report by a Norman ill-wisher who was close to Roger I, the conqueror of Sicily. Roger did not condone too many disputes with the Muslims in case it spoilt his good relations with Egypt and the North African potentates, and he declined Pisa's proposal that he participate in the attack. Today the full importance of this episode has been appreciated, and it is seen as much more than a straightforward retaliation to a commercial snub or a corsair raid. With Mazara, Al-Mahdiyah was the premier port of call on the east–west route across the Mediterranean between Almeria and the Nile ports. This gives some idea of how high the stakes were.

In fact, it appears that the expedition, which was unusually generously equipped with material, men and ships, was the subject of lengthy preparations and was carried out with the agreement of Pope Victor II. Indulgences similar to those bestowed by Alexander II before Barbastro were granted by the Pope to those taking part. Although Pisans predominated, the fleet represented a coalition with the people of Genoa and Amalfi, and others; Benedict, Bishop of Modena, seems to have played an important role. Was he representing the Pope? It is more likely to have been his membership of the entourage of Matilda of Canossa that gave him political weight. A poetic composition from Pisa, which seems to be a reliable source of historical information, makes reference to the *signum* of St Peter on the *scarsellae* worn by the sailors, which may have been similar to the *signa super vestes* worn to indicate that a vow of pilgrimage had been made; it may also have had a connection with the papal offer of indulgences. This would lend weight to the evidence of a chronicle from Cassino, which describes the Pope handing his *vexillum* to the fleet, according to a custom that came back into practice with the reforming Popes, but which pre-dates by a decade Pope Urban II's gesture – considered epoch-making – in Clermont (a town on the road to Santiago) in Auvergne, when he gave the *signum crucis* to all those who had accepted his request to go the assistance of the Eastern Christian Church when it was threatened by the infidel.

The Pisans joined the 'first crusade' somewhat late, sending an expeditionary force which left the coast of Tuscany in the spring of 1099 and arrived at the Syrian port of Laodicea the following September, by which time Jerusalem had already been taken. Although the fleet was carrying the new papal legate – Daimbert, Archbishop of Pisa – they lingered on the way, stopping to loot a few Byzantine islands; it is difficult to believe these raids were purely opportunistic. The Venetians joined the fray even later, waiting until the crusade looked as if it might disturb their monopoly over relations with Byzantium and Alexandria. As soon as the crusade was over, the Pisans, the Genoese and the Venetians began competing to establish commercial colonies in the coastal towns of Syria, Lebanon and Palestine. A few years later, in 1113–15, the Pisans joined forces with Ramon Berenguer III, Count of Barcelona, and took part (without the Genoese this time) in a short-lived conquest of the Balearics. This gave rise to another Pisan celebratory piece, the *Liber Maiorichinus*. Once again, the Pope presented the leaders of the attack with a *vexillum*.

The Christian occupation of the Balearic Islands did not last long. The episode could nevertheless be regarded as the culmination of the phase begun in the Mediterranean by the Muslim conquest of Ifriqiya. As always in history, however, a climax is also a point of departure. Apart from a few isolated incidents, very few Saracen sails were to be seen henceforward (until the sixteenth century) in Mediterranean waters west of the Sicilian Channel.

The conquest of Sicily by the Norman Roger I de Hauteville, the younger brother of Robert Guiscard, was made possible (as had happened in Spain) by the collapse of the emirate of Palermo; this was followed by disorder and confusion amongst the petty potentates of Sicily, until one of them, Ibn al-Thummah, who controlled the area between Catania, Noto and Syracuse, appealed to the Normans for help. Although Messina was captured almost immediately, in 1061, the conquering army's progress across the island was fairly slow, in spite of the fact that, according to Western sources (although it is not easy to place much confidence in them) the Christian population was in favour of the new arrivals. In 1063 the victory of Cerami, due in part to the appearance of St George in full armour to support the Normans, gave new courage and enthusiasm to the invaders. These were two portentous years for the Christian armies: the Pisan attack on the port of Palermo, the Barbastro expedition and the conquest of Coimbra. It was not until Guiscard, who was fighting the Byzantines in Apulia, got the better of his opponents in 1071, and fresh troops were taken to Sicily from the mainland, that the Saracens eventually suffered a defeat. Palermo was besieged in August 1071 and fell to its attackers the following January. The victors entered the city without loss of life and the great mosque was transformed into a temple dedicated to the Virgin Mary.

The conquest of the island nevertheless proceeded quite slowly, in spite of the reign of terror instigated by the Normans. Once he was the overlord of Sicily, Roger made an effort to be on good terms with his Muslim subjects; this included guaranteeing the continuation of their relations with their neighbours across the Channel. In fact, there was no other option but to live side by side: at the time of the Norman conquest, the island was almost entirely inhabited by Berber Arabs and by an arabized indigenous population who had converted to Islam. Only in Palermo and in a few restricted areas of the north-east were there Greek Christian communities of any size. During his military campaign, Roger I had assured the islanders that they would have freedom of worship. He introduced large numbers of Saracens into his army. At the same time, however, he was planning to repopulate the island with Latin Christians; when he felt a little more secure, he deliberately changed his attitude towards the Muslims, becoming much more severe. There were certainly Arab officials who continued in their jobs throughout the Norman period, some of them even in the *diwan*, the office from which taxation was organized.

# 4

# The Role of the Holy City

### Al-Quds

In the early years of the seventh century there was a terrible crisis in the Near East. In the year 614 the Persians conquered Syria and destroyed the great basilicas of Jerusalem. *Basileus* Heraclius managed to recapture the city: in 629 he marched into Jerusalem, barefoot, carrying the relics of the True Cross which King Khosrow II, the Great, had carried off triumphantly to Ctesiphon and which he, Heraclius, was now returning.

The Arab-Muslim offensive was launched from the Arabian Peninsula immediately after the death of the Prophet Mohammed in 632; it was able to turn the crisis existing between the two empires to its own advantage. In the space of a few years it had absorbed the Persian Empire and put Byzantium under severe pressure; as we know, the Muslims reached the walls of the Byzantine capital.

The indefatigable Heraclius led his troops eastward again, hoping to put a stop to the Arab advance. As had happened in 614 at the time of the Persian assault, all those who were dissatisfied with the heavy yoke of Byzantine rule, from Jews to heterodox Christians, joined forces with the Arabs. This time an element of passionate religious enthusiasm had found its way into the attacking armies, and many Christians converted to Islam. The inexorable driving force, therefore, behind the Islamic conquests in Syria, Anatolia, North Africa and Spain could be said to have been conversion. Heraclius attempted to stop the Arabs on the river Yarmuk, but when he realized the difference in the size of their armies he withdrew, taking with him the True Cross and other relics from Jerusalem. After withstanding attack for two years, Jerusalem at last opened its gates to the Prophet's successor, Caliph Umar ibn al-Khatthab, in 638.

Dressed in the garb of a humble nomad, with a patched cloak, the caliph met Patriarch Sophronius on the Mount of Olives; then, riding an old camel, he entered the city with the patriarch, after having given him assurances that the lives and property of the Christian population would be respected and their holy places left intact. He visited the church of the *Anastasis*, leading prayers outside the building to prevent the Muslims claiming ownership of the church. He next asked to be led to the Temple, and was saddened to see it being used as a rubbish dump. Assisted by his companions, he began to clean it with his own hands (other sources claim that he also enlisted the help of the patriarch). They laboured until the sacred rock of the *Moriah* appeared from underneath the thick layer of filth, then they covered the rock with a simple wooden oratory.

The Muslims called (and still call) Jerusalem *al-Quds*, 'the Sacred': they consider its central and most sacred place to be the rock of the *Moriah* where, according to Jewish tradition (which was accepted without demur by the Christians but is hotly contested by Islam), Abraham offered his son Isaac as a sacrifice to God, an angel appeared during a great plague at the time of King David and, finally, the Ark of the Covenant was located: in other words, this was the *Sancta Sanctorum* of the Temple built by Solomon. (In the opinion of others, the rock served as a plinth for the sacrificial altar.)

According to a tradition described in the seventh *sura* of the Koran (the *sura* of the *Night Journey*), one night in the year 619 the Prophet Mohammed was transported from Mecca to Jerusalem: he set off on his ascent to heaven from the rock of the *Moriah*, riding on his human-headed horse al-Buraq.

On the rock of Abraham, where the oratory built by Umar used to be, Caliph Abd al-Malik ordered the construction of the building correctly called *Oubbet as-Sakhra*, 'the Dome of the Rock', in 687. The Muslims responsible for commissioning the building probably employed local craftsmen, but their architects were definitely from Damascus (and therefore of the Byzantine school); with its glorious gilded dome, the building still seems to dominate Jerusalem. The architects drew their inspiration for the dome from the cupola of the *Anastasis*, the basilica built by Constantine in the fourth century in the place where the Calvary and Holy Sepulchre had been located, and they aimed to rival it in size.

South of the Great Mosque, and also built on the level area called *Haram esh-Sharif*, is the mosque named *al-Aqsa* ('the Distant One'), the name given to Jerusalem in the Koran. *Al-Aqsa* is built against the Royal Gateway of the Herodian era; with its seven naves in the Byzantine style and its silver domes, it completes the splendid group of Muslim religious buildings. The construction of the mosque and its subsequent alteration took several centuries, from the Umayyad to the Ayyubid periods (the seventh to the thirteenth centuries).

The Jewish *aliyah*, or ascent to the Temple, brought pilgrims flocking to Jerusalem, and the city was also the focus of a pilgrimage undertaken by followers of Jesus. The practice of pilgrimage may already have existed in Judaeo-Christian communities, for whom the ascent to the Temple helped them remember the Messiah; it was certainly well established by the second century and possibly earlier (it may have been established immediately). Between the fourth and fifth centuries it was sanctioned by the Christian emperors. Tradition holds Empress Helena responsible for the *inventio*, the discovery of the True Cross and the other relics of the Passion. From that time forward, innumerable Christian sanctuaries were established in Jerusalem and all over the Holy Land, and they attracted pilgrims in large numbers.

For Sunni Muslims, *al-Quds* is the third Holy City of Islam, after Mecca and Medina, and it is also one of the most important religious sites for Shiites. Although the pilgrimage to Jerusalem is not obligatory in Islam, it is strongly recommended. At certain times, for example when Mecca could not be reached for political reasons, a pilgrimage to Jerusalem was suggested as an appropriate substitute for the great *haj* to the city of Kaaba.

When the Muslims took possession of Jerusalem, they had the firm intention of respecting the Jews and the Christians. As 'people of the Book', these non-Muslims had the right to their own forms of worship, although with some limitations. From the seventh century to the early eleventh century, life in Jerusalem proceeded peacefully in the main. The Christian pilgrims continued to visit their holy places undisturbed (the many surviving accounts in Latin of the journey testify to this). The partition of the city into quarters was under way, organized so that members of different faiths could live near their sanctuaries. The Muslims occupied the northeastern and central areas, around the *Haram esh-Sharif*. The Greek Christians settled in the north-west, in the area overlooking the basilica of the *Anastasis*; the Western Christians seem to have established hostels in the same area from about the ninth century. The Armenians and Georgians settled in the south-west, near Sion and around their large, beautiful and highly venerated church of St James. The Jews huddled together in the south of the city, between the Eastern Christians and the 'western wall' of the Temple enclosure. Apart from the period of occupation by the crusaders, between 1096 and 1187, this ethno-religious partition of the city has been respected throughout innumerable conflicts, at least until the Arab–Israeli wars of 1948–67.

The Christian pilgrimage resumed after an interruption enforced by a long period of war during the first half of the seventh century. Apart from a few trivial incidents, no obstacles were put in the way of the Christian pilgrims. If there was a problem, it was the irregularity and infrequency of naval contacts, which seemed to exist on the Middle East's sole behalf (as far as Western Europe was concerned); all boats were bound for Southern Italy.

The general attitude towards pilgrimage changed, meanwhile, perhaps in response to the upsurge of Celtic 'itinerant' monasticism and its practices with regard to penance, which by now had spread to the continent. After the wave of enthusiasm connected with the building of Christian Jerusalem, another phase was beginning, one that was closely bound up with penitential discipline. A pilgrim was regarded primarily as a repentant sinner, whose rights and duties were clearly and carefully laid down by the Church. The wandering monks making their way to and from Jerusalem became increasingly indebted, because of their need for assistance and security. All along the way, particularly in Italy, there were hostels and minor sanctuaries where it was possible to gain indulgences and obtain hospitality. If the descriptions of the church of the *Anastasis* at this period are compared with descriptions written before the Persian invasion, it becomes evident that the building suffered immense damage, but that repairs were carried out swiftly. On the other hand, a pilgrim (a monk by the name of Bernard) noted in 870 that a hostel had been opened for pilgrims of the Latin rite (and Latin speakers) near the Holy Sepulchre; this seems to have been the hostel inaugurated at Charlemagne's wish and with the permission of the Caliph of Baghdad, Harun ar-Rashid. It was built at the same time as the church of St Mary, called the *Latina*, and was staffed by monks from the adjacent Benedictine monastery; it was situated a little to the southeast of the church of the Sepulchre.

The internal battles within Islam did not spare the Holy City for very long. As well as the fragmentation of the caliph's power, dynastic struggles and hostility between Sunni and Shiite Muslims, there is also a geo-historical element all over the Middle East and the so-called fertile crescent which crops up at (irregular) intervals and which we are familiar with from the Bible. The area lying between the Eastern Mediterranean and Jordan, Lebanon and the Red Sea is an area of frontiers and of slow-moving caravans, usually the subject of a dispute between whoever is in power in Syria and Mesopotamia and whoever is in power in Egypt. This long-running dispute crops up again at the end of the tenth century, when Egypt was the centre of the Fatimid dynasty. Jerusalem quickly fell to the Shiite Caliphs of Egypt; one of these caliphs, al-Hakim (held to be the founder of the Druse sect), began a campaign of persecution which was aimed at Jews and Christians as well as at Sunni Muslims. He closed synagogues and churches, emptied monasteries and banned pilgrimages. Finally, in 1009, he ordered the destruction of the church of the *Anastasis* and of the small building of the Sepulchre beneath the dome. The caliph's orders were sketchily and badly carried out, possibly because they were opposed by the Muslims of Jerusalem, who were mainly Sunni. In addition, the suspension of pilgrimages was an economic disaster. The buildings were damaged, however, and archaeological excavation has proved that the damage was extremely severe.

Once the whirlwind that was al-Hakim had passed, the same Muslim authority requested that the damaged buildings be rebuilt and pilgrimages resumed. Constantine Monomachus, the Emperor of Byzantium, who was considered to be the natural protector of the local Christians (called Melchites or 'people of the king', from the Arabic word *malik*, the translation of the Greek word *basileus*, 'emperor'), took over the restoration of the Holy Sepulchre. By the middle of the eleventh century the sacred building had been completely restored. Between 1030 and 1040 the people of Amalfi, who for many years had been a powerful and welcome mercantile presence in Jerusalem, restored Charlemagne's old hospice; now the hospice and some new churches occupied a well-organized area known as *Muristan* ('hospice') south-east of the Sepulchre.

It is possible that the local Christians, and pilgrims in particular, suffered further harassment; as Palestine passed alternately between Fatimid and Abbasid rule in the eleventh century, the Caliphs of Baghdad used Seljuk Turkish militia, who were newcomers to Islam and somewhat heavy-handed. Tales of violence and theft often reached the West, but these stories may in fact have been a kind of *a posteriori* explanation for the crusade, an etiological-cum-legendary excuse. The accounts of skulduggery and visions by Peter the Hermit, a pilgrim to Jerusalem, come under this category; they are assumed to have been used by him, on his return to Europe, to encourage people to join the holy enterprise. There were dangers awaiting pilgrims and travellers, in Jerusalem as anywhere else; the areas surrounding the city were turbulent, there were brigands and bandits everywhere and, in order to reach Jerusalem and the church of the *Anastasis*, tolls often had to be paid. In spite of all this, in the second half of the eleventh century pilgrimages started again, in fact becoming more numerous and more frequent than they had been before, and often being accompanied by an armed escort. Conditions on the journey were evidently not so bad as to discourage travel and pilgrimages altogether.

## The Crusade

In Western Christianity, fear and anxiety connected with the end of the world, in addition to far-reaching environmental and social changes due to an increase in population and to political and religious strife, made people turn their thoughts with increasing intensity towards Jerusalem, where the human race was supposed to meet its end: according to the pseudo-prophets, the last Christian emperor would surrender the vestiges of his power in Jerusalem, handing over his role as vicar general to the Lord of the End of the World. The prophets predicted that Christ's second coming would be preceded by the advent of the Antichrist.

In 1033, the millennium of the Death and Resurrection of Christ, apocalyptic anxiety was reawakened and droves of worried believers made their way to Palestine. The existing good relations with Fatimid Egypt were not sufficient to assuage the conscience of Western Christians, who were horrified by the sight of their greatest treasure, the Holy Sepulchre, in the care of the infidel. Whilst the whole of Christendom, from the Emperor of Byzantium to the Dukes of Normandy, was contributing to the reconstruction of the basilica, which had been profaned and destroyed in 1009, pilgrims in ever-increasing numbers took to the road in the hope of being present at the end of the world somewhere near the valley of Jehoshaphat. The imminent end of the world spread successive waves of fear throughout Europe. Scholars bent their heads over astronomical calculations and scriptural exegeses, pondering the end of the world with mounting fervour. In 1065, a year in which the date of the Incarnation and Holy Saturday both fell on 25 March, coinciding (according to some calendars and some traditions) with the date of the Creation, a group of pilgrims left Germany with the aim of reaching Jerusalem in time for the Day of Judgement. The enthusiasm with which Europe greeted Pope Urban's appeal in 1095 is difficult to comprehend unless one remembers these facts, and unless one is familiar with the long history attached to the spiritual significance of pilgrimage.

In November 1095, in Clermont, Pope Urban II certainly did not preach a 'crusade', since this was a term that arrived in the Latin and vernacular languages of Europe at a much later date. In his sermon he again deprecated the violence that was staining Christianity with blood, and appealed to the knightly aristocracy – of France in particular – to respond to the request being made to the West to come to the assistance of the beleaguered Eastern Church. This meant enlisting as a mercenary in the military campaign that was being waged against the Seljuk Turks by *basileus* Alexius I Comnenus in the Anatolian Peninsula. Engagements of this type were common in the eleventh century; the Norman troops had often agreed to take part and their assistance in Asia, after the disastrous defeat at Manzikert, was much appreciated. These Western border fighters, who often acquired a somewhat ambiguous identity, enabling them to function as mediators between Christianity and Islam and between different cultures, were not very different from the mercenary-adventurers populating Spain at the time (El Cid Campeador was their most illustrious example); or from the Byzantine warriors described in the epic poem *Dighenis Akrites*; or from the *boghatyry* who, although fighting the pagans on the Steppes in the Russian *Bylyne*, were familiar with their customs and characteristics; or from the hero of the *Knight of the Tiger Skin*, the great Georgian chivalric romance by the national poet Chota Rustaveli; or, finally, from the Turkish *ghazi* of Anatolia.

Between 1095 and 1096 the aristocracy of Europe responded to the appeal made by Pope Urban II in a most unexpected fashion. The knights who took part in the expedition have variously been called *déracinés*, fortune seekers or *milites*, stripped of their rightful heritage by feudal natural selection (which operated to maintain the cohesion of family lineages) and forced to lead the life of an adventurer. This was a stock theme, which was powerful enough to set in motion shortly afterwards the whole complex mechanism of chivalric romance; in romance, the genuine forms of the *aventure* (which, although not always very chivalrous or dignified, reflected the reality of service as a mercenary soldier in the crusade) were sublimated and idealized. In fact, the leaders who organized the departure of several thousand warriors for Constantinople and places beyond in Asia (once agreement had been reached with the *basileus*), and who included in their number an unknown (but certainly high) percentage of *pauperes* wishing to make the pilgrimage to Jerusalem, were anything but the drop-outs of aristocratic society of the day. They included princes such as the Marquis of Provence, who ruled over a large area of Southern France, the Duke of Normandy, brother of the King of England, the Duke of Lower Lorraine and the Count of Flanders, who between them controlled most of the populous areas near the lower reaches of the great rivers that run into the North Sea from France and Germany; and the eldest son of Guiscard. The upper echelons of the aristocracy were certainly in crisis at the time, either because of disputes with relatives or with awkward neighbouring powers, or because over the preceding years they had chosen to support the losing side in the conflict between the papacy and the Holy Roman Empire. This aristocracy wanted and needed a change of scene for a year or two – or for ever – and wished to discover, in the words of the Apocalypse, 'new skies and a new land', to amass riches and power elsewhere. This exodus of *domini* and *milites* fostered, among other things, the birth of a Europe of great feudal monarchies.

This great crowd of armed warriors and pilgrims, called the *cruce signati* after the symbol of pilgrimage and penitence given them by Urban II at Clermont (it was also the symbol of the spiritual indulgences and temporal privileges accorded them by the Pope), crossed Anatolia and Syria in a march that took two long years and was fraught with vicissitudes and unspeakable suffering. They finally attacked Jerusalem between the spring and early summer of 1099, capturing the city on 15 July of the same year. The city wall was breached at its most vulnerable spot, on the northeastern side; the 'Franks' (as the Byzantines, Eastern Christians, Jews and Saracens called the Westerners) rampaged through the city, massacring nearly all its Jewish and Muslim inhabitants. If the Saracen governor had not expelled the Eastern Christians from the city before the attack (he did not trust them), they would probably have met with the same fate because it is doubtful whether the Western assailants would have managed to recognize them. The city was repopulated by the Eastern Christians who had been expelled and by Syrian and Armenian Christians. Muslims and Jews were banned from staying in the city, at least at the outset.

Although no irrefutable proof exists, it has been suggested that the plan of the Western Christians who had captured the Holy City might have been to set it up as an ecclesiastical dominion, or to hand it over to the Church of Rome's rule. A Latin patriarch was appointed forthwith (it was considered inadvisable to appoint a Greek prelate since the two Churches had been in schism for the past forty-five years); the military leaders, after a period of disagreement, finally chose as their leader an ailing prince who was lacking in energy and wielded no real authority. This was Godfrey of Bouillon, Duke of Lower Lorraine; it was he who claimed (it may have been suggested to him by a member of the clergy) that he should not 'wear a golden crown in the place where Christ was crowned with thorns'. In other words, he was elected as *Advocatus Sancti Sepulchri* rather than as king; Bouillon was lay procurator for the day-to-day management of the church of Jerusalem, whose patriarchal seat was the Basilica of the Holy Sepulchre. When Godfrey died in 1100 his brother Baldwin of Boulogne was crowned king, although it was not clear on what authority a king could be appointed. This was how the 'Frankish kingdom of Jerusalem' came about: an elective monarchy with intermittent dynastic characteristics, whose crown could pass down the female as well as the male line.

Eight kings succeeded one another in Jerusalem before the Muslims, having finally recovered from the shock they had received when the city was captured in 1099, retook the city. After the battle of Hattin, near

Lake Tiberias in Galilee in July 1187, the Emir of Syria and Egypt, Yusuf ibn Ayyub Salah ed-Din (the 'Saladin' of the Western chronicles), took back the Holy City in October of the same year. The history of the kings and kingdom of Jerusalem continued after that date, but action shifted to the coast where the crusaders were still in occupation. The court took up residence in the magnificent stronghold of Acre.

The crusader kingdoms of Jerusalem and Acre, like some of the 'crusader' principalities of Spain, have sometimes been described as early experiments in colonialism. The kingdom's real power, however, was to be found in cities where the preponderant influence was the 'commercial colonies' from the coastal towns of Italy – Genoa, Venice and Pisa; the violent enmities existing between the cities on the mainland (or they may have originated in Jerusalem) kept these settlers at each other's throats. The trading cities on the coasts of Syria and Palestine (Beirut, Tyre, Acre, Haifa, Caesarea, Jaffa and Ascalon) were important because it was here that the caravans that linked the Mediterranean shores with Central Asia and the Silk Route, via Damascus, Aleppo and Mosul, arrived. The Italian merchants residing in these ports had access to the most valuable oriental product – spice – and could monitor and control the European markets. It was not until the thirteenth and fourteenth centuries that attempts were made to penetrate the continent of Asia; these coincided with Mongol expansion and brought peace to the area thanks to the missionary zeal of the Latin Church in these parts.

The relatively brief life of the crusader kingdom of Jerusalem, between the twelfth and thirteenth centuries (with its capital in Acre between 1197 and 1291), was complicated by the presence of a number of 'separatist' (either in form or in substance) bodies which prevented the crown from exercising power. These separatist bodies included seigneuries with extensive legal immunity, self-governing commercial communities like miniature municipalities and, finally, the military Orders. The latter were religious organizations with their own rule, each harbouring a qualified nucleus of warriors who made a vow to defend the Holy Land and pilgrims: the Templars, the Hospitallers of St John of Jerusalem, and the Hospitallers of St Mary, known as the 'Teutonic Order' because membership was open to Germans only. The continual disputes between seigneuries, commercial communes and military Orders contributed strongly to the disintegration of the kingdom. In spite of this, however, it should be remembered that as time passed a culture of compromise and dialogue developed with the Muslim milieu. In fact, the soldiers and pilgrims disembarking from Europe were scandalized by this society of *poulains*, 'crossbreeds', whose population was often crossed with Syrian and Armenian families, who spoke Arabic, Armenian and Greek and who dressed, ate and lived according to local custom. The Western visitors found 'colonial' crusader society corrupt and almost entirely Islamic; they imagined that every crusading expedition would be a struggle to the death. On the other hand, the 'overseas Franks', who had over the past two centuries required the periodic assistance of their European brothers and co-religionists, considered the visitors as uncouth and dangerous, and in general preferred to make diplomatic agreements with the Saracens rather than receive military assistance sanctioned by papal decree and led by princes and adventurers hungry for plunder and resistant to any kind of conciliation, or advice on tactics or logistics.

An intelligent Syrian-Arab writer, Usama ibn Munqidh, Emir of Shaizar, who lived in the mid-thirteenth century and travelled extensively in the crusader kingdom of Jerusalem, both on diplomatic missions and on social visits to friends, has left in his memoirs a vivid, eye-witness account of a society in which there was a very clearly defined difference between those already accustomed to oriental manners, who felt extremely comfortable there, and those (whether soldiers, merchants or pilgrims) who reckoned to stay only a short time and who did not succeed in adapting to local manners or to the local mentality. Usama is very helpful in identifying as the cause of the region's many problems what would today be defined as ethnocentricity and a clash of cultures. For instance, he describes a visit he made to the sacred enclosure of the Temple in Jerusalem, the *Haram esh-Sharif*. Although now occupied by Franks, the Temple was not forbidden to Muslims (or at any rate to Muslims of standing); they were allowed to enter and to say prayers there. The Templars, whom Usama describes as his friends, now occupied the *al-Aqsa* mosque, which had become part church and part military quarters. They invited Usama in as usual to pray according to the Muslim rite in an oratory adjacent to the building. They apologized profusely when a Christian fanatic, probably newly arrived from Europe, disturbed his devotions by shouting at him to pray in the Christian manner.

All this may alert us to a feature of life that was very important to Western culture. Accusations of sympathy for the Muslims, or even complicity with them, were part of a package of rumour and calumny that was in circulation, particularly in the latter half of the thirteenth century, and was directed against the Templars. During the case brought against the Order between 1307 and 1312, at the instigation of Philip IV of France, 'proof' of their heretical beliefs is said to have emerged; the 'proof' seems to have varied from allusions to Islam to the reiteration of old anti-gnostic and anti-Cathar charges. Even the idol they were accused of worshipping, 'Baphomet', had a name that sounded just like one of the various versions (in Latin or in the vernacular) of the name of the Prophet. The proof was ridiculous and inconsistent with the truth, but this was really of no importance since the trial was patently a political stunt. Those standing accused of heresy and attachment to Islam probably behaved with deliberate coarseness, partly in order to feed the curiosity of French public opinion about the affair (and in the early fourteenth century it is already possible to speak of public opinion in cities like Paris), and partly to bring home to the Pope that, as far as the condemnation of the Temple was concerned, the king would not have yielded to, nor even heeded, scruples of any kind; any attempt at defence or mediation was doomed to failure.

In the twelfth and thirteenth centuries, in any case, crusaders from Europe generally paid scant attention to the opinions of the 'overseas Franks', and this was one of the principal reasons for the failure of the many crusading expeditions that followed the first one. In cultural terms, the tendency today is to modify the impression of sterility conveyed by the kingdom of Jerusalem. The centres from which Arab scholarship found its way into Western culture were undoubtedly those in Spain; although there were centres on the coast of Syria and Palestine, for example Damascus, the area counted as a provincial part of the Islamic world. The *scriptoria* of Jerusalem, Acre and Tyre had a respectable output, but it is only in recent years that scholars have learned to recognize this and to give their output the credit it deserves. Another important centre of culture was the kingdom of Cyprus, which came into being at the end of the twelfth century and was governed by the Lusignan family. The Lusignans also had to adapt to continuous conflict between the municipalities in the Italian coastal cities and between the rival orders, the Templars and the Hospitallers.

The importance of Jerusalem in the Christian world, however, the symbolic and spiritual standing that made it irreplaceable, and the familiarity and respect that had developed for the city in Christendom thanks to travel and pilgrimages, meant that it played a fundamental role in generating the reciprocal awareness that grew up (whether it was amicable or not) between Europe and Islam.

### From the Ayyubids to the Mamelukes

Saladin's vast personal empire did not survive for long after his death in 1193. His descendants split the empire between them, giving new impetus to the geo-historical constant that was a feature of life in the Near East, namely, tension and rivalry for control of the area by the person governing Syria (or Mesopotamia) and the person in power in Egypt. The sultans of the Ayyubid dynasty, descendants of Saladin, divided the two regions between them: Jerusalem belonged to the Ayyu-bid of Cairo, al-Malik al-Kamil, who appears to have inherited many of Saladin's good qualities. Intelligent, moderate and true to his word, he is famous for an encounter with St Francis of Assisi which seems genuinely to have taken place, although Western sources treat it as if it were legend (there are comparable accounts in Muslim sources); he is also celebrated for having negotiated a truce with his neighbour and diplomatic/political counterpart, Emperor Frederick II who, although he was leading a crusade, was ruler of Sicily and Southern Italy and it was in his interest to maintain friendly relations with Egypt. He and Frederick also had some scientific interests in common.

The truce arranged by the sultan with Frederick in 1229 stipulated that all military fortifications in the Holy City be dismantled, that the Christian holy places be returned to followers of Christ and that the Muslim holy places in the *Haram esh-Sharif* be controlled by Muslims. This admirably equitable solution was confirmed in 1240–1 by Richard of Cornwall, brother of the King of England and another apparently peace-loving crusader.

The weakness of this solution, which has often been quoted as a model of diplomatic wisdom, was, however, its fragility. The agreement was based on the persistence of good diplomatic relations between the Christian powers in the Holy Land and the Ayyubid sultans in Cairo. The Christians, however, enjoyed relations that were far from peaceful, and matters were complicated by external events such as the Mongol advance throughout Central Asia. Because of this threat, some felt it appropriate to enter into alliance with the Ayyubids of Damascus; this disturbed the pattern of political relations and elicited counter-measures from the ruler in Cairo – one measure was the recruitment of about ten thousand mercenary soldiers from the Kwarezm, the area of southern Central Asia around the lower reaches of the Amu Darya, between what are now Uzbekistan and Turkmenistan. In July 1244 these mercen-aries attacked and ransacked Jerusalem, indulging in murder and dese-cration.

Meanwhile, a large Jewish community, encouraged (in the Muslim tradition) by Saladin himself, had become established in Jerusalem. This community was composed mainly of families who had fled from France and England, where restrictions and persecution were already beginning to take place. There are several instances of Jews being accused of desecrating the consecrated host, and of ritual infanticide. At the same period, and for similar reasons, many Jews were escaping (particularly from France) to Muslim Spain. Jerusalem was visited during the crusad-ing period by a number of illustrious Jewish visitors, including the great Maimonides and Benjamin of Tudela. During the Ayyubid period the organizer of Jewish culture in Jerusalem was another celebrated Spaniard, Moshe ben Nahman, known as Nahmanides.

The Kwarezmian desecration of Jerusalem in 1244 prompted Louis IX of France to act speedily and to send the crusade he had been planning for some years to attack Ayyubid Egypt. The king was beaten and taken prisoner. During his imprisonment, in 1249, he witnessed the coup d'état which overturned the sultans descended from Saladin and replaced them with a dynasty raised from a military division consisting mainly of slaves of Asian and Caucasian origin (Turks, Kurds, Circassians, Tartars); this dynasty was known, appropriately enough, as the Mameluke dynasty (from the Arabic word *mamluk*, 'slave').

The first phase of Mameluke power over Jerusalem, during which they kept tight control over the city, was military. The Mamelukes exploited the internal rivalries in what remained of the crusader dominion (and particularly the rivalry between the Venetians and Pisans, and the Genoese, and between the Templars and the Hospitallers). In 1260, the Mamelukes vanquished the Mongol/crusader coalition and began a systematic military campaign to get rid of the last 'Frankish' garrisons in Syria and Palestine. In fact, the 'Frankish' presence by this time existed only in the coastal cities and in a few fortresses occupied by the military Orders. Having succeeded by the end of the century in what they set out to do (the last crusader stronghold, Acre, fell in 1291), the Mamelukes applied themselves equally systematically to dismantling the harbour installations around the coastline, reducing agricultural productivity by encouraging depopulation and desertification, and deflecting caravan traffic. In a few decades they succeeded in impoverishing an area that had previously been thriving.

This impoverishment was the result of deliberate policy rather than neglect or mismanagement. The Mamelukes were well aware that the Christians were interested in Jerusalem for religious and political reasons, but they also knew that for at least the past two centuries, economy and trade had been linked with religion and politics as a justification for crusading expeditions. If it were possible to reduce the financial and commercial incentives, the crusades would lose a lot of their support.

In addition, as rulers of Egypt and therefore controllers of all traffic crossing the Red Sea and the Nile to reach the Nile Delta and the trading posts of Alexandria and Damietta, the Mamelukes regarded the coastline of Syria and Palestine as providing direct competition to their trade. If the Syrian ports were rendered unusable, traffic on the Nile would increase. For these tactical and economic reasons the Mamelukes were the instigators of a demographic and environmental decline which still persists; it is only in the last few decades that initiatives have been introduced to try to improve the situation.

As far as Jerusalem was concerned, the slave-rulers were attentive to Muslim needs, but they also respected the rights of Jews and Christians and behaved correctly towards pilgrims. Between the thirteenth and the sixteenth century pilgrims arrived in large numbers and shipping lines based in Venice were set up to transport them; the sultan's coffers and the purses of Muslim merchants were well-lined. The Mamelukes enhanced the appearance of the city by restoring the walls, restructuring the area of the *Haram esh-Sharif* and building a large number of madrassahs.

The Mamelukes had no hesitation in setting one subject community against another, if it were politically expedient. In fact, they acted generally with moderation, but preferred Christians to Jews; of the Christians, they liked the Franciscans best because they were supported by the Angevin rulers of Naples, who were such good neighbours to the sultans of Cairo. In 1309 the sultan gave formal permission to the Friars Minor to establish themselves in the basilica of the Holy Sepulchre, on Sion and in Bethlehem. Later, in 1333, Robert, king of Naples, acquired from the sultan ownership of the building situated immediately outside the walls south of the city, traditionally connected with the Last Supper. He handed it over to the Minorites in 1342. This marked the beginning of Franciscan custody of the Holy Land (the guardian of the Franciscan monastery on Mount Sion later became Custodian of the Holy Land), and permitted the rebuilding (in Gothic style) of the room in which the Last Supper took place. It can still be seen today. The Mameluke governors applied Muslim rules relating to the restoration of places of worship with the utmost rigour: it was forbidden for subject communities to repair or restore places of worship, and as a result many Christian churches appeared to travellers and pilgrims to be in a parlous condition (they might have appealed to the taste for romantic decay of travellers in the nineteenth century). They lent the landscape an air of desolation which can be detected in descriptions and drawings made during the sixteenth to nineteenth centuries.

During the fifteenth century, the Mameluke government began to deteriorate for reasons connected with the internal politics of Egypt. Diaries written by Western pilgrims from the mid-fourteenth century to the early sixteenth century show Jerusalem in a state of progressive abandon, with an increasingly neglectful and corrupt administration, a dwindling and increasingly impoverished population, and too enfeebled to withstand natural catastrophes such as famine, plague or earthquakes. It has been calculated that the population of Jerusalem was nearly fifty thousand in the mid-thirteenth century, but that it had dropped to about ten thousand two and half centuries later.

# 5

# Conflict and Encounters in the Twelfth and Thirteenth Centuries

## Gesta Dei per Francos

The term 'crusade' has been used sparingly so far, and an accompanying adjectival numeral has almost always been avoided. The Latin word *cruciata* – obviously retranslated from the vernacular languages – came into use relatively late; to use the word to refer to a period before the thirteenth or fourteenth century is anachronistic, although it is sanctioned by long-standing historiographic practice. Source material relating to the first crusade uses the expression *cruce signati*, but prefers terms that are more precise and more comprehensive, like *peregrini*. Military expeditions sanctioned by papal proclamation took place in quick succession until well after the thirteenth century (and were in fact still being contemplated as late as the end of the eighteenth); their aim was to bring assistance to the crusader Holy Land, or to recapture it after its fall. In fact, Popes and canon lawyers tended to proclaim each expedition as equivalent to the rescue or recapture of the Holy Land, even when the immediate aim was very different. The terms most commonly used were *iter* ('military expedition'), *via Hierosolymitana* or *peregrinatio* ('pilgrimage'). The words *auxilium* and *succursus*, which refer specifically to the urgent and defensive nature of the expedition, came later. Finally, *passagium* was a term that alluded mainly to the sea-crossing necessary to reach the Holy Land; thanks to its strong symbolic sense and evocative ring, the term was a great success and remained permanently in the vocabulary of some of the vernacular languages.

A *passagium* was *particulare* if it was organized and led by an individual or a group; its stated aims could be quite narrow, providing that the ultimate aim was the liberation of Jerusalem. Or the *passagium* was *generale* or *universale* when it was proclaimed by the papal authority and regarded as a duty for all Christians, who were invited to lend direct support as soldiers or by making a financial contribution (tithes, alms, sums paid in penance or legacies). By the middle of the thirteenth century, canonists like Henry of Sousa (better known as Cardinal Ostiense) or Sinibaldo Fieschi introduced expressions like *crux transmarina* and *crux cismarina* to distinguish between expeditions directed towards the reconquest of the Holy Land and expeditions against the Muslims and pagans (the latter including crusades in Spain and in Northeastern Europe against the Slavonic and Baltic peoples), and expeditions against heretics. A typical example of the latter is the so-called Albigensian crusade of the early thirteenth century. Later, in the early fifteenth century, there were expeditions against the Hussites, or against political enemies of the papacy such as the Swabians or the Aragonese in the thirteenth century, or the Ghibellines of Italy in the fourteenth. Finally, there were expeditions against forces considered antisocial or threatening to Christianity as a whole, such as the *Stedinger*, the peasants who rebelled against the Archbishop of Bremen and were the target in 1233 of Gregory IX's bull *Vox in Rama*; or the mercenary troops in the fourteenth century. In the twelfth century the initiative behind the crusades belonged to the sovereigns of Europe; when a succession of Popes beginning with Innocent III took over the reins, and claimed the proclamation of a crusade as their exclusive right (crusaders were able to obtain plenary indulgence for taking part), crusades became an exceptional means of exerting pressure and of organizing the legal, military and financial administration of Christianity, with the assistance of one particularly powerful tool: the doctrine of the vow. This doctrine allowed the threat of excommunication to be used against anyone who, having promised to go on a crusade, delayed or cancelled his departure; excommunication in fact constituted a kind of 'civil death'. The doctrine also allowed the objective of a vow to be changed: by paying a fixed sum of money, or by choosing another expedition that was officially declared to be of equal (theological) value, the person who had made the vow was allowed to change the goal of his crusade. As time went by, expressions such as *causa crucis* or *negotium crucis* appeared in canonical writings and councils.

These doctrinal arrangements were widely abused, and the abuses combined with the petulant, arrogant manner in which the crusades were preached (usually by the mendicant orders after the thirteenth century) gave rise to a mood of weariness and opposition – or even of furious denunciation. Except on very rare occasions, however, the denouncers were not repudiating the war against the infidel. They were almost always inveighing against the growing tendency to push the original aim of the crusades (the defence or recovery of the Holy Sepulchre) into second place, substituting for it a set of completely different aims – ones which were politically or economically more advantageous to the papal Curia. The crusades cannot anyway be regarded as wars of religion. There are no recorded claims by theologians or canon lawyers that the ultimate aim of the crusades was the conversion of the infidel, nor that suppression of the infidel could in itself be considered legitimate.

The crusade, therefore, is a single entity with many facets. It has to be understood through its internal dynamic. Although the subject of strict and consistent legislation, it consisted of a plurality of manifestations that were (in phenomenological terms) different from one another; it could change according to the changing spectrum of proposed objectives, or according to the time and context of its proclamation. The crusade is protean, a sort of white whale within Christianity: a legal and political device, a powerful and inspiring idea, an inexhaustible source of metaphor, a myth, the endless subject of apologia, censure, argument and misunderstanding; it cropped up in many different situations and was prone to unexpected revivals.

Amongst those present at Clermont in November 1095 there were a number of Spaniards; the Pope, however, had discouraged them from going East from the outset. They had their own pagan peril on their doorstep. After the defeat of Zallaqa in 1086, the King of Castile made certain that his cry of desperation was heard in Rome. In 1089 Urban II rewarded the people engaged in the rebuilding of Tarragona (they were making it a barbican against the Saracens of Spain) with the same indulgences as he had granted to the pilgrims bound for Jerusalem: this was sanctioned by the first Lateran Council in 1123. Urban may have been surprised by the enthusiasm with which his message at Clermont was received; he did not want too many of his supporters to leave for the Orient because the struggle with Henry IV had not yet reached a conclusion. He spent the three years after 1095 issuing bulls and sending forth trusted legates, in an attempt to regulate the stream of people departing for the East. He favoured and encouraged military expeditions and naval sorties from the cities along the Tyrrhenian coast, but he was strongly opposed to any departure that might destabilize society in any way – for example, departures by monks or by married people, who were enjoined to seek advice from, respectively, the abbot or their spouse; he advised the elderly and infirm against making the journey. We do not know how successful his recommendations on these matters were. He was beginning to realize that the military *iter* he had preached was in the process of merging with the streams of pilgrims who had joined the ranks between 1096 and 1097. This was partly due to a fairly familiar and generalized phenomenon, namely that the large pilgrimages of the eleventh century were frequently accompanied, at least for part of the way, by armed militia; there was, however, an additional and very disturbing reason. The massacres by pilgrims of Jewish communities along the Rhine and Danube in 1095 showed just how dangerous the millenarian ferment affecting these crowds could be; but they also demonstrated that a large pilgrimage was the vehicle for many different needs and cravings, linked to social mobility and to the religious anxieties that beset the populace during those difficult years. In conclusion, however much we feel the need to identify the 'roots' or the 'origins' of the crusade, the concurrence of events which caused it to explode, and the convergence of contributory causes, whether close at hand or distant, constituted a most extraordinary event.

The news that found its way back to Europe from the expedition to the Anatolian Peninsula between 1097 and 1098 was extremely contradictory and dubious; it was not until the Council of Bari in October 1098 that the Pope was able to gain a slightly clearer idea of what was going on along the coastline of Asia.

A Norman prince from Italy was involved in this crusade, and indeed was one of its principal protagonists. This was Bohemond de Hauteville, the eldest son of Guiscard and the nephew of the great Roger, who, as it happens, disliked him thoroughly and viewed him with the greatest distrust. He must have been pleased that his nephew was becoming embroiled in the muddle and mess in progress in Anatolia and Syria: but he had decided not to exert himself to help him or anyone who could compromise the good relations he enjoyed with the potentates of Africa. He required peace and calm to terminate and consolidate his conquest of Sicily; he had even turned down the opportunity afforded by the coalition with Mahdia in 1087. Once Roger had become overlord of the ports of Sicily, the conquest of Mahdia gave him complete control over the straits through which all the traffic between the eastern and western basins of the Mediterranean had to pass. He was aware, however, of not having the strength to sustain a conquest of such importance: it would have made him responsible for a coalition of Almoravids, Zirids and Fatimids. For the same reason, in spite of the wishes of the Pope (who had guaranteed and given legitimacy to his Sicilian venture), he had no intention of compromising his position by undertaking the *iter Hierosolymitanum*. Ibn al-Athīr, the famous Iraqi chronicler whose life straddled the twelfth and thirteenth centuries, informs us that the Frankish leaders invited Roger to take part in the expedition, offering the use of their harbours for his ships, provided he allowed them to occupy Africa. Roger had no intention of jeopardizing his good relations with his neighbours, the Zirid Emirs of Tunisia; he invited his bellicose co-religionists to turn their sights towards Syria. Writing about a century after the event, the Arab historian gives us a very different and arbitrary aetiology of the crusade: according to his account, the Franks wished to take possession of Africa, using the Sicilian ports as their base. Roger's advice, apparently, was to set their sights on Jerusalem instead. Apart from this, however, the position of the conqueror of Sicily is presented with remarkable insight.

In 1128 the Council of Troyes more or less opened the way to the creation of military-religious Orders; the fraternity of knights who assisted and protected pilgrims visiting the 'Temple of Solomon' was transformed into a proper *militia* governed by a set of rules. A succession of Popes continued to bestow the same indulgences accorded by Urban II to those departing for the East in 1095; those eligible for indulgences included anyone going to fight in Spain, or anyone combating enemies of the apostolic see of Rome *pro libertate Ecclesiae*. This latter category was established at the Council of Pisa in 1135, while the campaign against Roger II of Sicily was being waged.

*Causa XXIII* of Gratian's *Decretum*, published in about 1140, was intended to give the war a legal framework. Five or six years later, between 1145 and 1146, two different editions of Eugenius III's encyclical *Quantum praedecessores* appeared, summarizing what the Popes had compiled from decrees made by Alexander II at the time of Barbastro, and developed thereafter on the subject of war against the infidel; these formed the basis of the legal provisions relating to the crusades. Two years later, in a new encyclical, *Divina dispensatione*, the Pope referred simultaneously to the crusade in the Holy Land, the crusade in Spain (after Alfonso 'the Battler' of Aragon had reached Malaga from Saragossa between 1118 and 1126) and the crusade against the pagan group known as the Wends, who lived in Northern Europe. The expedition in Syria was a disaster, the campaign against the Slavonic Wends yielded very little, but the crusaders in Spain (including sailors from Genoa and Pisa) conquered Almeria and Tortosa.

Almeria soon fell into the hands of the Moors again. This took place in 1157, by which time al-Andalus (once the power of the Almoravids had collapsed) had already been colonized by representatives of a new, even stricter, religious movement for ten years. These were the Almohads, or *al-muwahiddin*, 'champions of the unity of God', who were by now established all over the Maghreb.

Meanwhile, the military-religious Orders had established themselves in the Iberian Peninsula, even giving rise to some local Orders (as had happened in Germany and Livonia). In general, these were modelled on the Templars. While the Templars and the Hospitallers of St John continued to predominate in Aragon, matters developed differently in Castile, León and Portugal. In 1157, when, in the presence of King Sancho III of Castille, the Templars rejected the task of protecting the castle of Calatrava, its defence was entrusted to a *fraternitas* of volunteers who were later absorbed into the Cistercian order. This marked the birth of the Order of Calatrava, the successor to similar Orders in Santiago, Alcantara and Aviz. In general the small Orders born from local circumstances were absorbed by the larger ones.


### Victory in the West, Defeat in the East

In the second half of the twelfth century the Christians began to withdraw from the confrontation with the might of Islam: in the Iberian Peninsula, the arrival of the Almohads halted the *Reconquista* in its tracks, whilst in Syria the rule of Saladin discouraged new crusades after the failure of the great expedition of 1189–93 led by Emperor Frederick I (he perished on the journey), King Philip Augustus II of France, and the King of England, Richard the Lionheart. The failure of an expedition led by all the leading Western sovereigns lent credibility to those who claimed that no crusade could succeed if it were not accompanied by the thorough purging of Christianity of its sins; it also persuaded Lotario dei Conti di Segni, who had become Pope Innocent III (1198–1216), to promulgate the right of the Pope to assume direct control of the crusading movement. Military leadership would, of course, be delegated to others.

By this time the first ferments of quite pronounced national identities – French, German and Castilian/Aragonese – were beginning to manifest themselves clearly within the *corpus christianorum* as the troops went off to the crusades. This put the 'feudal monarchies' under a certain amount of pressure. By the time of the third crusade, the insistence on these distinctions had grown so strong that the soldiers, united by a common cause and by their vows, pursued a practice that had begun during the crusade against the Wends and wore crosses of different colours on their clothes: red for the French, white for the English and green for the Flemish. The rivalry that had broken out between Philip of France and Richard of England under the walls of Acre in 1191 was only the opening chapter in a history of confrontation that was to last for centuries.

The weakest point of the pontificate of the great Pope Innocent III was, in fact, the outcome of the crusades, which had been one of the building blocks of his programme. The expedition proclaimed in 1202 concluded two years later with the capture of Constantinople by the crusaders and the Venetians, and the dismemberment of the Byzantine Empire; the Livonian crusade in the Baltic and the Albigensian crusade in Southern France achieved results which the Pope cannot have viewed with satisfaction, although he had given them his blessing at the outset; details of the 'children's crusade' in 1212 remain obscure, but its outcome was probably only of advantage to the slave traders of the Mediterranean. Only the campaign against the Almohads in Spain brought positive results.

The Almohad caliph, Abu Yusuf Yaqubal-Mansur, conquered Alfonso VII, King of Castile, in the great pitched battle of Alarcos on 16 July 1195. Only eight years had passed since the defeat of Hattin and the Muslim capture of Jerusalem: Christianity seemed to be held in a vice-like grip. This feeling of imminent danger must surely have played a part in the choice of a Pope like Lotario dei Segni, who was determined to relaunch the crusade. The Aquitanians, who had made a solemn vow to set off on a crusade to the Holy Land, were authorized to alter the vow and to make an expedition to Spain. The capture of the castle of Salvatierra by the Almohads in 1210 encouraged the Pope to launch another crusade, proclaimed this time in France. A campaign involving Kings Alfonso of Castile and Peter of Aragon, joined later by Sancho of Navarre and a quantity of knights from Spain, Portugal and France, resulted on 17 July 1212 is the great victory of Las Navas de Tolosa, between Castile and Andalusia.

By one of those strange chronological coincidences that seem to occur so often in history (and not only in the history of relations between the East and the West), the thirteenth century in the Orient witnessed the slow death of what was left of the Latin kingdom of Jerusalem, reduced by this time to a nominal (although still hotly disputed) crown, plus a constellation of seigneuries, mercantile communities and military Orders all at each other's throats. In the West, on the other hand, the *Reconquista* was once again in progress.

By now any hope of retrieving Jerusalem from the Muslims by force was fading, the more so because the recapture of the city by the infidels neither staunched nor slowed down the influx of Christian pilgrims. The crusades of 1217–21 and 1248–54 (the first to be led by Louis IX of France) were directed at the Nile ports. St Louis was taken prisoner by the Muslims in April 1250, and after his prompt release he spent at least four years on the coast of Syria-Palestine (all that was left of the crusader kingdom by this time), repairing fortifications and trying to mediate between the warring factions now dominating this languishing overseas strip of Europe.

In the meantime, many alternative solutions were sought. In 1228–9, in compliance with the truce signed by both parties, Frederick II received from the hands of the Sultan of Egypt a city that had almost been demolished and was impossible to defend. Later, between 1240 and 1290, great faith was placed in assistance from the Tartars, who had invaded and conquered large tracts of Central and Western Asia, reaching as far as Southern Russia and Persia. The whole political landscape of the Near East was about to be brutally redefined, however. In 1244 the Kwarezmian nomads entered Jerusalem, as has already been described; they found a city that had been demolished (as the truce between the Holy Roman Emperor and the Sultan of Egypt had decreed) and they expelled all Christians (about six thousand of them), killing two thousand or thereabouts in a hideous massacre which is now seldom remembered. In 1250 the Mameluke warrior-slaves who were in the service of the Ayyubid Sultan of Egypt overthrew their ruler in a surprise attack and usurped his position, swearing vengeance against the crusaders who would have preferred the old order to have remained in place. Finally, in 1258, Hulagu Khan's Mongol hordes conquered Baghdad and murdered the last Abbasid caliph. In the course of a few years the equilibrium of the 'fertile crescent' was completely disrupted.

In 1274, at the second Council of Lyon, Pope Gregory X, who had spent years in the Holy Land already as papal legate, requested that detailed memoranda should be drawn up and sent to him concerning the possibility of organizing a new and effective crusade. This gave rise to a rich and often very interesting literature *de recuperatione Terrae Sanctae*, characterized by a huge quantity of strategic advice – on tactics, geography, logistics, economics and finance. A number of the authors of these (sometimes) weighty tomes were already famous – for example, the grand master of the Order of the Knights Templars, Jacques de Molay; Pierre Dubois, Philip IV of France's famous lawyer; the Genoese admiral Benedetto Zaccaria; or the Venetian Marin Sanudo Torsello. A large number of solutions to the seemingly insoluble problem of the crusades was put forward: a siege of the Nile ports aimed at forcing the Mameluke sultans (the lords of Jerusalem) to surrender the Holy City in exchange for the lifting of the blockade; the unification of the military Orders; various ways of reorganizing the system used for raising finance for future expeditions. None of these solutions, however, could prevent the Mameluke Sultans of Egypt from destroying the remaining fortresses on the coast of the Holy Land that were still in French hands. The last one, Acre, fell as we know in 1291.

Although endowed with a complex agenda of its own, the Jubilee Year (1300) proclaimed by Boniface VIII could be interpreted as an attempt to substitute a pilgrimage to Rome for the traditional pilgrimage to

Jerusalem, with its attendant indulgences (which remained solidly in force): thus the Tomb of the Apostle would replace the Saviour's Sepulchre. In fact, during the fateful year 1300, when the pilgrimage to Rome was reaching its climax, a false rumour was circulated which claimed that the Mongols had moved from Persia and had conquered Jerusalem; they were preparing to hand Jerusalem back to the Christians. For a while this tall story was believed in Europe. But the suppression of the Order of Templars, during the celebrated (though still obscure) events that took place in 1307 and 1312, had epoch-making implications – which must surely imply that it was no accident. The Order survived the fall of Acre and, unlike the Order of St John in Rhodes, which failed to adapt to the new circumstances, the Templars were beginning to carve out a new role for themselves. Over and above the reasons behind the French king's decision to suppress it, however, and the papal Curia's endorsement of the decision, the Order of the Knights Templars seems to have outlived its usefulness, except in the Iberian Peninsula, where it managed to maintain its position in Aragon and Portugal, and where the 'suppression' was something of a *fictio iuris*.

Spain was always a case apart. The increasing tendency of the kings of Castile and Aragon to consider the *Reconquista* as an entirely Spanish affair seemed, following Las Navas de Tolosa, to have been backed by the Popes. Nevertheless, both Innocent III and Honorius III expressed the opinion that the Spanish campaign should not divert troops from the Orient. In the Iberian Peninsula, in fact, things seemed to have begun to go well again, whereas in the Mediterranean the situation was going from bad to worse. The Southern French, meanwhile, continued to take part in the Iberian campaign, whilst the routes of the crusaders heading to Syria by sea from England, the Low Countries and the Rhineland all intersected off the coast of Portugal, and the travellers would often stop and compete in the capture of one Saracen coastal stronghold or another. In addition, the Almohads reached a crisis point in the second quarter of the thirteenth century: no further Muslim auxiliaries reached the Iberian Peninsula from Africa, and the Castilians and Aragonese took full advantage of this. The Almohad Caliph al-Mamun (1227–32) needed the indirect support of the King of Castile in order to impose his authority on the remaining *taifas* of al-Andalus, and his army owed its efficiency partly to a strong presence within it of Christian mercenaries.

With constant assistance from the Spanish military Orders and the support of indulgences granted by the Pope, James I of Aragon succeeded in conquering Majorca with an expedition that lasted for two years, from 1229 to 1231, and between 1232 and 1253 in taking possession of the kingdom of Valencia. Ferdinand III, King of Castile, who, like St Louis, was later canonized, successively captured Badajoz, Jerez, Córdoba and finally Seville between 1230 and 1248. These victories procured him immense fame: he was the only Christian conqueror of Islam in a world in which Muslims and Mongols seemed everywhere to have the upper hand. However, the fact that, in 1246, the Pope authorized and even gave his blessing to a crusade organized to capture Seville (one of the largest cities of the day), whilst at exactly the same time Louis IX was putting enormous effort into preparing his great expedition into Egypt and the Holy Land, proves once again that, although the Iberian crusade represented the 'Western branch' of the whole crusading campaign, the idea that the Spanish crusade was an exclusively Spanish affair was beginning to catch on. In fact it caught on to such an extent that St Ferdinand was able to finance his crusade by drawing on the *tercias reales*, one third of the tithes collected by the Church of Castile.

By the middle of the century even Portugal was free of the Muslim yoke and a new balance of power seemed to have been achieved. Morocco was in the hands of a new dynasty, the Merinids, who conquered Marrakesh in 1269. The Merinid sultan, Abu Yusuf, had acted swiftly to reinforce (as far as was possible) the garrisons in what remained of al-Andalus. In Castile, plans were afoot for a crusade to conquer the Maghreb. Alfonso X (1252–84), however, who had succeeded his father as King of Castile, preferred to consolidate his continental conquests. He expelled the Muslims from Murcia but left the last big city in al-Andalus, Granada, in their hands. The border between Christian and Muslim Spain in al-Andalus was a very difficult one to supervise; it was here, between 1271 and 1273, that a group of Christian nobles preferred to pay feudal homage to the Moroccan sultan rather than submit to Alfonso X. On the other side, the Nazirid Emirs of Granada turned out to be unwilling to submit to the Merinid sultan, who had hoped to present himself as their last hope in the war against the Christians. In 1279 Emir Abdullah Mohammed II signed a commercial treaty with the Republic of Genoa which gave some economic advantages to the Ligurians who, as a result, established their own colony in Granada. The emir, seeking to assume an independent role internationally, was eager to adapt to prevailing circumstances.

Now that al-Andalus was encircled by Castile, the Aragonese began to feel slightly liberated and less involved in the Spanish crusade. Their former close relationship with Southern France and with the Western Mediterranean encouraged them to consider the possibility of collaborating jointly in other exploits against Islam. It was in this spirit that James I of Aragon became directly (although very cautiously) involved in preparations for St Louis' second crusade. His ship set sail from Barcelona on 1 September 1269, but was forced back into port by a storm. In December a modest contingent from Aragon appeared in Acre, but left again shortly afterwards, having achieved nothing.

The English had also promised their support to the King of France, but the departure of their contingent was repeatedly postponed. Louis weighed anchor on 2 July 1270, having already decided (for reasons which are not clear) to make a stop in Tunis before proceeding to the Holy Land. Was this a manoeuvre connected with the policy towards Africa of his brother Charles d'Anjou, King of Sicily? Unfortunately Louis died, possibly of typhoid, on 25 August 1270 on the coast of Tunisia, near the ruins of ancient Carthage. His brother Charles arrived at the crusader camp on the very day he died and ordered the expedition to retreat. Edward, son of Henry III of England, had also recently arrived in Africa; he at first agreed to withdraw to Sicily, but in April 1271 he resumed his journey to the Holy Land and landed at Acre on 1 May. He remained there for almost a year, then in September 1272 he beat a retreat, discouraged and sick. Prince Edward was the last scion of an illustrious dynasty to lead a crusade to the shores of the Eastern Mediterranean. Henceforward, in spite of the strong commitment to crusading of Popes Gregory X and Nicholas IV, most of what remained of the crusader kingdom was abandoned to the fate that finally befell it in 1291.

## Amors de terra londhana

In the early twelfth century the cleric Foucher de Chartres, who wrote an eye-witness account of the first crusade, produced a passionate paean to the wealth and *joie de vivre* of the new conquerors of Palestine, who all came from the harsher climates of Northern Europe. Foucher seems to have expressed the gratified desires and the innermost feelings of all *pieds noirs* – or, at any rate, of the few who managed it – who, through the ages, far from their native soil, over the mountains and across the sea, have found good fortune and wealth. In Foucher's poem we also find casual mention of the words 'Orient' and 'Occident', and we happen upon an Orient that is highly prized; indeed, it is something to dream about and to love, as well as something to possess. What did Europe gain from the crusades? Leprosy, replied Voltaire. What was the finest fruit of the crusades? The apricot, according to Jacques Le Goff.

Although both replies are light-hearted, there is some truth in both of them: they seem to explain the crusade as a historical and political (or 'colonial') event seen in its historical context, and from the point of view of the cultural and economic *rapprochement* between Europe and Islam.

Out of the resumption (or inauguration) of close relations that seems to have fuelled the economic, financial, technological, scientific and intellectual developments of the thirteenth century, one of the most prosperous and enlightened centuries in the entire history of the Mediterranean was to emerge.

At the root of these positive developments, which were achieved through a complex series of causes and events (of which the crusades were the military aspect), and which also contained social and religious elements (as we have seen, this was also the case with pilgrimages), we should also take account of the gradual discovery of the Other by Western Christians.

Was this discovery reciprocated? As far as knowledge of one another was concerned, Christianity and Islam did not begin from a level playing field. The Prophet himself had had contact with Christian hermits, and the earliest Muslims, except for the Bedouin tribes whose religious faith had emerged from pagan syncretism, were for the most part converted Christians. The many venerable and flourishing Christian churches in the East were a familiar sight to the Muslims; and the Eastern Christians in their turn soon showed that they knew how to cope with the new religious phenomenon. Things were different amongst the hierarchies, the monks and scholars of the Greek Church who received their first intimations of Islam indirectly, mainly from Syriac sources. It is possible that they for many years underestimated the problem of the new religion, regarding it as an eccentric and uninteresting form of barbarity. The Muslims, on the other hand, may have been familiar with, or they had certainly heard a great deal about, the *rumi*, the Byzantines, but could not conjure up much interest in the distant boorish *faranji*, with whom only the Berber Arabs who occupied Spain came into contact in the first twenty years of the eighth century. The fact that the *faranji* were Christian, however, constituted a perfectly intelligible point of reference for the Muslims.

Conversely, the Western Europeans had no clear nor reliable notion upon which to base their understanding of who these new arrivals might be, or what was their way of thinking. In the ancient Latin tradition, which had been preserved in large measure (although it was not very widespread), the *Arabes* were *molles*, effeminate and corrupt. Their country, *Arabia felix*, was the mysterious country from which spices came; it was connected with the myth of the Phoenix and the Biblical story of the Queen of Sheba. Some decades later things had certainly begun to change: Saracen raids along the coastline of Europe and in the Western Mediterranean certainly did not provide the most appropriate opportunity for amicable encounter, but they must have provided a means of gaining information. Episodes like the diplomatic missions between Charles and the *walis* of Spain or the Caliph of Baghdad, the letter written by Bertha of Tuscany to the caliph, the ambiguous relations between the Saracen corsairs and Hugh of Provence, are evidence of glints of reciprocal knowledge glancing through the curtain of ignorance – an ignorance that was, more over, reciprocal, although not equally distributed between the two parties.

An interesting example is the exchange of ambassadors and information between Pope Gregory VII, in 1076, and the Hammadid Emir en-Nasr, lord of Bugia, on the subject of the Christian community of Bugia. The Pope's words on that occasion emphasize his awareness that 'although in a different manner, both of us recognize one God and each day we praise and adore Him as Creator and ruler of the universe'.[1]

Bearing all this in mind, the picture of Islam that emerges from the texts at the time of the first crusade is at first disconcerting; it is gleaned from the epics rather than from the chroniclers, who are parsimonious with this kind of detail. The epics were compiled or collected in areas that were predominantly (or entirely) secular, and yet they contain propaganda aimed at laymen and the *illiterati*. Information about Islam was scarce, confused and incomplete amongst Western Europeans in the eleventh century; but above all it was articulated at different levels of awareness and was subject to concerted mediation which coordinated and manipulated it to suit the environment and the purpose for which it was intended. Although in a clerical environment, amongst the elite, the monotheistic nature of the Saracens, religion was well known, this knowledge was far from widespread; there are some instances of contact and direct experience, but these were few and far between.

In the oldest of the epics, the adjective 'pagan' is the one usually used to indicate the religion of those who, at different times and with many variations, are called Saracens, Hagarenes, Ishmaelites, Arabs, Moors, Berbers, Turks, Persians, 'Azopards' (Ethiopians), or names that are even more fanciful. The names of the 'pagan' heroes usually have some connection with magic or the devil: Loquifer, Agrapart, Noiron, Orgueilleux. They are rarely depicted as mere human beings, but are endowed with a ferocious, contorted kind of humanity: in general they are either superhuman, inhuman or anti-human. The pagan is often a giant, recalling an ancient tradition found in Latin classical literature and also the Biblical giant Goliath; gigantism is often the characteristic of a demon. When they are not giants, the Saracens often have a monstrous or diabolical appearance: they are black, with horns, and they gnash their teeth – aspects which were to remain in the iconography

---

[1]  Gregorii PP. VII, *Registrum*, L. III, ep. CL, ed. E. Caspar, *M.G.H., Epistolae selectae*, pp. 287–8.

for a very long time. The black skin of the 'pagans' is an important feature. It was probably the result of observing the Africans who served so frequently as slaves or soldiers, especially in Egypt and Spain. It was only later that African characteristics such as curly hair, thick lips or flattened noses came to be associated with black skin colour: the black of the 'Hagarenes' was initially based on the skin colour of the Yemenis, the Nubians and the Saharans. It certainly possessed diabolical connotations, which derived from the patristic and apologist tradition of depicting demons as Egyptians or Ethiopians. It was from this image, which quickly became established, that the word *Maurus* (indicating an inhabitant of Mauretania) acquired an ethnic dimension (the 'Moors') and also (with minor variations in neo-Latin languages and German) the dark brown of the epidermis and the hair. Even the flags attributed to the Muslims in Christian fantasy are alarming, with magical or diabolical heads of Moors, snakes, dragons or scorpions.

From time to time the pagan hosts also include Amazons (Ariosto and Tasso were to recall this) and *sagittarii*, centaurs. In the *Chanson de Roland* the emir is assisted by giants; in the *Coronemenz Louis*, a *chanson* that may be dated to the period between the first and second crusades, the Christian hero William has to do battle with the Emir Corsolt, a giant whose princedom is situated beyond the Red Sea. William has a friend and 'brother-in-arms' who is another giant, Raynard, who is naturally a good Christian but who is son of the Saracen King Deramé, which explains his enormous size. Proof of the fact that the Saracen is a devil-worshipper is provided by the amazing characters who accompany his death: crowds of demons rush forward to steal his soul when he falls in the fray. While the Christian weapons are protected by the power of relics and blessings, the Saracens owe the strength of their weapons to magic, precious stones and herbs with mysterious powers.

In the epics (and therefore in propaganda) Islam is false and wicked, and this, as we have seen, might correspond with the scholarly view of the subject. Scholars who produced apologetics or debates did not, however, rely on these tales of falsehood and evil. Epic poetry had absorbed information that was fairly vague and had amplified it and filled it with fanciful detail: the Saracens worshipped monstrous idols like the golden colossus of Cádiz, which appears in the *Chronicle* of the Pseudo-Turpin; they worshipped Mohammed as their God and included him in 'anti-trinity' blasphemy with the pagan gods of old and with divinities bearing fantastic names or names derived from a long inventory of demoniacal or pseudo-scriptural designations.

The 'pagan' ethical system was supposed to be the complete reverse of the Christian system, particularly as regards carnal pleasures: it was held that the Saracens were encouraged by their faith to commit every kind of abuse and lechery because of the atrocious morals of their religion's founder who, to avoid shame, had made such practices obligatory by incorporating them in the law. In the early thirteenth century, Jacques de Vitry was able to claim that the more cultivated and intelligent Saracens, well versed in the classics and in the Christian scriptures, would certainly have converted if they had not been forced to remain within Islam by the sexual permissiveness recommended by Mohammed. Views such as these were repeated and sanctioned with great authority by Thomas Aquinas, according to whom the Prophet had lured his flock with the promise of unbridled lust, apparently passing a law authorizing all acts of lechery. In spite of such absurdly exaggerated stories and the sometimes comical and grotesque outcomes, it would be a mistake to think of them as completely arbitrary. Sometimes at the heart of a series of bizarre assertions can be found an authoritative detail, an intuition or a submerged memory.

With regard to the devil worship practised by the Muslims, for example, the mistake may have arisen from a slight change in the meaning of certain words or concepts. Before the emergence of Islam, when the Saracens were simply the Bedouins who lived in the desert, St Jerome, who knew them well, pointed out in his *Vita Hilarionis Heremitae* that they were devoted to the cult of Lucifer. Between the fourth and the fifth centuries this still meant the planet Venus. It is common knowledge that astral cults were widespread in Arabia: the goddess Alat is identified with the planet Venus. On the other hand, it was St Jerome himself who identified the morning star, Lucifer, mentioned in the Book of Isaiah, with the leader of the rebel angels in the apocalyptic tradition. In the light of this information, it may seem less strange that (according to Nicetas of Byzantium) Mohammed imposed upon the Saracens worship of an idol whose characteristics are certainly reminiscent of Venus, but who could be adapted to fit any of the mother goddesses known and worshipped around the 'fertile crescent' and *Arabia felix* before Christianity reached the area, and whose worship, connected syncretistically to para-Biblical tradition, continued to be practised by the nomadic tribespeople.

With regard also to the demoniacal, monstrous aspect of the Saracens and the heroic, pious deaths of the Paladins, the fact that the epic hero falls in battle against creatures of diabolical mien confers an apocalyptic character on the war waged against the pagans. We are in the sphere foreshadowing the final battle between the forces of Light and the forces of Darkness, as endorsed by the intervention of the deity or of angels in the wars in Spain, Sicily and Syria. The struggle of the warrior-hero with the infidel is also an emblem of the battle to be waged with the *arma lucis* mentioned by St Paul, or of the internal conflict against sin and evil experienced by all believers in their heart of hearts. In the fourth century this *pugna spiritualis* was expressed in epic-allegorical terms by the Christian poet Prudentius in his *Psychomachia*; in language recalling the *Iliad*, the *Aeneid* and Statius' *Thebais*, Prudentius describes the battle between the pagan virtues and the Christian vices. The poem was to become a fundamental source for literature as well as for sculpture and painting in the Middle Ages. It provided one of the firmest foundations for the prestige of the medieval knight and the state of mind which motivated the crusading movement.

In the early 1340s, soon after the Council of Troyes at which the new experience of the Order of the Knights Templars within the Church was sanctioned, Bernard of Clairvaux compiled a short treatise, *De laude novae militiae*, about the Templars. After a topical comparison between the 'new cavalry' of the Templars and the secular cavalry, the latter eliciting irremissible censure for the way the chivalrous life was conducted, the Cistercian abbot dwells on the mission of the *novi milites* and, finally, on the spiritual and allegorical importance of the holy places. Along with the thorny problem of the legitimacy of killing the enemy in a context in which the legal framework of *bellum iustum* was no longer adequate (it was a debate about how a conflict could be conducted devoutly, rather than about how a war could be presented as legitimate), Bernard introduced the idea of 'malicide', although not without some embarrassment. Slaying the enemy became a necessity and therefore a duty to the extent that, objectively, the enemy is the bringer of evil and sin which cannot be checked unless the person responsible for bringing them is killed. This was a difficult contention to support, only justifiable in such exceptional circumstances as the defence of the Holy Land or the founding of the military-religious Orders: it would have been untenable (apart from its theological argument) if it had not been based on the model of the *pugna spiritualis*.

Similar themes run through the whole epic output devoted to the crusades: few *chansons* are ascribed to the twelfth and early fourteenth centuries, yet those that existed succeeded in influencing European public opinion profoundly. Many of them are based, at least in part, on myths connected with the figure of Godfrey of Bouillon. The historical inspiration of the cycle seems to be slight and very sporadic; the literature should be read with contemporary crusading propaganda in mind, since this is the spirit in which all the *chansons* were composed. Also vehicles for propaganda (and also occasionally of enthusiasm, disillusion and disappointment) are the many crusading songs which emerged from France, Spain, Germany, Italy and, less frequently, from other countries. These accompanied the crusading themes arranged so carefully by Innocent III, and endlessly repeated and renewed after the thirteenth century by preachers – mainly Franciscans and Dominicans. Surveillance by the Inquisition, economic pressure and public sermons were the weapons used by the papacy from the thirteenth century onwards to exploit the crusades in support of their own supremacy, including temporal supremacy, to influence the policy of different governments, to condition public opinion and to dampen the fervour and efficacity of heretical tendencies.

As far as the production of texts is concerned, this complex *iter* produced chronicles and hagiographies as well as literature and treatises.

The failure of the crusades to the Holy Land and the increase in opportunities for contact between Christians and Muslims gradually modified the demonizing of the Muslims by the Christians; elements of sympathy and appreciation began to creep in. In fact, even in the *chansons* and the chronicles of the first crusade, the courage and loyalty of the Muslims often earned praise, even sometimes being contrasted with the cowardliness and bad faith of the Christians. The anonymous Norman knight who was in the train of the Prince of Taranto during the first crusade, author of the *Gesta Francorum*, begins by observing how brave in battle the Turks are, referring soon afterwards to the legend according to which Turks and Franks were both descended from the Trojans and were therefore both natural enemies of the despicable, disloyal Greeks. This marks the arrival of the first stock theme in literature, used later to justify the antipathy felt generally towards the Byzantine Empire; it was to return at full strength between the medieval and the modern period. If the Turks were only to convert to Christianity, the anonymous writer concludes, no nation would be their equal.

In a Latin composition, the *Ludus de Antichristo*, issuing from a monastery in Bavaria in the 1150s to 1160s and written to celebrate the aspiration of Emperor Frederick I to fulfil the role of ruler with an apocalyptic mission, the character of *Rex Babilonis* (easily recognizable as the typification of a supreme Muslim ruler) is naturally pagan and idolatrous: yet he is presented as a reasonably magnanimous figure. He is only persuaded to submit to the Antichrist – who has deceived the whole of Christendom – by the strength of his armies. Several decades later, at the beginning of the thirteenth century, in Wolfram von Eschenbach's *Parzifal*, the figure of the pagan Feirefiz is shrouded in a fascinating aura of magic, to the extent that this has been described as the first real manifestation of exoticism in medieval culture. Feirefiz is seen in a strongly positive light, in fact, and his good looks, courage and magnanimity are all admired. At almost the same time Jean Bodel, the great poet of Picardy, composed the *Jeu de Saint Nicholas*, an extraordinary synthesis of all the prejudices and arguments of the day; it was probably written to be recited in Bodel's native Arras on the night of the feast of St Nicholas, between 5 and 6 December. It contains portraits of the *cornu Mahomet*, thus named because (like the devil) he wears a pair of horns, and the god Tervagante; there are crusaders who are 'vagabonds, profligates, dissolutes', but who die like martyrs when the time comes; the magical practices of the infidels are contrasted with the Christian miracle; and finally there are the Emirs of 'Konya', 'Orcania', 'Oliferne' and 'l'Arbre Sec', in which historical and geographical references to the first crusade merge with folklore and semi-scriptural fantasy, and with the imaginary geography borrowed from tradition based on the romances belonging to the Alexander the Great cycle: cruelty and generosity, madness and wisdom all mingle. Finally, the king and the emirs are all converted thanks to the virtue of l'Arbre Sec, who refuses to repudiate his faith, proudly reprimands his colleagues and returns the king's lands to him with contempt, denouncing him as a traitor. He does submit in the end, but against his better feelings: he is, in fact, the most attractive of all the characters.

The magical and astrological context in which Wolfram von Eschenbach places his pagan hero Feirefiz is the reflection, in a lay and only moderately cultivated environment, of the arrival (via Arabic, and at a higher intellectual level) of philosophy and science. In the twelfth and thirteenth centuries this was to change the face of Western learning. Oral and written literature and secular culture in general were given a heavy overlay of magic by the new scientific speculation and the innovations that followed: magic as in 'the marvellous'. In the Provençal story *Daurel e Beton*, composed at the end of the twelfth and the beginning of the thirteenth centuries, a young exiled prince who has been betrayed in the vilest manner by a false friend of his father is lodged for twelve years in Babylon, where the pagans extend to him the courtesy and hospitality he sought in vain in his own country. One of the many upshots of the crusades was the arrival in Europe of the oriental romance from Byzantium, and also from Georgia, Armenia and Arabia/Persia. These were the successors to the Hellenistic tales and were therefore full of long journeys and fabulous adventures. Sometimes the themes were those transmitted through Celtic folklore (which produced the typical Arthurian *féerie*); at other times, however, an oriental flavour was sought and then Islam was bathed in the magical atmosphere of India inherited from the literature devoted to Alexander the Great. This would eventually lead to exoticism. The travel literature born in the wake of missionary and merchant forays into the heart of Asia in the thirteenth and fourteenth centuries (before the fragmentation of the Mongol Empire made such journeys impracticable) gave new stimulus to this subject matter; Giovanni Boccaccio's *Filocolo* is a classic tale of oriental adventure.

Three figures stand out as symbols of the change in the Western attitude towards Islam, and of the permanence of this change. Mohammed is portrayed in a series of slanderous legends as a heretic or a sorcerer: the image never really left him. In Voltaire's play about Mohammed, the Prophet is the symbol of fanaticism and tyranny. Saladin was at first the enemy of the Cross, to the extent of being presented (like Mohammed) as a forerunner of the Antichrist; gradually, however, he progressed to being the symbol of all the virtues, in addition to courtesy and magnanimity. By the eighteenth century he had become, in the work of Lessing, the symbol of tolerance. Thirdly, there is the fascinating figure of the Shiite religious leader known as 'the Old Man of the Mountain' who, as time went by, became the *Idealtypus* of the nascent exoticism.

# 6

# The Treasure of the Pharaoh

*La belle prisonnière*

To the Fathers of the Church, the ancient *auctores* were at once a solace and dilemma. Although they were a source of wisdom, to be venerated, they were also contaminated by the absence of the light of faith. Taking their inspiration from Exodus and Deuteronomy, in the footsteps of Origen and St Jerome, they would interpret certain passages as allegories: for example, the removal of the treasure of the Egyptians by the Jews who departed with Moses in search of the Promised Land, or the story of '*la belle prisonnière*'. It was regarded as permissible, indeed just, to rob the ancients of their treasures – the truths that were scattered throughout their writings.

Could there be any truth in the writings of the Saracens, as there was in the writings of the pagan authors of antiquity? If there was, would it be permissible and just to take possession of that as well? The Saracens' sacred books had been familiar to Eastern Christians and the Mozarabs in Spain for many years; there were also books by ancient authors which had been studied and translated by the Muslims but which the Christians had lost much earlier. By the mid-twelfth century it was beginning to be realized that such treasures were worth acquiring. Towards the end of the century Daniel of Morley, an English translator from the Arabic, had managed to arrive at the theory that God ordered the New Israel (Christianity) to divest the Egyptians of their treasures in order to enrich themselves, as had happened with Moses: 'Let us therefore rob the pagan philosophers of their wisdom and their eloquence as the Lord commands and with His help; let us rob these infidels and enrich our own faith with the spoils.' 'Philosophers' was the name given by Latin scholars to the Arabs who, to the *illiterati*, were simply 'pagans' and 'infidels': Abelard himself, when challenged by Bernard of Clairvaux, threatened to take refuge with 'the philosophers' in order to preserve his liberty and his dignity.

Although the *chansons* spoke of idolatrous Saracens, and legends about the heresies of Mohammed abounded, there was never any shortage of people who understood matters more clearly. The *Historia de vita Caroli Magni et Rolandi eius nipotis*, by the Pseudo-Turpin, is a fanciful document in many respects, and it goes into the fullest and strangest detail on the subject of Saracen 'idolatry', yet it contradicts itself frequently: in one disturbing passage, the dispute between Roland and Ferracute, which was to provide another epic topos, quite inaccurate theological information is provided. In fact, as early as 1120, William of Malmesbury had stated with assurance: '*nam Saraceni et Turchi Deum creatorem colunt, Mahomet non Deum sed Eius prophetam aestimantes*'.[1] Also in England, at about the same time, the *Dialogues* of Pietro Alfonsi were in circulation. Alfonsi was a Spanish Jew from Huesca, baptized in 1106, who became doctor to Alfonso I of Aragon and to Henry I of England. Thanks to this intermediary, information passed at first hand between the Iberian Peninsula and the British Isles. Pietro Alfonsi was extremely learned in matters concerning religions based on the Old Testament.

In the Iberian Peninsula the crusader ships were just setting sail for Syria. The time was ripe for one of the leading Church personalities of the day, Peter the Venerable, Abbot of Cluny, to join in an extraordinary initiative centring on Toledo, restored to Christianity only half a century previously. Raymond of Sauvetat, Archbishop of Toledo, acted as guarantor and 'Emperor' Alfonso VII of Castile backed the Abbot of Cluny's proposal. While wholeheartedly supporting the *Reconquista*, Peter the Venerable was working to improve the West's comprehension of Islam.

A team was formed which, with advice from Muslims and Jews, furnished the first translation of the Koran; the translation bears the name of Robert of Ketton in Rutland, and appears to have been prepared from a series of earlier translations (from Arabic to Hebrew and Castilian Spanish, and thence into Latin). Although the result is confused and incomplete, it was such an important step forward that this translation remained in use for the next four centuries. The translators of the Koran should not be thought of as a structured group, however: they were more likely to have been a widely scattered network of people loosely connected to one another through their studies.

---

[1] Willelmi Malmesbiriensis, *De gestis regum Anglorum*, ed. W. Stubbs, in *Rerum Britannicarum Scriptores*, Vol. XC, p. 230.

The team coordinated by Peter the Venerable did not cease their labours when the translation of the Koran was completed. Although there was intense activity in at least three centres, Spain, England and Southern Italy, the role of the Iberian Peninsula was central and vital. For years, the Islamic texts turned into Latin versions by translators such as John of Seville, Domenico Gundisalvi, Herman of Dalmatia, Plato of Tivoli or Gerard of Cremona, and the writings about Islam compiled with reference to this new material, formed the basis of the best body of knowledge on the subject of Islam available in medieval Europe. Peter may not have exploited these studies to their fullest extent, but nevertheless, as can be gathered from his two treatises, the concise *Summa totius heresis saracenorum* and the much longer *Liber contra sectam sive heresim saracenorum*, important progress was made, progress which found resonance in works such as John Damascene's *Diàlexis sarrakenù kài christianù*. (Peter the Venerable could not, however, have been familiar with the pamphlets of John Damascene, at least at the outset. They were not translated by Burgundio da Pisa until 1148–50.)

While Robert of Ketton was translating the Koran, Herman of Carinthia was busy with a genealogy of Mohammed, and Mark of Toledo, a Mozarab Christian, was translating a work of apologetics, al-Kindi's *Risala*, with the help of Peter the Venerable's secretary, Peter of Poitiers. All these different texts were assembled together to form a collection which for centuries remained the most comprehensive and authoritative body of Islamic writing in the West. It was known as the *Corpus cluniacense*, or the *Collectio Toletana*. Later, Mark of Toledo presented a version of the Koran that was even better than the previous one; and besides translating the holy book, Mark also translated from the Arabic the works of Galen, plus a controversial text probably written by a Muslim convert to Christianity, and a mystical work by Ibn Tumart, the celebrated Almohad scholar.

In many respects the character of Mark of Toledo is typical of the period. Scholars like him were not motivated solely by a love of pure knowledge: their aim was a practical one, to refute Islam. They wanted to learn more about Islamic doctrine in order to dispute it more effectively. Although this attitude is comprehensible in an area where the methods of reasoning promoted by Peter the Venerable's great friend Abelard held sway, it is less easy to see how it could bear fruit in an extreme missionary environment; in Islamic lands it was strictly forbidden to preach anything but the Koran.

The number of Muslims outside the *dar al-Islam*, however, was constantly growing: these were the inhabitants of Syria and Palestine, and the Iberian Peninsula, who had been conquered by Christian merchants and prisoners. It may have been the intention to direct missionary propaganda at them because they lived in countries controlled by Christians where such activity was possible. The infidel could not be forced to convert to Christianity, but would do so if convinced by persuasive argument. Francis of Assisi, as we shall see, provided a new example and pointed a new way: even within his Order his teaching was often in conflict with other types of attitude. Thomas Aquinas, who had devoted part of his *Summa contra gentiles* to Islam, shared Peter the Venerable's intention of participating in whatever way possible in the conversion of the Muslims. In his short *De rationibus fidei contra Saracenos, Graecos et Armenos*, he set out four propositions against Islam that were to remain the traditional way of refuting it for years. Islam was the distortion of truth; Islam was the religion of violence and war; Islam was the religion based on sexual licence; Mohammed was a false prophet.

The literature of religious controversy prospered in the thirteenth century. In the Iberian Peninsula there were works such as the *Quadruplex reprobatio* by the Dominican Ramon Martí, the faithful interpreter and executor of Ramon de Penafort's missionary project; and the *De origine et progressu Machometis* by Pedro Pascual, a friar of the Order of Mercy (the Mercedarians), who devoted his life to the liberation of Christians taken prisoner by the Saracens. In Syria and Palestine there were texts such as *De statu saracenorum* by William of Tripoli, and the *Contra legem sarracenorum* by the Florentine Dominican Ricoldo da Montecroce, who travelled as far as Baghdad and was therefore in a position to witness the beginning of the conversion to Islam of the Mongols of Persia, and the death of one of the great dreams of Western Christianity – the conversion of the Tartars to Christianity. If the latter had taken place, a grand crusade could have been mounted with the West, and the Mameluke Sultan of Egypt crushed by a pincer movement from East and West.

Meanwhile, another truth was beginning to dawn. The study of Arabic was beginning to appear increasingly necessary, not only because it was a sacred language, the language of revealed Scriptures (though whether these were widely accepted as such is another matter), but also because it was the language of an extensive culture. The leading examples of the wisdom of Ancient Greece had all been translated into Arabic; and, although these were accessible through translation from Greek (much less accessible in the West at that time, for example in the Byzantine world, than the Arabic versions available to scholars in the Iberian Peninsula), the translations into Arabic were greatly to be preferred, on account of the excellent commentaries supplied by the Arab translators and scholars, the abundance of new studies undertaken by them and, finally, because Western scholars were beginning to realize that through Arabic they could gain access (however indirectly) to the wisdom and technology of countries even further afield – from Persia to India and even China.

The Iberian Peninsula was the real home of the scientific revival in the West, and also of the propagation of one of its most important material supports. It is known that paper, which originated in China and had spread throughout Central Asia by the eighth century, was present in Muslim Spain from the tenth century. Paper mills were to be found in Toledo and particularly in Jativa, in the province of the Levante, where James I of Aragon established a kind of monopoly for the whole kingdom of Valencia. In the thirteenth century this valuable new material spread from Aragon all over the Western lands.

Scientific knowledge, diffused through the Muslim world via the language of the Holy Koran, had made a promising start in the Iberian Peninsula thanks to an earlier scholar, Gerbert of Aurillac, who had travelled to Catalonia as a very young man. Between 967 and 970, he had learned the rudiments of Arabic (and possibly Greek) arithmetic and astronomy in the bishop's curia in Vich and in the monastery of Ripoll. Having subsequently become head of the episcopal college in Reims and then Abbot of Bobbio, Gerbert was able to share his learning before ascending to the papal throne, with the fateful name of Sylvester II. The influence exercised by Gerbert on Fulbert, Bishop of Chartres, in the years between 1008 and 1028 is important in the subsequent development of the School of Chartres, whence came the vital Latin translation of the Arabic version of Ptolemy's *Planisphaerium*, prepared by Herman of Dalmatia. Translators of the Koran and of scientific texts made their names known; interest in religion was nourished and sustained by interest in philosophy and science, with language as the intermediary.

This process, which began mainly in Spain, and in which Peter the Venerable's team of translators undoubtedly took part, would have been less straightforward and certainly much less rapid and productive if contact with Arab culture (through the Arabic language) had not suddenly been made indispensable by a sudden overwhelming growth in the economy and in trade. Thanks initially to the inhabitants of Amalfi, and later the Venetians, Pisans and Genoese, a number of key texts soon became known, although this was seldom through systematic translation, more often through vernacular versions and abridgements; these were Arabic texts that were useful on a practical level – the writings of geographers, mathematicians and doctors. From the Arabic were translated Ptolemy's great treatise, the *Almagest*, the writings on algebra of al-Khuwarizmi, and works of astrology and astronomy such as the *Liber de aggregatione scientiae stellarum* by Abu'l Abbas al-Farghani ('Alfragan'); Alfragan's great work was familiar to Dante. Also translated were the works of Abu Ma'shar (Albumasar in the West), the *Introductrium in astronomiam* and *De magnis coniunctionibus et annorum revolutionibus ac eorum profectionibus*. The Latins did not simply receive this vast body of knowledge, they elaborated it enormously, as can be observed, for example, in the *Liber abbaci* compiled in 1202 by Leonardo Fibonacci (1170–1240) of Pisa. Fibonacci produced a brief outline of elementary arithmetic and, in his *Practica geometriae* of 1220, introduced the use of algebra to the West. Even more important from a practical point of view (and revolutionary in conceptual terms) was the introduction of the numerals called 'Indian' by the Arabs and 'Arabic' by the Latins; this was accompanied by an even more epoch-making innovation, the adoption of the figure nought.

Medicine was for a long time a favoured subject for translation. Alfano, a monk from Montecassino, translated several texts from Greek in the eleventh century. In the latter half of the eleventh century, however, another monk from Montecassino, Constantine the African, who came from what is today Tunisia, increased the medical libraries of the West enormously by translating into Latin from Arabic and from Greek books such as Hippocrates' *Liber aphorismorum* with Galen's commentary, his *Prognostica*, and al-Gazzar's *Liber graduum*. One important centre of medical studies was Salerno, where scientific knowledge was obtained from Greek culture, from the Arab world (via Sicily and North Africa) and from Jewish culture.

The books on mathematics and medicine, and their translations, were a response to practical and technical needs. Philosophy was a different matter, however, but it had assumed great importance for Western scholars on theological grounds. This was how they were able to gain access to the work of Aristotle: theirs was a quite different type of Aristotle, one who had been translated and reworked under the Abbasid caliphs in the eighth and ninth centuries and who was profoundly imbued with elements of Neoplatonism garnered mainly from Plotinus and Proclus. Of fundamental importance to Europe were the translations of the *Liber de intellectu* by al-Kindi and the commentaries of al-Farabi, who collated Aristotle's theories with the theories of the Neoplatonists, particularly those of Porphyry. Most important of all were the translations of Ibn Sina, Avicenna in the West, to whom we owe the celebrated *Canon*, a medical book which was reprinted several times in the sixteenth century and was still in use in the universities of Europe in the seventeenth. Avicenna (with ar-Razi) was the most famous author of medical texts in the West after the classical authors Hippocrates and Galen. Also irreplaceable in universities in the thirteenth and fourteenth centuries were Avicenna's philosophical treatises, particularly his *Kitab as-Sifa*. Without these, the philosophical writings of Thomas Aquinas and Bonaventura da Bagnoregio would have been inconceivable. Naturally these translations infused Latin culture with traces of the controversies that were then rife in the Muslim world, itself divided between authors who were more sensitive to 'pagan' Greek philosophy and its arguments, and those who were anxious that such influences should not eventually compromise the body of prophecy on which Islam was founded. Famous in this respect was the violent critique of al-Farabi and Avicenna by al-Ghazzali in his *Destructio philosophorum*. Avicenna nevertheless made a powerful mark on Muslim philosophy, which was increasingly preoccupied with the rationalization of faith and revelation. In authors such as Ibn Bajja ('Avempace' in the West) or Abu Bakr ibn Tafayl ('Abubacer'), the imprint of Avicenna is very strong; but it is just as strong in all the Latin philosophers, both Platonist and Aristotelian, from the thirteenth to the sixteenth centuries. Only one other Muslim thinker can compare with Avicenna in the influence he had on Western thought: this is the Córdoban Ibn Rushd al Hafid, famous in the Latin world under the name of Averroës, condemned as 'godless' and 'the enemy of Christ' by some theologians but venerated by others, who considered him to be the true interpreter of Aristotle. Albertus Magnus himself, the teacher of Thomas Aquinas, thought of him in this way, although the strong Neoplatonic component in his work took him a long way from Averroës. As well as the Arab authors, Jewish thinkers were also, of course, of great importance in the West. Notable amongst these were Salomon ibn Gabirol ('Avicebron'), Judas ha-Levy, Abraham ibn Ezra and, above all, the great Moshen ben Maymon ('Maimonides') from Córdoba, Saladin's personal physician; commentators on the work of Maimonides, in particular on his admirable *Guide to the perplexed*, revived the influence of Averroës in the Jewish world as well as in the world of Islam and Christianity.

By the second half of the twelfth century, less than half a century later, a bureau of translators in Toledo had managed to produce Latin versions of all the writings on astronomy of Albategnius, Alcabitius and Alfragan, the *De intellectu* of al-Kindi, part of the *Kitab as-Sifa* of Avicenna and the writings of Algazel. Of admirable quality (in spite of accusations of haste, errors, misunderstandings and barbarisms) were the indefatigable labours of Gerard of Cremona (d. 1187), who translated Avicenna's *Canon*, Ptolemy's *Almagest* (of which there was already an anonymous translation from the Greek, compiled in Sicily in about 1160), the writings of al-Kindi and also possibly of al-Farabi, a large quantity of Aristotelian writings and the pseudo-Aristotelian *Liber de causis*; he also added to the works in Arabic such Hebrew writings as *The Book of Definitions* and *The Book of Elements* by Isaac Israel, the Neoplatonist who was inspired by al-Kindi and who was also translated by Domenico Gundisalvi.

Gerard's vast undertaking was continued at the court of Emperor Frederick II in Palermo by the philosopher, astrologer, doctor and 'magus' Michael Scot (1180–1235), who had spent time in Toledo, Bologna and Rome. He translated a number of texts by Aristotle with their commentaries by Averroës, Alpetragius' *De Sphaera* and Avicenna's *De animalibus*. Meanwhile, between 1240 and 1256, another translator from Toledo, Herman the German, translated other important commentaries by Averroës, including the commentary to the *Nichomachean Ethics*. The renaissance of philosophy and science in the West, which bears the traces of Neoplatonism and incipient Aristotelianism and which lies at the base of modern thought, owes its origins to this early close union between Latin and Islamic culture.

The years between the mid-twelfth and the mid-thirteenth centuries were among the most important in the long intellectual adventure of the Mediterranean world. With the school of Abelard and the establishment of scholasticism, logic and the dialectic method were born. Whilst the inquisition and various outbreaks of heresy were in confrontation, the religious life and the Church were enjoying a revival thanks to the contribution of the Mendicant Orders. The *Studia* in the universities was just entering its most flourishing period. The duel between the crown and the clergy was slowly becoming spent as the feudal monarchies and independent city-states became established. As a monetary economy began to prevail the use of gold coinage returned to the West. These were also the crucial years of the crusading movement: it would be a mistake to look at this movement out of context as it naturally includes a strong military component. As we have seen, the crusades played an essential role in the relationship between Europe and Islam, but this relationship cannot be regarded as being exclusively military.

### Frederick II of Swabia and Alfonso of Castile

Was the thirteenth century pro-Islamic? It was certainly one of the greatest centuries in European history and crucial to the building of the cultural identity of the continent. It also remains one of the moments in history when Christianity and Islam – in spite of the crusades, or perhaps because of them – were closest together.

The relationship between the two civilizations, or their association, shows both societies in a favourable light. Western European civilization (without Byzantine or Eastern Christianity, although both were important) enjoyed the collaboration of princes, secular and regular clergy, knights, merchants and translators, some of them worthy of special attention.

Frederick II was the 'emir', or the 'baptized sultan'. These epithets, used to denigrate the emperor by his adversaries in the papal Curia and by Guelph propagandists, have stuck to him over the centuries. They were revived, but as a compliment to the emperor, by the extraordinary nineteenth-century Arabist Michele Amari, and have been repeated to this day by almost all the biographers of the man who is called by Arab sources 'al-Imbiratur'. Information from the Muslim world relating to Frederick II tells us that, in Palermo, he was raised by the leaders of the Islamic community; Western sources assure us that, as well as Latin, he spoke Greek and Arabic. Between the months of February and March 1229, the emperor succeeded in reaching agreement with the Ayyubid Sultan of Cairo, al-Malik al-Kamil, to the effect that Jerusalem (demolished and without the Muslim holy places, i.e. without the *Haram esh-Sharif*) was his until a ten-year truce expired, including Bethlehem, Nazareth and a few less important places with access to the sea. Notwithstanding the fact that he had been excommunicated, Frederick celebrated this in the Basilica of the Resurrection, becoming King of Jerusalem in a ceremony which involved crowning himself. The Arab chroniclers Ibn Wasil and Sibt Ibn al-Giawzi mention the fact that, during his visit to the Holy City, he seized every opportunity to express his sympathy with Islam and his admiration for its customs, whilst speaking scornfully and with rancour of the Latin ecclesiastical world. With a touch of romantic Orientalism *avant la lettre*, he asked to hear the muezzin's call to prayer during the night.

Frederick II's 'diplomatic crusade' should not be regarded as proof either of any particular pro-Islamic feeling on his part, or of any dislike of the crusading movement or the idea of the crusades as such. He was perfectly well aware that the *iter Hierosolymitanum* had by this time become a political tool in the hands of the papacy; as emperor, he was eager to regain personal control, something that his great forefather, Barbarossa, had hoped to do forty years earlier. Frederick II took on the crusade in Aix-la-Chapelle during the ceremony held there on 25 July 1215 (the feast of St James the Apostle), when he was crowned King of Germany, and therefore 'King of the Holy Roman Empire'; he was waiting to receive the imperial diadem from the hands of the Pope himself.

There was no possibility, therefore, of his renouncing the crusades. To attack Egypt, however, would in no way have conformed with his current interests or preoccupations since it would have alienated al-Malik al-Kamil, a political and diplomatic ally who was not to be trifled with. His alliance with Cairo was the more important because of the manifest enmity of Pope Gregory IX: the turbulent unreliability of the Franco-Syrian barons meant that neither his authority nor his permanence in the Holy Land could be relied upon. By continuing to pursue the policies of his Norman predecessors (which would later also be pursued by those governing Sicily after he had gone: Manfred, then the Angevins, then the Aragonese), and perhaps in response to some kind of objective geopolitical principle, Frederick's aim as King of Sicily was to maintain neighbourly relations with the Sultans of Egypt as well as with the dynasts of North Africa. Such an aim may tell us something about the diplomatic policy of a Mediterranean ruler, but it certainly reveals no general desire to understand or to collude with Islam. During the crusades, in Syria and in the Iberian Peninsula, we know that several instances of diplomatic agreement and even of sympathy occurred. Similarly, Saracen mercenaries were common property during the crusades, to such an extent that even the military arm of the religious orders made use of their services.

Frederick had been familiar with Islamic culture from boyhood and quite probably admired it. In this he was continuing a tradition begun in Norman times: Roger II furthered the geographical and cartographic studies being undertaken by Idris, and the two Williams promoted the translation of works on astronomy and mathematics. Frederick II vigorously pursued his interest in the more speculative fields of philosophy and natural sciences. The Norman court, although aware of Arab culture and science, paid most attention to Greek scholarship. In his *Magna Curia* Frederick pursued quite a different tack, one partly dictated by his own tastes and interests, partly made more accessible and more necessary by circumstances. After the fourth crusade the Byzantine Empire split up into kingdoms in which the decline and decadence of Hellenic scholarship was inevitable; in exchange the political and diplomatic activity of the emperor, particularly after his visit to the East in 1228–9, encouraged him to delve more deeply into the world of Islam.

Michael Scot arrived at Frederick's court in 1227. British by birth, Toledan by training, he soon became a naturalized Sicilian. He seems to have epitomized all that was best in the strenuous activity of the translators from Arabic in the twelfth and thirteenth centuries. He had already completed the translation of the celebrated *Kitab al-hay'a*, the 'Book of the Sphere', by Abu Ishaq Nur ad-Din al Bitruji ('Alpetragius' in the West), in which the movement of the sun and the planets was explained in a manner that conformed with Aristotelian physics. Scot also translated a number of Aristotelian texts from Greek and Arabic, one of which was particularly relevant to the emperor's penchant for natural history. This was the *Historia animalium,* to which Scot added (with a dedication to Frederick) the *Abbreviatio Avicennae de animalibus*. The fact that Sicily at that period became a centre of Aristotelian thought, filtered principally through the work of Avicenna and Averroës, was due to Michael Scot. He himself was interested primarily in astrology and in two sciences that were akin to astrology in many respects, alchemy and physiognomy. He wrote copiously on the two latter subjects, heavily influenced in his work by ar-Razi, Abu Ma'shar and al-Farghani.

In the middle of the 1330s another high-powered scholar made his appearance in the *Magna Curia* in Palermo. This was Theodore of Antioch, who may have been sent there by the Sultan of Egypt. He was set to work in the chancery writing letters to the Muslim courts. We know that there was an Arabic department within the imperial chancery, and it has also been noted that the style and formal composition produced by the chancery, including their output in Latin, was perceptibly influenced by Arabic. Theodore, who was a Monophysite Christian from Syria (a Jacobite), interpreted texts and information about the Near East and the Maghreb, and spent his time translating books on medicine and hygiene, also apparently translating a famous Arabic treatise on falconry, compiled by the falconer Moamit, expressly for the emperor. Frederick had developed a passion for falconry while on a crusade. It was owing to the books translated by Michael and Theodore that he was able to build on his experience as a hunter, breeder and observer and write his celebrated *De arte venandi cum avibus*. Not content, however, with the scholars whom he had gathered round him in the *Magna Curia*, or with those who lived elsewhere in his kingdom (in the new university of Naples, for example, or in the venerable old school at Salerno), the emperor organized for himself a series of investigations into an extraordinary variety of scientific topics involving the whole of the Mediterranean area. Admirable testimony to this can be found in the manuscript of the *Kitab al-masa'il as-siqilliyya* ('Book on the Problems of Sicily') compiled by one Ibn Sab'in, from Murcia in Andalusia, a Sufi mystic who had been handed by his sovereign – the Almohad Emir Abd al-Wahid – a series of questions sent by the emperor to all the major Islamic countries of the Mediterranean and the Near East, with instructions to reply.

In spite of this intellectual engagement by the ruler, known as *Stupor mundi*, none of Frederick's cultural centres – Palermo, Naples and Foggia – could rival the level of familiarity with Arabic culture that was prevalent in Spain. Intellectual life in Christian Spain at the time centred on Toledo and Seville; its hunger for everything Arabic or Jewish bore the seal of the great King of Castile and León Alfonso X, son of St Ferdinand, who came to the throne in 1252, two years after Frederick's death. He is traditionally known in Spain as *el Sabio* ('the Wise') and he is, with Frederick, the great intellectual ruler of that great intellectual century. It could be claimed that what associated Frederick with Alfonso was this shared passion for Arabic culture. The Spanish ruler absorbed the message of the great school of translators in Toledo and monitored its coherent progress, even though he was obliged by events to take up arms; as a crusader he carried more conviction than Frederick II. Enterprising but not always very shrewd, nor favoured by fortune in his dreams of greatness (one only has to think of his foolish attempt to assume the crown of the Holy Roman Empire), the Wise King was more fortunate, and his fame remained more radiant, as a scholar and keen promoter of respect and understanding towards non-Christian communities in the lands of the *Reconquista*. This attitude soon began to be modified by others, and by the end of the fifteenth century had disappeared entirely.

Besides *el Sabio*'s support for the translation of Arabic and Hebrew texts, amongst his other most obvious services to society were the establishment of Castilian as the language of culture – prose and poetry – and the particular attention he paid to texts and themes in philosophy, astrology and the natural sciences.

The extraordinary *rapprochement* between Europe and Islam during the thirteenth century had other causes as well. Bearing in mind that some of its leading protagonists wore the habit of the Friars Minor, this may be an appropriate moment to recall a text and event whose consequences were of critical importance.

## St Francis of Assisi and the Franciscan Order

The Lord said: 'Look, I send you out as sheep amongst wolves: therefore be as prudent as snakes and as wise as doves'. For this reason, if any friar wishes to travel amongst the Saracens and other infidels, let him go, with the permission of his Minister and his servant [...] When the friars are amongst infidels they may choose between two modes of spiritual conduct. The first is that they should not cause arguments or disputes, but should be submissive to all human beings for the love of God, and should confess to being Christians. The second is that, when they see that it is pleasing to the Lord, they should pronounce the word of God, so that they too will believe in God the omnipotent Father, the Son and the Holy Ghost, the Creator of all things, and in the Son our Redeemer and Saviour, and will be baptized and will become Christian, for he who is not reborn through water and the Holy Spirit may not enter the Kingdom of Heaven.[1]

---

[1]  *Regula non bullata*, XVI, in *Fonti francescane* (Assisi, 1986), pp. 21–42.

The *Regula non bullata* was promulgated during the Whitsun Chapter of the Order of Friars Minor in 1221. Francis had returned from the journey undertaken in 1219 to Syria and Egypt, during which he preached to the crusaders taking part in the siege of Damietta and also visited the sultan, al-Kamil. His encounter with the sultan is described in slightly different terms in Franciscan and non-Franciscan Western sources, and is indirectly confirmed in an epigraphic Arabic source. For the sultan to have offered the hospitality of his tent and a few kind words to this Sufi (a 'man of God', wearing the characteristic hooded woollen robe – *suf* in Arabic – of the ascetic), for him to have bidden farewell to him with a few small gifts is perfectly credible and would be perfectly in accordance with Islamic tradition. Less credible is the episode of the ordeal by fire, mentioned only by Bonaventura di Bagnoregio; although it is reminiscent of similar incidents in the history of medieval Christianity, it does not seem to fit into the context of an encounter with Islam (although the Franciscan scholar Giulio Basetti thinks otherwise).

With regard to the encounter with the sultan and the passage in the *Regula* that is undoubtedly closely connected with it, the role of St Francis in the history of the missions has been highlighted and his attitude to the crusades discussed at length. The saint from Assisi repeatedly stresses that the central point of his 'Christian proposal' is the renunciation of all forms of power, including the desire to put forward arguments, or specialized knowledge or technical expertise, in order to convince. Such behaviour would also have signified the exercise of power. The display of knowledge can itself be a manifestation of strength.

Similar considerations necessitate caution about the saint's attitude towards the crusades: this was not a missionary war, nor was conversion of the infidel its aim. St Francis, although obviously not in favour of war, would never have risked trying to halt its development; this would have meant violating the vow of obedience that obliged him to respect the orders of the Pope. Since the time of Innocent III, the crusades clearly depended directly on the Pope. What would be really interesting to find out is the extent of St Francis' knowledge of Islam: what idea did he have of it, how did he imagine it to be? He had been familiar with various texts from his youth and may have known some of the oral tales of chivalry; he had made the pilgrimage to Santiago (and probably knew the Pseudo-Turpin). Other information may have reached him via the Friars Minor who, from 1217, were in the Holy Land.

In St Francis' meeting with the sultan, neither the sultan's cordiality nor the mutual sympathy between him and St Francis was new or unexpected; as has already been noted, such cordial relations between the opposing sides were quite common. What is new, however, is the recognition (and this is evident in the text of the *Regula*) that Islam is part of God's grand design and therefore part of the plan set out in Revelations. The Saracens are like 'wolves': but 'brother wolf' is still a brother.

The Minorite scientist Roger Bacon regarded love as the incentive for scientific knowledge and this regulated his view of the Muslim world. It has been said that the great Franciscan tradition of the School of Oxford can only be understood fully if one bears in mind that, apart from its contribution to human understanding of the natural world, its innermost inspiration rests on St Francis' *Cantico di Frate Sole*. A similar observation could perhaps be made regarding the missionary commitment (which altered over the years and latterly became linked to the aims of the crusades) that runs through the Order of St Francis in a continuous line from Roger Bacon to Ramón Lull. In preparing the tools for the propagation of the Christian faith, although ecclesiastical tradition had hitherto always made controversy the pivot, the subjects and methods of controversy were not abandoned. Indeed, they recur frequently in Minorite writing. Alongside controversy, however, a different kind of appeal was being made, one still aimed at convincing the Muslims through debate and discussion (the debating techniques of scholastic logic came in very useful), but based above all on example and on love. In some Minorite circles, preaching for the conversion of Islam also became important as a sign of the times: according to the *Lectura super Apocalipsim* by Pietro di Giovanni Olivi, the Franciscans were expected to convert the Muslims before the coming of the Day of Judgement. In his *Opus maius*, written between 1266 and 1268 in order to furnish Pope Clement IV with the arguments needed to bring science into Church reform, Brother Bacon, *doctor mirabilis*, laid out all the objections he held against the practice of crusading in the Holy Land; as will be remembered, the crusades had recently experienced an impressive series of failures. Bacon's objections are almost identical to those Humbert de Romans, grand master of the Dominican Order, had reported as being extremely widespread (and not only in heretical circles) amongst the Christians.

Bacon did not condemn crusading as such; his objections to it were that it did not fulfil its function, either because armed expeditions against the Muslims were so frequently defeated, or because, if they did succeed, their effect was shortlived since no one or almost no one wanted to stay on to defend the conquered territory. In addition, crusading failed to observe the principle of charity because the infidels were not converted but killed; war therefore inspired even greater hatred of Christianity in their hearts, which meant that their souls were, damned.

God would prefer them to live and be converted rather than die and burn in hell. A new element was becoming more prominent. The crusade and the religious mission were both now taken into account as factors in the conversion of the infidel; conversion to Christianity was not the original aim of the crusades, although it is nowadays often seen as such. This represents a fundamental change in the Christian attitude towards the infidel.

Amongst the spate of activities undertaken by Ramón Lull (about 1232–1315) of Majorca, crusading amd missionary activity, desire for martyrdom and longing for the conversion of the whole world to Christianity constantly alternate and overlap – or conflict. Ramón Lull wrote works of theology, philosophy, alchemy and poetry, writing equally fluently in Latin, Catalan and Arabic. He led a tumultuous life both as a man and as a member of the Franciscan Third Order, as well as a missionary and scholar. Notwithstanding the continual changes of view that characterize his attitude to the crusades, going beyond what could be justified simply by the crises assailing the Catholic Church in the early days of the Avignon Popes, he stuck firmly to his support of missionary activity and his opinion that those preaching Christianity should learn the languages used by the infidel, beginning with Arabic, which he knew and admired (he also admired the beauty and poetry of the Koran). His work can be enjoyed in the *Libre del gentil*, in which the *gentil*, a pagan, is instructed in the monotheism of Abraham by three wise men – a Jew, a Christian and a Muslim – and is convinced by the arguments over which all three agree, suspending judgement over the points on which their opinions diverge; the solution has something of the atmosphere of the 'fable of the three rings'. It endorses Lull's strongly held belief in the excellence of the three sister faiths. In the *Liber de quinque sapientibus*, four different modes of being Christian – Latin, Greek, Monophysite and Nestorian – are compared with Islam. Once again, Latin Christianity emerges as the winner, but the validity of the other three is recognized.

Between 1314 and 1315, when he was already eighty-two years old, Ramón Lull set sail for North Africa for the third time. While preaching the gospel he was assaulted by the crowd. The crew of a Genoese ship picked him up, dying, in Bugia and took him in the direction of Palma de Majorca. He died just as his home town came into view. The man who termed himself *doctor phantasticus* or 'Ramón lo Foll' remained faithful in death to the two role models he had most loved during his lifetime: St Francis of Assisi and the 'holy fool' Perceval, both examples of Divine Folly at odds with the 'wisdom' of the world.

# 7

# The Lords of Fear

## The Shadow of Sorcery

As a result of pilgrimage, trade and the crusades, oriental customs penetrated deeply into late medieval Europe – along with the spices and other commodities that were imported from the East. At this period, many details of dress and of general taste were imported from Byzantium, Asia or from Muslim Spain, a testimony to the scale of Europe's debt to the Islamic world. Tradition has it that when St Albert the Great arrived in Paris in 1245 he was wearing Arab dress; this was no mere act of provocation, but rather a way of underlining his role as a scholar. By now the Muslims were 'philosophers' rather than 'pagans'. The most sought-after fabrics sold (and frequently copied) in the West often bore the name of the city in which they were manufactured: muslin from Mosul, baldachin from the Italian name for Baghdad (Baldacco), damask from Damascus in Syria. Carpets were imported from Egypt, Syria, Persia, Turkestan and the Caucasus; precious gilded and painted leatherwork from Córdoba and Morocco. Textiles made of woven silver came from Almeria, silks from Murcia and Malaga. The Arab-Muslim genius for decorative inscriptions was enormously admired: fake Arabic inscriptions had already been reproduced on Western coins, and 'kufic' calligraphy was to be used on fabrics, manufactured goods and paintings right up to the fifteenth century. Some of the most prominent features of the Gothic style, particularly in ornamentation, were the patterns known in Spain as *moriscos*, or, because they were typically used by Muslims living in minority communities in reconquered Spain, *mudéjares*.

The vogue for things oriental in late medieval Europe had many paradoxical features, however. Trade with the East intensified dramatically in order to satisfy Europe's requirements, and the balance of trade between East and West gradually shifted towards the West. This took place in an environment in which the idea of the crusade was constantly being revived, putting the Europeans in the perplexing position of a people who loves and dreams constantly of their enemy.

The area in which attraction and repulsion, fascination and a sense of danger collided most dramatically was, however, the area of the occult. The translators of Arabic texts had ensured by their efforts that large numbers of texts on astronomy and alchemy, as well as treatises on the occult, were in circulation in Europe (having passed through the filter of Platonism that infused Islamic philosophy). These texts provided an introduction to the disturbing world of the evocation of spirits. In its anxiety about the spread of the Cathar heresy, the thirteenth-century Church equipped itself with the inquisitorial powers necessary to confront ceremonial magic with increasing ferocity. Although such magic was thought to have disappeared from the West, or to have become extremely rare, after the collapse of the ancient civilization, i.e. after the fourth or fifth century AD, it now seemed to be re-emerging.

These Arabic texts rekindled the belief that the occult arts not only provided further proof of the diabolical doctrine promulgated by the heresiarch Mohammed, but were also a means of disorientating and corrupting Christianity. At the same time, however, the reputation this body of knowledge enjoyed for potency and efficacy helped confirm the Arab-Muslim world as the home of 'philosophy' *par excellence.*

Besides owing a great deal to Greek tradition, Arabic astrology's greatest debt was to Persia and India. It made extraordinary strides between the ninth and the eleventh centuries thanks to authors such as al-Kindi, Abu Ma'shar and al-Biruni. The greatest alchemist of the Arab-Muslim tradition, Jabir b. Hayyan (known in the West as Geber), lived between the eighth and the ninth centuries.

These authors and their writings permeated Christian Europe slowly but inexorably. Abu Ma'shar's *Introductorium* was translated in 1133 and Ptolemy's *Tetrabiblos* in 1138. Meanwhile the *Centiloquium*, a collection of pseudo-Ptolemaic astrological aphorisms, enjoyed a huge vogue. As might have been expected, many Hebrew versions combined with the Arabic texts in the gradual construction of a body of learning which, because it was frowned on by the Church, was transmitted by unconventional routes but was nevertheless much sought after. In addition to its value as speculation, astrology also had a very topical and practical function: it was used for the *electiones*, for consulting the stars before an important decision was made, or before a new activity was started. *Electiones* were also a feature of medical training: every organ of the body was presided over by a particular constellation. Particular importance, especially with regard to kingdoms and government, was given to the branch of astrology which studied the conjunction between the planets. In Italy, astrology was held in high regard in the seigneurial courts. It was said to be more highly esteemed in Ghibelline than in Guelph society because Emperor Federico II paid it particular attention, and also because the Church regarded it with such suspicion. This may have been only propaganda, however. The assistance of astrological science was frequently sought, especially when an auspicious moment was being chosen for the foundation of a city or a building, the consummation of a marriage (to make sure that any children conceived would possess certain gifts), when embarking on a business transaction or a journey, or when joining battle. An element of anxiety, however, hovered over astrology when its determinism had to be reconciled with the principle of free will. Or when, under the guidance of Albumasar, the prospect of a 'horoscope of religions' presented itself (similar to the horoscopes drawn up for individuals); logically, this would have implied that faith was also dominated by the stars, and the validity of Revealed Truth would have had to be re-examined under the chill light of the stars. There were some who even dared risk drawing up a horoscope for Christ.

Robert of Ketton, the translator of the Koran, also supplied the Latin version of one of the first treatises on alchemy to be circulated in the West. Since the Koran was the great model for language, style and philosophy (as well as for religion), its translation was extremely useful as a preparation for tackling texts on philosophy, medicine, astrology and alchemy. The association between planets and metals provided a very close link between astrology, alchemy and medicine; some of the greatest minds of the fourteenth century were at work in this field, for example the great Arnaldus of Villa Nova. The books translated from Arabic were often written in a style designed to preserve their secrecy (with parts in code, or in fake alphabets etc.). One of the most celebrated of these was the pseudo-Aristotelian treatise *Sirr al Asrar*, the *Secretum Secretorum*, possibly first translated by the Roman *curialis* Philip of Tripoli and thence translated into a number of vernacular languages; it contained Aristotle's teachings to Alexander the Great. Roger Bacon wrote the first commentary on this treatise, which exerted a considerable influence over the development of Western medical science.

The Inquisition watched apprehensively as these sciences spread, although there is no concrete evidence of the oft-quoted ecclesiastical condemnation of the *Secretum Secretorum*. In fact, the contribution of scholars such as Petrus Hispanus, Campanus of Novara, Witelo, William of Moerbecke, Simon of Genoa and John Peckham helped make pontifical Rome an important centre for the production and diffusion of scientific texts in the second half of the thirteenth century. These texts ranged naturally from astronomy and astrology to alchemy, mathematics and optics. Their diffusion is evidence of the Pope's interest in research into matters relating, for example, to 'drinkable gold' – a tried-and-tested cure for leprosy and also necessary for the *prolongatio vitae* praised by Arnaldus of Villa Nova (it is still not known whether this came to the West via Arabic science or via Chinese alchemy). These subjects, along with other theologically slightly suspect subjects, occupied a position on the borders of the occult.

An even more interesting example of a book of magic which passed from Arabic into European culture initially via a Castilian intermediary, then via a subsequent translation into Latin, was the so-called *Picatrix*. As far as we know, the book was translated in 1256 by order of Alfonso X, from Arabic into Castilian, and thereafter from Castilian into Latin; the translator was Jewish, Jehuda ben Moshe.

The origin of the *Picatrix* was the *Ghayat al-Hakim fi'l sihr* ('The function of assay in magic'), an apocrypha attributed to the great tenth-century mathematician and astronomer, al-Madjriti; the book assumed the Latin title by which it is known as a result of a series of misunderstandings. The *Picatrix* was not only the most famous treatise on magic in the Western world, it was also the subject of an extraordinary number of reworkings and falsifications. The aspect of the book which has attracted most notice over the years is the section giving technical information on methods of constructing talismans; also highly influential were the sections on the names of stars and the spiritual forces to be invoked while performing magic, and the section dealing with the practical aspects of a science whose aim is the attainment of power over souls and objects.

The pre-eminence of the Arab-Muslims in the arts of necromancy was very widely recognized, indeed legendary. The sorcerer was often depicted as a Muslim – as is clear in a theatrical text, the *Ludus Theophili*, in which the character who calls up demons is named Saladin. Such preconceptions were in fact little more than the 'popular' aspect of the custom of considering the Arabs as philosophers *par excellence* which took hold amongst learned folk in the early scholastic period. For this reason, Muslim culture was regarded as generally sceptical and incredulous – quite undeservedly, as we know. This misunderstanding ran completely contrary to the truth, yet it fits quite symmetrically with the contemporary Western prejudice which views Islamic culture as fanatical and integralist. The short circuit between the partial disappearance of any Islamic presence from Western culture between the eighteenth and twentieth centuries (except at the level of Orientalism) and the characteristic process of secularization of that culture accounts for this reversal. Overwhelming proof, perhaps, of the chronic misunderstanding of Islam by the West, and of the endless, contradictory ways in which it is perpetuated.

## Threats and Eclipses

The Arabs, as has been shown, were the possessors of fearsome might. During the trial of the Knights Templars, the suspicion emerged that, amongst other crimes, they may have been colluding with the infidel to bring about the destruction of Christianity. They were alleged to worship (an obvious calumny perpetrated by their accusers) a little-known god called Baphomet. The name bears a close resemblance to the name of the Prophet, which Ramón Lull always wrote as 'Mafumet'. One of the commonest forms assumed by this idol, it was said, was a head. Heads were also customary in reliquaries, the so-called 'cephalotecs', and they were traditionally used in divination. The talking skull was a component of the necromancer's tool kit. According to legend, Albert of Cologne, the 'magus' and teacher of St Thomas, had, with the assistance of magic arts learned from the Arabs, built a strange automaton, a talking head. St Thomas inherited it but he was obliged to destroy it because its loquacity disturbed his meditation. As the shadow of magic lengthened over late medieval Europe, there was growing suspicion that the infidels might use the occult arts of which they were the masters to harm Christianity. When 'popular' movements, looking somewhat like pilgrimages, armed or unarmed, threw Europe into confusion (there were 'crusades' of the 'innocents' or the 'shepherds' in 1212, 1251 and 1320), plenty of voices were raised complaining of Muslim conspiracy. The conspirators in these Muslim plots to ruin Christianity were sometimes beggars, lepers or Jews. In 1321 in the south of France an alarming plot was uncovered, with the aim of spreading leprosy by means of a mysterious powder that was to be poured into wells and watercourses. The plot had been hatched by the heads of various leper hospitals, with the support of the Jews. Behind them all, however, were no lesser figures than the Sultan of Babylon and the King of Granada. Later the names of the King of Tunis, the Kings of Jerusalem, of 'Azor' and of other improbable Saracen monarchs appeared. In exchange for large quantities of gold (but most importantly out of hatred for Christianity), the lepers were prepared to renounce their faith; with Europe fatally weakened by the spread of the contagion, the Muslims would have the opportunity to attack and conquer. Compromising missives were found, naturally, which provided proof of the conspiracy.

It is known that, after a few sporadic warning signals in the Middle Ages, persecution of the Jews began in earnest in the fourteenth century:

Although it fluctuated in its severity, it was on occasions as dramatic and as violent as a witch hunt. Added to this picture were also recurrences of slanderous attacks on the Muslim world, kept alive by renewed attempts at crusading. A prolonged period of crisis and anxiety was beginning in Europe, culminating in the great plague of 1347–50.

The attractiveness and nobility of the Arabs were essential components of this world, one which was now in the process of revealing its fragility and its illusory quality. The Arab was the 'philosopher', the fearless and generous opponent of the heroes of the chivalric romances, the sorcerer who knew the secrets of nature and who could cure bodily ills by scrutinizing the stars at night, the shrewd dealer in the commodities that were hotly in demand all over Europe and, finally, the dreaded enemy who had snatched Jerusalem from the Christians. What remained of all these attributes?

Jerusalem was closer now. The Jubilees proclaimed by the Roman Curia (soon to move to Avignon) had removed some of the strength of Jerusalem's attraction as the source of indulgences, since these could now be gained without the need to make the expensive and dangerous journey across the sea. Pilgrimages continued to be made, nevertheless: evidence of this can be found in a rich series of diaries describing the experience of the journey. Besides notes about sanctuaries, prayer and spiritual matters, the diaries also list stopping places en route, itineraries, exchange rates and the cost of goods and services. They were 'account books' as well as travel diaries. Further evidence is provided by the gradual appearance of shipping lines to and from the Holy Land, particularly from Venice. There were a few crusading expeditions, it is true, and many proposals and plans for more. Peter I of Lusignan, King of Cyprus, devised and carried out an attack on the port and the city of Alexandria; his *coup de main* (carried out with the assistance of a strange mystic, Philippe de Mézières, who was passionate about chivalric ceremony) was intended to be the prelude to a *passagium generale* of the whole of Christianity. This, in fact, had been proclaimed the previous year by Pope Urban V in Avignon in the presence of the Holy Roman Emperor, Charles IV of Bohemia. In the event, the King of Cyprus' attack was nothing more than a sack of the city, which provoked a loud outcry from the Christian merchants (predominantly Venetians) living there; they were the people who probably suffered the most serious damage. The consul to the colonists of St Mark in Venice, Andrea Venier, met his death during the attack.

The themes of the 'sea crossing' and the 'banner of the Cross' recur frequently in the letters of Catherine of Siena, particularly in her letters to the Pope. In her view, the crusade was first and foremost a means of forcing Christianity to abandon its fratricidal wars and to acquire internal peace and agreement. The idea of the crusade as *opus pacis*, paradoxical to us from this distance in time, was in fact the most commonly held view of the matter in the medieval world and persisted until the early modern period. In the last ten years of the fourteenth century, Philippe de Mézières, who was tutor and mentor to Charles VI of France, successfully sought the support of a number of aristocrats from France, England, Spain and Italy for his plan for a new expedition to the Orient: he was of the opinion that the crusade would have helped resolve and terminate the long war between France and England.

The island of Cyprus was a forward post of the crusading movement, although the Mameluke occupation in 1337 of the port of Ayas on the coast of Cilicia – where the caravan routes from the Black Sea and the Persian Gulf converged – had served to reduce its importance. Cyprus was ruled by the very unstable Lusignan dynasty and was under continual threat from the Genoese. Its weakness had become so evident that in 1426 an expeditionary force from Egypt (probably with the connivance of Genoa) ransacked the island, taking the king hostage and forcing him to recognize the sovereignty of the Mameluke sultan.

In spite of these successful ventures, the sultanate of Egypt was experiencing progressive economic decline which, in the second half of the fifteenth century, culminated in collapse. The spice trade, between the Indian Ocean and the Nile ports, using the great waterway as its principal route, continued nevertheless. Portuguese enterprise, however, was already laying the foundations for the circumnavigation of Africa. The Infante Enrico, later Henry the Navigator, had founded a school of cartography and navigation in the Algarve which would wrest from Alexandria and Damietta what remained of their semi-monopoly over the spice trade between the Far East and the Mediterranean. Gold from the Sudan continued to arrive in Egypt and the balance of payments was healthy, but manufacturing was in irreversible decline and the country was flooded with products from Europe and the Far East. It seems that the excessive extravagance of the Mameluke ruling classes, plus heavy military expenditure, were crucial factors in the economic collapse.

The Baghdad caliphate had been eliminated in the mid-thirteenth century and was no longer in existence. The Moors in Spain, wedged in and around the Nasrid emirate of Granada, were a distant reality. The Berber Arab principalities of North Africa, dominated by the thalassocracies of Genoa and Catalan Spain in the Western Mediterranean, had long since lost their ability to influence Mediterranean life, and had to endure repeated attacks by Christians during the crusade of 1390 against al-Madiya, led by Louis II, Duke of Bourbon, in which the English, the Germans and the Italians took part. Anatolian Turks and Tartars from Russia and Persia had by now long replaced the Arabs in the hegemony over Islam. Egypt itself, always slightly spurious as an 'Arab' country, was ruled by a dynasty of warrior-slaves who were basically of Turkish origin with an admixture of Circassian and Slav. Arabic remained the sacred language of Islam, although as a language of culture it had been in competition with Persian for a long while. The Arab peoples, however, now reduced to the inhabitants of the cities of the 'fertile crescent', plus a few nomadic tribes, had virtually disappeared from European consciousness. In the travel writings of the fourteenth and fifteenth centuries, Arab is synonymous only with Bedouin.

The ethnic and cultural eclipse of the Arab peoples, which proceeded with a symmetry more or less corresponding to the Arabization of the countries that had embraced Islam from the seventh century onwards, was accompanied by a strong devaluation of Arabism as an intellectual phenomenon. The substance of this movement was a growing intolerance of the stale, inflexible scholastic tradition which by this juncture was doing little other than reproduce itself.

Arabs were too prevalent in people's minds in Europe during the thirteenth and fourteenth centuries, and they were physically present as well. Following a fashion launched by the Saracen soldiers in the service of Frederick and Manfred in Lucera, the overlords of Italy, particularly the Ghibellines, often dressed their bodyguards in Moorish dress. In 1241 Saracen soldiers employed in local skirmishes in Italy attacked the convent of San Damiano, near Assisi, the home of St Clare; legend has it that they were frightened off by the sight of the saint holding a monstrance containing the Holy Sacrament.

Francesco Petrarch may have been in dissent (and therefore ahead of his time) when he wrote to his Paduan friend Giovanni Dondi in 1370 to express his violent dislike of everything Arabic, or anything connected with Arabic matters. The poet's antipathy and scorn were primarily directed towards Arab medicine, which he considered as being held in far too high esteem in Italy and France, to the disadvantage of Latin and Greek science. His feelings also extended to literature and philosophy. The poet made no mention of mathematics and astronomy, subjects in which the predominance of books in the Arabic language was indisputable. Neither subject was of great interest to him and his opinion of them was tinged with scorn. Although in his letter to Dondi Petrarch left the final judgement on Arabic medicine to his friend, in his *invectiva contra medicum quemdam* he went further, also speaking of *Arabum mendacia*.

Petrarch's haughty but hardly objective criticism brought together various disparate elements. First there was his well-known aversion to the medical profession, second his indignation at the lack of esteem accorded to Latin compared with Arabic medicine, and third his irrational anti-Averroism. The latter occurs in many letters and in the treatise *De sui ipsius et multorum aliorum ignorantia*. Of course, Petrarch's antipathy towards Averroism was based on the image of Averroës promulgated by the 'Averroists' of Padua. Nowadays we are aware of just how far removed they were from the authentic message of the master. This does not, however, alter the prejudice, arising from ignorance and misunderstanding, which fuelled Petrarch's position; the poet was probably aware of the irrationality of his views and tried to ennoble them through poetry. Whether he had any knowledge of Arabic poetry at all, either direct or indirect, is not known. According to his letter to Dondi, Arab poetry was *blanda, mollis, enervata*, charges which hark back to the old view of Islam as depraved and lustful. These labels were introduced to justify the Prophet's unnatural leanings (the subject of a venomous page in *De vita solitaria*); they are closely connected to the topoi of Catullus and Horace in respect of the *Arabes molles*, with which Petrarch was familiar.

This anti-Arab feeling was deeply ingrained, however. Contrary to what a kind of mass-media Vulgate would have us believe, the crusades cannot be considered as the cause of the split between Christianity and Islam, largely because no such split ever took place. Nevertheless, it would be impossible to deny that repeated military expeditions eventually provoked a spiral of reciprocal ill-feeling, tempered by other values. The ironic or satirical imitations of Arabic sometimes found in literary texts, from the *Jeu de Saint Nicolas* to the garbled speech of the giant Nembrot in Dante's *Divine Comedy*, betray signs of weariness with the Arab invasion of European intellectual life between the twelfth and fourteenth centuries. In addition, the doctrinal censure passed by the University of Paris in 1277 dealt a severe blow to the status of Arab culture. Egidius Romanus devoted his *De erroribus philosophorum* mainly to refuting the work of the philosophers *par excellence*, the Arabs. During the fourteenth century, particularly in Italy, these instances of anti-Arab feeling grew more frequent until they became an important element in the nascent humanism. The texts which had survived the centuries in the libraries of Byzantium gave direct access to the venerable voices of the past, in versions that were philologically more precise than the translations made from Arabic texts. The Arabic versions now began to look contrived and confused. One only has to remember the highly Platonized version of Aristotle contained in many of these treatises, which nevertheless constituted the core of scholastic philosophy. The humanists rejected scholastic methods and rebelled against the tradition of the Arabic 'philosophers'. Diatribes against Arabic texts were a pretext. This did not alter the fact that the anti-Arabism ingrained in a certain section of European culture had found something new to attack; the effect of changing its nature was to perpetuate it further. First there was the false Prophet and the religion which excused violence and vice; then there were its monstrous, idolatrous, demonic followers as depicted in the *chansons*; finally, following a long period when the Arabs were venerated as 'philosophers', came the scornful attitude of Francesco Petrarch, the father of humanism.

Meanwhile, however, as the Arabs departed from the Mediterranean stage, a new Muslim enemy made an appearance. Between the thirteenth and fourteenth centuries, the crusades had turned their attention towards the pagans of Northeastern Europe, the remnants of Islam in the Iberian Peninsula, the Cathars, the Ghibellines in Italy, political enemies of the papacy and even against mercenary troops. Now their services were needed again to oppose the waves of Muslims coming from the East. In the eleventh century the first *peregrinatio Hierosolymitana* evolved along the pilgrim routes as the indirect consequence of the spread towards the Mediterranean of the neo-Muslim Seljuk Turks. Between the fourteenth and fifteenth centuries a new Turkish menace was to cause a further change in the appearance and aims of the 'white whale' that was the crusades.

## The Sons of Othman

One of the most important results of the fourth crusade, with the conquest of Constantinople in 1204 and the restoration of the Byzantine Empire (in radically altered form) under the Palaeologi in 1261, was the total loss by Byzantium of any remaining control over the Anatolian Peninsula. After the arrival of the Mongols in the Near East, the area had become a buffer zone between the Armenians, Tartars, Mamelukes from Egypt, the kingdom of Cyprus, which was trying to retain bases in Cilicia, and the Knights of St John who, from their new base on Rhodes, were trying to control some part at least of the former Phrygia, Lydia and Caria. The simultaneous collapse, in the middle of the fourteenth century, of the Tartar ilkhanate of Persia and its rival khanate of the Golden Horde gave freedom to a number of Turco-Mongol groups, who celebrated their new-found independence by settling in the Anatolian Peninsula, where a series of *ghazi* sultanates grew up possessed by an almost mystical sense of *jihad*. This strong sense of mission seems to have produced powerful groupings, such as the sultanate of Aidin and the two Turkoman confederations, the *Aq-Qoyunlu* (White Rams), who were Sunni, and the *Qara-Qoyunlu* (Black Rams), who were Shiites. Between the fourteenth and fifteenth centuries, the two groups fought for possession of the area between Eastern Anatolia and Western Persia.

This new explosion of Turkic peoples in the Northeastern corner of the Mediterranean brought with it unexpected problems for Europe. The danger from Anatolia could not be underestimated. Between 1344 and 1346 a 'crusading league', formed between Venice, Genoa, Cyprus and the Knights of Rhodes, joined in a *passagium particulare* against the city of Smyrna, which had become a nest of Turkish pirates. Pope Clement VI, a fervent supporter of the idea of new crusades, had the *succursus* for the conquerors of Smyrna preached all over Europe, but the only positive response to this appeal came from a Burgundian noble, Humbert, Dauphin of Viennois. The Kings of France and England took great care not to be diverted from the conflict they had just begun and Genoa soon showed her hand; she was less interested in Smyrna than in the recovery of the island of Chios (an important producer of mastic), which the Byzantines had snatched from its overlord, the Genoan Martino Zaccaria, in 1329. The Venetians also had their eye on Chios. At the end of spring 1346, a fleet of Genoan ships landed on Chios as well as on Zaccaria's former possessions on the mainland, Old and New Foça, which produced alum, a commodity that was crucial to the cloth trade as it was the most effective mordant for fixing colour on cloth. The fleet stopped here, abandoning any further thought of a crusade. The expedition had merely served to unleash the greed of all the European powers.

An outbreak of plague brought the conflict to a rapid conclusion. In 1350 the Knights of Rhodes were acknowledged as lords of Smyrna, but the Turks were given control of the citadel and the Venetians won important commercial privileges. The innocent hero of the crusade, Humbert of Viennois, had to renounce any gains and was in any case soon to be robbed of all his possessions by a gang of English pirates. Tired and disillusioned, he turned his back on the world and its parades and became a Dominican friar. Fortune smiled on him in his ecclesiastical garb: he became the Latin Patriarch of Constantinople and later Archbishop of Reims.

Meanwhile, the real protagonists in the Muslim history of the Mediterranean were making progress in Anatolia. This was a Turkic tribe which, in the 1230s, had been pushed westwards by the Mongol expansion and had offered their services to the Seljuk Sultan of Konya, who allotted them a small area not far from Constantinople. At the end of the thirteenth century, their khan, Osman or Othman (1291–1326), took advantage of the crisis afflicting the sultanate of Konya, which was tightly enclosed between the Mongols of Persia and the Mamelukes of Egypt. Later, Othman's successor Orkhan exploited the struggles for imperial power in Constantinople and gradually managed to appropriate Bithynia and Bursa (formerly Prusa) from the empire, Iznik (the ancient Nicaea) and Nicomedia and, finally, Gallipoli on the European coast of the Dardanelles; this gave him control over the Straits and access to the Balkan Peninsula. By the time Byzantium realized that this little group of allies, whose various factions all hoped to gain power, had the capital surrounded and almost in a stranglehold, it was too late. Tightly squeezed between Thrace and Bithynia, both Ottoman, the Byzantine Empire was virtually reduced to the capital and the area surrounding the Bosphorus. Meanwhile, Turkish pirates were roaming the Aegean making life difficult for Genoese and Venetian shipping.

Now that the Ottoman peril had, with a bound, spread almost to the Danube, the realization suddenly dawned in Europe that there was no time to lose. However, the conference summoned by Pope Innocent VI in Avignon was a fiasco.

Europe was by now seething with new crusading zeal. In 1370 Cardinal Pietro Roger was elected Pope and, as if deliberately, chose the name Gregory XI. Gregory was the name of at least three great former Popes with crusading ambitions. He almost immediately proclaimed a new *passagium generale* in 1371, while he was preparing for the return of the papacy to Rome. These were to be the two main features of his programme, and both won the support and encouragement of the two great Christian *prophetissae* of the day, Bridget of Sweden and Catherine of Siena. A new crusade was proclaimed in July 1375. Catherine hoped to persuade members of the professional mercenary companies to take part in order to give the soldiers the opportunity to make their peace with God. She was also convinced that the crusade would procure peace, or at least a truce, in the endless conflict between France and England. The Sienese saint had managed to rally the brother of Charles V of France, Louis, Duke of Anjou, to the cause of the *passagium*. Unfortunately, her hopes were destined to be dashed against harsh political reality. The Pope's return to Rome, far from giving the Church a much-needed boost, was the beginning of the so-called 'Great Western Schism'. Both England and France, drained by their conflict, had the misfortune to see a mere boy ascend to the throne: Richard II in England and the half-witted Charles VI in France. In 1381 England was shaken by the revolt of Wat Tyler; Flanders was devastated by the weavers' rebellion in Ghent in 1382, followed by uprisings in Paris and Rouen. Meanwhile, a new epidemic of plague was ravaging Europe.

The political and social upheavals in Europe, the frequent epidemics of plague, the great schism in the Church, fear of the advancing Turkish armies, propaganda from groups who hoped that the Church would return to the purity of an evangelical age, all nourished hopes and fears which were expressed in an outpouring of apocalyptic prophecies and in popular religious movements. Between 1378 and 1380 a prophecy spread around Europe which presented the Pope in Avignon and the King of France as protagonists in a movement of ecumenical renewal which aimed at purifying the Church; it was supposed to lead eventually to the liberation of Jerusalem. In 1386 a treatise along the same lines, bearing the signature of the hermit Telesphorus of Cosenza, was addressed to the Doge of Genoa, in the hope that he would be tempted to join the Franco-Avignonese alliance. This was a recurrence of the kind of apocryphal prophesying that had been rife in Europe for centuries.

Apocalyptic fantasies were a feature of texts such as *Le Songe du vieil pèlerin* by Philippe de Mézières, the founder of a new religious Order called the *Nova Religio Passionis Jesu Christi*, which, according to the unfulfilled notion of many theorists of the crusades over the years, was supposed to unite and supersede all the crusading Orders. Such fantasies were also cultivated by people such as Jean Le Meingre, the famous 'Maréchal Boucicaut' who made the pilgrimage to Jerusalem, planned crusades and invented orders of chivalry for the defence of women.

Meanwhile the Ottomans were advancing. Sultan Bajazet (1389–1402) routed the fledgling Serbian power in the ferocious battle of Kosovo in June 1389. The Ottomans, having subdued Walachia, Bulgaria, Macedonia and Thessaly and pushed the Walachians back to north of the Danube, conquered Thessalonica in 1394.

A new wave of terror ensued. *Basileus* Manuel II wanted to make a long trip through Europe in order to kindle interest in a new crusade, but as money was short, he turned to Venice and offered to sell her the island of Lemnos. This was a miscalculation. The Serenissima had no intention of falling out with the sultan and therefore sensibly urged the *basileus* to caution and prudence.

The King of Hungary, Sigismund, was beginning to feel anxious about the Turkish offensive in the Balkans. He put pressure on the two Popes, Benedict XIII of Avignon and Boniface IX of Rome, thereby obtaining the proclamation of a new crusade in which even the Venetians (against their better judgement) were to take part. The truce between France and England, pronounced in 1388, was prolonged until 1396 in order for the expedition to take place. Another wave of penitential and eschatological enthusiasm was rising in Europe. After seeing the Antichrist in a vision, the great Dominican preacher Vincent Ferrer managed to inject new life into the flagellant movement. The crusade found a patron with real authority in Philip II the Bold, Duke of Burgundy, who was able to raise a sizeable amount of money. He appointed his son John, Count of Nevers (later John the Fearless), leader of the mission. On 20 April an enthusiastic army, consisting of a mixture of French, German, English and Italian knights, left Dijon. When they reached Buda at the end of July they were joined by the King of Hungary with troops of *vojvoda* from Walachia (now his vassal), whilst a fleet of ships including Knights

Hospitallers of Rhodes, Venetians and Genoese reached the mouth of the Danube via the Black Sea. The number of combatants taking part has been estimated at around one hundred thousand, which may be no exaggeration.

On 26 September, however, near Nicopolis, where the great Bulgarian highway met the southern branch of the Morava, this formidable band of crusaders suffered a crushing defeat. This seems to have been due in part to the impetuosity of the Western knights and their unfamiliarity with the terrain and with Turkish military tradition. The defeat turned into a genuine massacre, made worse by the cold-blooded murder of all prisoners of war – apart, of course, from those who could afford to pay a substantial ransom. These fortunate survivors were repatriated in 1397.

The fourteenth century ended with strenuous efforts to raise money for ransoms, vague proposals for new crusades and ever more insistent apocalyptic prophecies, aggravated by a final epidemic of plague.

At this point a miracle occurred, or something that was immediately mistaken for a miracle. A Turanian prince appeared from Transoxiana and, taking advantage of the collapse of the Mongol Empire, proceeded to resuscitate the power of Genghis Khan. The origin of this prince's name, Timur, is still the subject of debate: it may have evolved from a Turkic-Mongolian word meaning iron. From his native Samarkand, this prince, known in the West as Tamerlane, led a series of military campaigns during the final ten years of the century, displaying a true genius for warfare and a well-judged ferocity. He quickly took possession of Persia and Georgia, with their great trading posts of Tabriz and Tiflis, and hurled himself at Mesopotamia, entering Baghdad in 1392 and pressing forward as far as Syria, where he conquered the Sultan of Aleppo. In 1395 he defeated the Khan of the Golden Horde in pitched battle. Turning eastwards, he took his banners to the Indus and destroyed the city of Delhi in 1398. He returned to Syria and finally arrived in Damascus, where in 1401 he encountered the great North African historian and philosopher Ibn Khaldun, who for years had been eager to meet him. They exchanged gifts and discussed history, religion and law.

By this time Timur's vast empire reached to the Caucasus and included the southern and central parts of the Caspian, the Aral Sea, and the entire area between the Syr Darya and the Indus. The only Mediterranean potentate in a position to stand up to Timur was the ruler of the Ottomans.

It was obvious, therefore, that at this juncture the interests of Europe coincided with those of the Khan of Samarkand. Moreover, Timur's rapid progress recalled the overwhelming surge of the Mongols a century and a half earlier. These memories reignited the foolish hope of an alliance between the peoples of the Steppes and Christianity to defeat the Ottomans, the only power able to contend against Timur's total control of the Ural-Altaic world. The defeat of Islam was not on the agenda – Timur himself was a Muslim. All over Europe the legends which had kept hope and illusion alive for nearly three centuries resurfaced: the legend of Prester John, of the Three Wise Men and of the providential assistance received by the followers of Christ from the heart of Asia. European merchants were also hoping for a renewal of the *pax mongolica* that would have reopened the fast, safe caravan routes leading from the Black Sea and Armenia across Persia to Eastern Asia, which during the thirteenth and fourteenth centuries had been used by such large numbers of adventurers, diplomats and missionaries. John, Prince of Byzantium, to whom *basileus* Manuel had entrusted the care of Constantinople while he departed for Europe, agreed with the Genoese podesta of Galata that relations with the khan would be established through the good offices of the Greek Emperor of Trebizond (a descendant of the Comnenus family). Byzantium by this time was paying taxes to Bajazet, now accepted by Prince John as his new ally. The King of France entered the fray as well, using Dominican missionaries (the Dominicans had always maintained good relations with the Mongols and knew Persia and Armenia well) to propose to Timur that he join with the Christians in an action against the Ottomans. This was a resurrection of the old dream nourished by Louis IX, with the added hope of strengthening the Genoese commercial empire in the Levant, now that France ruled the cities of the Ligurian coast. If Genoa and Venice had been able to offer the formidable Mongol leader naval support strong enough to block the Straits, the course of history might have run very differently.

The Mongols and the Ottomans met near Ankara at the end of July 1402. Fortune favoured the Mongols this time. The victor of Nicopolis was himself defeated and ended his days the following year as a prisoner, subjected to atrocious humiliation. In 1405, however, Timur died unexpectedly and his vast empire was broken up into small nations which were all at war with one another.

For the rest, the Ottoman sultanate, although drastically reduced by the defeat of Ankara, had not been engulfed by Timur. With its power reduced to more manageable levels, it became an interesting ally once again. The Venetians realized this at once, while the French and the Genoese, with the impulsive Boucicaut as usual to the fore, preferred to offer their support to the *basileus* of Constantinople. In the early fifteenth century this gave rise to new 'crusades' and skirmishes between the Venetians and the Genoese in the Eastern Mediterranean. The Europeans chose to ignore the fact that the Ottomans were regrouping their forces and, after a chaotic decade when three sultans followed one another in quick succession, they found a reliable leader in Mohammed I and his son Murad II who, in 1422, lodged a formal claim to the city of Constantinople and laid siege to it. The siege, which may have been mainly a show of strength or a declaration of intent, was lifted after three months without producing any immediate consequences; but the illusion could no longer be sustained. Manuel II abdicated in 1423 and John VII succeeded him two years later. The sultan, meanwhile, was paying court to the Venetians and the Genoese. He was aware of their economic and naval strength in Constantinople and hoped, by showing favour to each of them in turn, to provoke rivalry between them. In 1423 Thessalonica surrendered to Venice. Murad recaptured the city in 1430 with the assistance of the Duke of Milan, Filippo Maria Visconti, who was the enemy of Venice and who, through Genoa, maintained excellent commercial and diplomatic relations with another Muslim ruler, the Emir of Tunis.

The sultan himself had no intention of falling out with the West if he could help it. After the conquest of Thessalonica he compensated the Venetians with a very favourable commercial treaty. He encouraged the Genoese to invest their capital in Ottoman territory and in 1437 allowed them to exploit the alum mines in Anatolia. In 1433 a delegation from the Ottoman court arrived in Basel to visit Emperor Sigismund, who, as King of Hungary, had taken part in the battle of Nicopolis. The old crusader welcomed the delegation most warmly.

The crusading ideal was not yet dead. In 1422, the year in which Sultan Murad and his troops appeared threateningly under the walls of Constantinople, Henry V, the victor of Agincourt, died. Beside his death bed friars stood reciting the Psalms. When they reached 'Benigne fac, Domine, in bona voluntate tua Sion, ut aedificentur muri Jerusalem',[1] the sovereign who had spent his whole life trying to subdue France stopped them in order to announce that his greatest wish had always been, once things were sorted out in his kingdom, to liberate the Holy City of Jerusalem. Like St Louis, he died with the name of Jerusalem on his lips.

---

[1]	Psalms 50.19 (51.20).

# 8

# 'Inimicus crucis, inimicus Europae': *The Ottoman Threat*

### The Hunt for the Red Apple

Both nations and peoples have ancient roots and long histories; like others, the Ottomans had dreams and prophecies to realize. Two archetypal myths dominated the lives of the Ural-Altaic peoples: the great primitive beast, the Wolf, and the primordial object of desire and happiness, the Apple.

In Turco-Mongolian folk tales the image of the legendary city of Kizil-Alma, the 'Red Apple', recurs repeatedly. Over the centuries, the nomads of Central Asia had seen the city glinting through the whirling sandstorm and the icy gusts of snow-laden wind, between the Caspian, the Gobi and the Tien Shan. The City of the Red Apple was interpreted and popularized as an immense golden dome. For the descendants of Othman and their subjects, it was Santa Sofia in Constantinople, then the Dome of the Rock in Jerusalem, then, as time passed, Buda and Vienna, twice almost won in the seventeenth and eighteenth centuries, and, in the intoxication which follows victory, Rome itself. In homage to the old legends and the flickering dreams, the capital of Kazakhstan was named Alma-Ata, 'Father Apple'.

In pursuit of the Red Apple, the peoples of the Steppes arrived at the foot of the walls of the New Rome. By this time it was quite clear that their wish was to pluck the golden apple which gleamed above the misty waters of the Bosphorus.

In 1421 the new Duke of Burgundy, Philip the Good, son of John the Fearless, was dreaming of the East as his grandfather and his father had done before him. His father Guillebert de Lannoy was sent to the Levant to study the feasibility of launching a new crusade, now that the schism in the West had been settled and, since Agincourt, the conflict between England and France seemed to have drawn to a close. In 1433 the duke sent another local emissary, Bertrandon de la Brocquière. These two perspicacious observers were forced to draw the same conclusion: the Turks were a strong, disciplined people who would be difficult to vanquish.

Philip at this time was busy fighting Emperor Sigismund, who seemed keen to place obstacles in the way of his expansion towards Brabant, Limburg and Luxembourg. He was in need of an achievement that would increase his prestige and place him morally on a higher plane than the other Christian dynasties: above the languishing *basileus* of Constantinople, the sleepy Holy Roman Emperor and the allied Kings of France and England, who were preoccupied by the need to hold their dominions on the other side of the Channel together. The 'Grand Duke of the West' was not worried about any of the others, neither the vacillating Dauphin (later King) of France, Charles VII, nor the Iberian rulers. The crusade would have brought him the prestige he was looking for: he would have been its sole leader, with the support of the papal court, and could have presented himself as the *bellator rex* about whom the theorists had been arguing inconclusively for more than a century and a half.

By now, *basileus* John VIII was beginning to realize that his empire, reduced to little more than the splendid capital, was reaching a critical point. In 1437 he journeyed to Europe to ask for the support of the leaders of the Latin Church, who were holding another council, this time in Basel. He was well aware of the price that the Western ecclesiastics would make him pay: humiliation, the renunciation of the independence of the Greek Church and the end of the schism by subjugation. Furthermore, he was aware that in ecclesiastical circles, in particular amongst the Greek clergy, and amongst the inhabitants of the capital, who were ordinary believers, it was being hinted and sometimes openly stated that the Ottoman turban was preferable to the papal mitre of Rome. The Muslims would have left the Greek Christians, a *dhimmi* community (one that was protected and had freedom of worship), in peace, whereas the Latins would have stripped them of their freedom of discipline, liturgy and theology.

Meanwhile, the Turks were tightening the noose around Byzantium and were advancing towards the north-west, in the direction of Europe. In 1437, taking advantage of the death of Emperor Sigismund and the consequent problems of succession, Sultan Murad II attacked Transylvania and Serbia. In spite of the brave resistance offered by its despot, George Brankovich, a couple of years later the whole of Serbia was in

Ottoman hands, whilst Transylvania retained a precarious freedom thanks to the valour of the *voivode*, Janos Hunyadi. In Basel the ecclesiastics produced a new schism.

The union between the two Churches, the Greek Church represented by a vacillating monarch and a reluctant patriarch, and the Latin Church already the victim of schism, was nevertheless solemnly proclaimed on 6 July 1439 in Florence, whence Pope Eugenius IV and the prelates loyal to his cause had moved the council's headquarters, first from Basel to Ferrara, then from Ferrara to Florence.

In the spring of the following year, the Turks returned to the offensive, this time focusing on Transylvania and Hungary. They made a vicious attack on the city of Alba Greca, Beograd or the 'White City' to the Slavs: Belgrade. Belgrade put up such a strong resistance that in September the sultan was obliged to pack up and go. Janos Hunyadi, to whom the new King of Hungary, Ladislas Jagiello, had entrusted the defence of the section between the Danube and the Tibiscus, was so well able to stand up to the Muslim armies that even the Hungarian nobles temporarily forgot their squabbles and united in a kind of Holy League around their *voivode*, the champion of faith and liberty.

At the beginning of 1443 an encyclical from Pope Eugenius IV invited all prelates to pay a tenth of their income to support the war against the Turks. The Pope had set aside one fifth of his resources to equip an army and a navy. In Hungary, the crusade had a strong supporter in the cardinal legate Giuliano Cesarini; Poland, Walachia and Ragusa – the plucky republic of St Blaise – were enthusiastic in their support of the Pope. The mission could have been successful: the Epirot noble Iskander Beg was rallying the Albanians and Montenegrins against the infidel, whilst the tireless George Brankovich reorganized the Serbs. In Anatolia, too, the Christians found a valuable if unexpected ally in Ibrahim Beg, the Sultan of Laranda – the region between Lake Tuz and the Taurus; although he was the sultan's brother-in-law, Ibrahim Beg was determined to oppose his supremacy in Asia. Meanwhile, a personal 'crusade' was being waged by Constantine Palaeologus, the despot of Mistra, in the Morea (the Peloponnese). Having invaded the lands of the Florentine Neri II Acciaioli, Duke of Athens, who had declared himself a vassal of the sultan, Constantine Palaeologus was advancing through Greece and Thessaly in the direction of Constantinople, rallying the Greeks and Thracians against the Ottomans as he went.

Prospects looked good. In the West, however, in spite of being accompanied by a spate of rhetoric from preachers and writers, the call to the crusade went unheeded as usual. In France the Hundred Years' War had not yet ended; in Italy the conflict between the Angevins and the Aragonese for possession of the kingdom of Naples had only just finished, leaving a cloud of ill-feeling in its wake. In addition, Genoa, Venice and Florence were not over-enthusiastic about compromising their good relations with the sultan. The new Holy 'Roman' Emperor, Frederick III Hapsburg, who had not yet received his imperial crown from the Pope, was determined not to take part in an enterprise which would probably only serve to reinforce the position of Ladislas of Hungary. Using the still unstable position of Bohemia as an excuse (the Hussites had not yet been suppressed), he refused to join a crusade for the time being.

The invading army which assembled at Buda in the summer of 1443 was composed of stray soldiers in search of fortune. Nevertheless, their campaign got off to a brilliant start, with a victory near Nís and the capture of Sofia. At this point, however, the harsh Balkan winter and Turkish guerilla tactics gained the upper hand. The crusaders returned gloomily to Belgrade and then to Buda, while Brankovich – who, as the despotic ruler of Serbia, was the sultan's vassal as well as his brother-in-law – set about mediating the peace that Murad, who was anxious about the intentions of the lords of Karaman, so fervently desired.

The following April, Ladislas of Hungary asked the sultan for a truce. Meanwhile, however, in order not to displease Cardinal Cesarini and the hardliners surrounding him, he assured them that he would take up arms again in the summer. Almost no one believed him, except of course the sultan, who was kept well informed by his spies. One exceptional observer who was then on Ottoman soil was the humanist Ciriaco de' Pizzicolli from Ancona, who assures us that at Adrianopolis fortification work was proceeding at a feverish pace in spite of the truce. It seems, in fact, that Ladislas signed a ten-year truce in extreme bad faith. At the end of July a fleet commanded by Alvise Loredan and the cardinal legate Francesco Codulmer, the Pope's nephew, was setting sail from Venice in the direction of the mouth of the Danube. The sultan had hastened to Anatolia to fight against Ibrahim Beg, whilst Adrianopolis was thrown into confusion by a religious uprising fomented by a Shiite group and a rebellion amongst the Janissaries.

This presented a unique opportunity to crush the Ottoman serpent once and for all. It cannot have been difficult for Cardinal Cesarini to persuade the indecisive, disloyal Ladislas of this since he was always persuaded by the argument he had heard most recently.

On 4 August, at Szegedin, the king and the nobles of the kingdoms of Poland and Hungary swore that they would together achieve the expulsion of the Turks from Europe. Only the despot of Serbia lagged behind and agreed to proposals for a separate peace.

By this time Murad had almost defeated Ibrahim Beg; he signed a hurried treaty with the latter and made off on a forced march towards the Straits. The fleet led by Loredan and Codulmer was supposed to have blocked the Straits in order to prevent Murad's access to Europe. This did not happen. It appears that the ships were stuck in the Sea of Marmara whilst the sultan was crossing the Bosphorus, helped in his hour of need by the Genoese from Galata and a few Venetian vessels. This apparently is what Eugenius IV is referring to in a bull anathematizing the assistance given to the infidel by the usual 'bogus Christians'.

The battle took place near the city of Varna, at the mouth of the river Provadija. The crusaders suffered a resounding defeat, as they had at Nicopolis. The only person with adequate military capability, Hunyadi, was hindered by the unprofessional and inept Ladislas, who paid for his lack of prudence with his life. Giuliano Cesarini was also killed. The *voivode* of Walachia, Vlad II, known as Dracul (Devil) or 'the Impaler', saw the way events were going. He decided to establish his credentials with the sultan in advance, intercepting and holding amicable dialogues with his Transylvanian colleague. Tradition has it that another double-crosser, Brankovich, had prevented Iskander Beg from going to the assistance of the crusaders by blocking the way. For his part, the *basileus* had stayed out of the conflict in order to deny the sultan a pretext for unleashing a fatal attack against Constantinople. Realizing by now that it was only a matter of time, he hoped to gain a few more months.

Murad took advantage of the lull that followed the total destruction of the Christian front to abdicate. But his young son Prince Mehmed revealed himself to be so inexperienced that he had to take up the reins again at once. The Venetians made it plain, to Murad as well as to the Pope, that they had had enough of crusading. The new ruler of Southern Italy, and therefore of the Southern Adriatic, Alfonso of Aragon, was more interested in strengthening his still somewhat uncertain power over the kingdom of Naples. The Serbs and Walachians remained allies and were generally untrustworthy but would not have acted impulsively. Only Iskander Beg and Hunyadi, now Regent of Hungary for the boy Ladislas Posthumous, were determined not to submit. Following a long campaign waged against him by the sultan, Constantine Palaeologus was forced to accept defeat in 1446.

### The Mitre or the Turban?

The humanist Tommaso Parentucelli of Sarzana was elected Pope Nicholas V on 6 March 1447, consecrated on 19 March, and died on 24 March 1455. He was destined to preside as Pope over two extremely important events, each of which carried different weight in the history of the Church and of Christianity at the time. Both events were very different.

On 9 April 1449 Nicholas V had the great consolation of being able to end the so-called 'little Western Schism' when the Antipope Felix V abdicated after a decade and returned to being Amedeo VIII of Savoy. Four years later, on 29 May 1453, he had to confront anguish and shame when Constantinople fell to the Ottoman Turks. The consequence of this act was the disappearance of what had to all intents and purposes been the *pars Orientalis* of the Roman Empire for more than a millennium, since the division of the empire by Theodosius (the continuity was broken by an ambiguous – though temporary – settlement between 1204 and 1261).

The greatest problems faced by Nicholas V and his successors Calixtus III and Pius II were the collapse of the empire in the East, plus the continuation of the crisis in the Holy Roman Empire and the advance of the Turks. Hence it was necessary to mount a crusade that would endorse the new-found Church unity – the Hundred Years' War was fading as the schism died away – and place at the centre of this new equilibrium the Pope, who was now the only Christian leader possessed of real authority and prestige. As regards relations between Christians and the Ottoman world, and proposals for new crusades, the capture of Constantinople could therefore be said to have inaugurated a phase that was to end only eleven years later with the death of Pius II and the extinction of his plans for the repossession of Constantinople and – at least in theory – the reconquest of Jerusalem. On the other hand, Parentucelli must certainly have felt anxious about the advance of the Turks before 1453. It cannot have required the fall of Constantinople to make him realize that a renewed call to the crusade, made at such a difficult time in such painful circumstances, would inevitably lead to the firm establishment of the papacy as central to Christian society, and therefore to a further opportunity to advance the monarchical-pontifical programme, contested to no avail by conciliar factions within the Church, which was so typical of the papacy after the end of the Council of Constance. As had happened at the end of Lateran IV in 1215, the *causa unionis* and the *causa reformationis* were presented in close conjunction with the *negotium crucis*, which soon came to be considered as prejudicial to the resolution of the *causae*. This opinion was enhanced by the fact that the *causa unionis* seemed to have been resolved after the dissolution of the pocket of resistance formed at the Council of Basel, and the *causa reformationis* was then scrapped *sine die*, with consequences which were not immediately obvious but which were to weigh heavily on Christianity in the last twenty years of the fifteenth century, and even more heavily (as is well known) at the beginning of the sixteenth.

When he ascended the papal throne in 1447, Nicholas inherited the crusading problem which his predecessor Eugenius IV had to some extent confronted, but also dodged. The crusading front was vast and complex, extending from the Balkans to the Aegean, Spain and North-eastern Europe. It was surmounted by the colossal diplomatic and financial structure required for the collection of tithes and the sale of indulgences. In 1448 the Pope reduced the purchase price of indulgences in Castile to three florins; Martin V had fixed the price at eight florins and Eugenius IV had reduced it to five. He allowed King John II to use the income thus raised to organize a crusade against Granada. In 1453 he also granted the king the administration of the Order of Santiago. He looked favourably on the African conquests and the Portuguese exploration of the Atlantic, giving equivalent status to the *dilatatio fidei* and the *defensio fidei*. The papal bull, *Romanus Pontifex*, issued by Nicholas on 8 January 1454, legitimized the nascent Portuguese Empire by sanctioning the position of the Infante, Henry 'the Navigator'. Between 1448 and 1449 the Pope turned his attention to crusades in Prussia and Livonia, making provisions for the sale of indulgences; he also took an interest in the means of repressing the Hussite movement and heresy in general. He favoured the founding of the 'Company of the Cross' in Bologna in 1450 by Conrad, the Inquisitor from Germany.

In spite of lending his support to these various actions, Nicholas showed no burning desire to take up arms against the Ottomans while the defeat of Varna still rankled. However, the Regent of Hungary, Janos Hunyadi, the Albanian Iskander Beg and the despot of Mistra, Constantine Palaeologus, were all determined (despite claims to the contrary by Iskander Beg) not to bow their heads to the triumphant infidel (whose victory was by now apparently a foregone conclusion). They cherished fond hopes of revenge.

Hunyadi was unwilling to wait and wrote as much to the papal court in September 1448 before setting forth impulsively from Belgrade across Serbia. Iskander Beg, having made an agreement with Venice to secure the Serenissima's support planned to join the enterprise. The Pope gave some rather general promises but made no serious move to join the campaign, although he made sure that the Regent of Hungary was well supplied with indulgences. The Hungarian army, with reinforcements from Albania and Walachia, encountered the armies of Sultan Murad between 17 and 19 October 1448 on the plain of Kosovo – the very place which in 1389 had proved so fatal to the Serbians and the Hungarians.

The second day of the Kosovo campaign confirmed the plain's ill-omened reputation. Hunyadi's strategy was knocked for six, then his armies were decimated by the Ottoman artillery and subsequent waves of Janissaries.

A few days before this battle, on 3 October, *basileus* John VIII died. At a sign from the sultan, who was sure by this time that Byzantium had been won, the crown of the Byzantine Empire was placed on the head of Constantine, the despot of Mistra. The lessons learned at Varna four years earlier seemed to have subdued him completely. In fact, Murad may still have considered him as a threat, preferring to have him established in Constantinople – a gilded cage surrounded on all sides by Ottoman territory – rather than at liberty in Greece. Only Iskander Beg remained to be brought to heel; he was walled up in the formidable fortress of Kruja, hidden in the inhospitable mountains of Albania. In April 1450 the sultan tried to storm this invincible retreat, but after five months of unsuccessful siege he was obliged to withdraw.

The heroism of Iskander Beg aroused a fresh wave of enthusiasm amongst European supporters of the crusade. The Pope, the Duke of Burgundy, the King of Naples and the Regent of Hungary supported the enterprise with gifts of food and money, whilst in the same year two distinguished figures from the ecclesiastical world – Nicholas of Cusa and Dionysius of Certosa – began a long journey through the Holy Roman Empire; one of their chief aims was to preach the crusade. The message of Dionysius particularly impressed Philip the Good, Duke of Burgundy, who embraced the crusading cause with great fervour. Another strong supporter of the war against the Ottomans, Enea Silvio Piccolomini, the papal nuncio in Germany, wrote to the Pope from Wiener Neustadt on 25 November 1448 to warn him that the enmity and egoism of the Christian princes was smoothing the path to conquest for the Turks.

When Sultan Murad died in 1451 he was succeeded by Mohammed II, the young man who a few years earlier had proved so ineffectual when he acted as regent for a couple of years. The crisis which then followed the death of the great sultan, and the reputation for weakness of the prince who succeeded him, produced a wave of euphoria in the Christian world. Francesco Filelfo, a humanist who had spent a number of years at the court of *basileus* John and who had married the daughter of Crisolora, considered himself to be something of an expert on oriental affairs. He sent a letter to King Charles VII of France to encourage him to lead a new campaign against the Ottomans. According to Filelfo, the new sultan was a listless young man with very little military or political talent. Any campaign waged in Anatolia would be assured of easy success.

In fact, Filelfo's epistle was written in an irritatingly obsequious manner and expressed views on Byzantine and Ottoman affairs so erroneous as to suggest that he may have been aware that what he was saying was incorrect. More likely, however, is that his opinion echoed the prejudices and platitudes then rife in the West; Filelfo may have repeated these platitudes through ignorance of the true state of affairs, or out of a desire to confirm commonly held opinions by emphasizing them further. He made light of the dangers, difficulties and high costs of the crusade while exaggerating the power of Byzantium, which by now hardly existed. With regard to the new sultan, Filelfo (somewhat unoriginally) endorsed the general opinion of his inadequacy.

Filelfo's exercise in courtly letter writing should not be taken too seriously, particularly as the King of France at that moment had plenty to do trying to reclaim the portions of France that were still in English hands. This kind of writing, however, demonstrates the way the crusade tended to be used for rhetorical purposes.

Nicholas V was unable at that moment to take strong action, shaken as he was by the successive defeats at Varna and Kosovo. He was permanently torn between his duty as Pope and the logistical difficulty of organizing an expedition that would unify Christianity – the latter depended on internal unity in Europe and vast financial resources. Possibly in order to disguise his intention, the Pope took refuge behind the old Latin issue of union, proclaimed at the Council of Florence. The crusade could only have taken place as a consequence of the resolution of the schism between the Latin and Greek Churches, otherwise its only effect would have been to strengthen the throne of the schismatic emperor. This blatantly sophistical argument, with its implications of blackmail, merely served to damage the cause it was intended to support. In Constantinople, meanwhile, the number of people who openly declared that the Ottoman turban was preferable to the papal mitre was growing. Nevertheless, the Pope made a few gestures, for example offering indulgences to individuals in return for the defence of Mediterranean islands threatened with invasion by the Turks. One such concession was issued in 1451 to anyone who defended the island of Cyprus; this is probably the first example of a printed indulgence (it was printed in Mainz in 1454). The *basileus* continued with his appeals: one of his ambassadors, Andronico Leontaris Briennio, visited first Venice and then Rome with the specific task of negotiating the union of the two Churches on condition that Western assistance to the empire be provided without further delay.

A practical plan for intervention was contemplated by Alfonso the Magnanimous, King of Naples, but with a special agenda in mind. The Aragonese king ruled over a kingdom which projected into the Mediterranean and was the natural heir to the Norman, Swabian and Angevin policies regarding the Orient. Alfonso cast a covetous eye over Albania, whose acquisition would have given him complete control over the strait of Otranto; he had already succeeded in becoming formal overlord of the area. Like Charles I of Anjou in the past, Alfonso dreamed one day of wearing the imperial crown of Constantinople – which is why he had come to an agreement with Demetrius, the brother and rival of *basileus* Constantine. In July 1451, he declared himself ready to 'proclaim a crusade which he would also command'.[1] His proposal, however, concealed a threat to the Pope since, rather than inclining towards him, he was inclining towards the 'Church militant', with a distant plan for conciliation which was consistent with the king's own background. In spite of these ambitions he was ensnared by Italian politics, feeling quite insecure upon the throne of Naples and having no ships. In 1451 the Arsenal of Naples rapidly built a few ships to send to the assistance of the *basileus*.

The young sultan, meanwhile, was proving not to be the lacklustre individual that people had supposed him to be. He made haste to endorse the peace treaty with Venice and to offer a reasonably honourable peace to Hunyadi. When, in the late summer of 1452, he began to fortify the Straits, the Genoese and the Venetians (both of whose commercial interests in Constantinople and the Black Sea were equally compromised by this measure) were unable to react in unison because they were in conflict with one another. And although Genoa tended more towards the *basileus* while Venice, following the peace of 10 September 1451, towards the sultan, neither was willing to jeopardize its relationship with either of the warring factions.

The fortification of the Straits meant that the passage of shipping could be monitored and life in Constantinople controlled. The sultan's action was undoubtedly a prelude to the hostilities which broke out at the end of summer 1452 and continued into October with an assault on the Morea, which was later discovered to be a diversionary tactic. Using the skills of renegade Christian technicians, Mohammed had had a series of enormous cannons cast. It was obvious that the final attack on the city of the Golden Horn was only weeks away.

Christian Europe was in a growing state of bewilderment and fear. The cry for help from the Genoese colony in Pera was received in their homeland and relayed to those considered to be Italy's main allies, the King of France and Florence. During Frederick III's journey to France in the spring of 1452, Piccolomini preached the crusade to the Pope and to the emperor in Rome whilst Flavio Biondo did the same thing in Naples before Frederick and Alfonso. (Biondo was exiled from Rome because he was in temporary disgrace with the Pope.) Keen to practise what he

---

[1]   R. Fubini, *Italia quattrocentesca* (Milan, 1994), p. 197.

preached, in 1453, after his return to Rome, Biondo dedicated a short treatise, *De expeditione in Turchos*, to the King of Naples. Mohammed II made it clear, however, that he had no intention of slowing down his attack. Between March and August 1452 there was a massacre of the inhabitants of Epibation; this was the inspiration (probably in September) for George of Trebizond's oration to the Pope, *Pro defendenda Europa*. On 16 November 1452 the senate in Venice wrote to the Pope and his cardinals to request more energetic action.

The Pope did not hide his anxiety, but he nevertheless remained firm on one point: the union of the two Churches should precede the crusade – in fact, it was a precondition of the crusade. He was not the only person to promote this position. The Chancellor of the Golden Fleece, Jean Germain, took the same stance and talked of a great expedition in the future which would involve Greeks and Latins fighting together, united in one Church. The Ethiopians and 'Prester John' would be fighting beside them – Prester John was no longer identified as an Asiatic prince but was the Negus of Ethiopia.

This time there was no choice but to accept the Roman revenge. On 12 December 1452, the end of the schism was solemnly celebrated in Santa Sophia in the presence of the Cardinal of Santa Sabina, in other words Isidore of Kiev, the Latin Patriarch of Constantinople now joined to Rome. This was a remedy that could not have been more unsuitable. Although the act of union was accompanied by a review clause, as soon as the Ottoman threat receded Greek monks and citizens of Constantinople started to protest on the pretext that the sacrilegious agreement had provoked the wrath of God.

### How the New Rome Fell

Constantinople was living in the shadow of discord and apprehension. The strength of its defence consisted of about three thousand Latins, mainly Venetians and Genoese, and it was doubtful if they would have acted in partnership. The sultan had a redoubtable 'fifth column' at his disposal in the shape of the Greek anti-unionist party led by George Scholarios; many of his followers were already well trained in espionage, sabotage and betrayal. What happened thereafter is well known. At the end of May the sultan marched into Constantinople, and the last *basileus* was killed defending his city.

Suddenly the West seemed to shake itself out of a long torpor. The death of Constantinople was a death long foretold. To judge by the immediate reaction of Christian Europe, it seemed as if no one had ever seriously believed that the city on the Bosphorus might fall. Its collapse was seen as presaging the end of the world, proof that the Turk was invincible and his advance impossible to stop.

Although the Ottoman advance over the Balkans and through the Aegean had made the Europeans aware that their continent was no longer safe from the infidel (apart from the Iberian Peninsula, there had been no invasion since the eleventh century), it was not until the fall of the New Rome that the idea of a crusade against the infidel began to be linked with the idea of the defence of Europe. Enea Silvio Piccolomini made the matter quite clear:

> In the past we received our wounds in Asia and in Africa – in foreign countries. This time, however, we are being attacked in Europe, in our own land, in our own house. You will protest that the Turks moved from Asia to Greece a long while ago, that the Mongols established themselves in Europe and the Arabs occupied part of Spain, having approached through the Straits of Gibraltar. We have never lost a city or a place comparable to Constantinople.[1]

The King of Bohemia, George of Poděbrad, also stressed the needs of Europe, sketching a rough outline for political union between the European countries that would serve as a permanent institutional base from which the struggle against the Turks could be organized. Poděbrad, however, although a moderate in a somewhat ambiguous position, was a supporter of the 'calixtine' heirs of Hus, and the Pope would soon be preaching a crusade against him along the lines of the crusade he wanted to organize against the infidel.

The continent was flooded with *excitatoria*, and appeals and plans for crusades. This time Nicholas V appeared to wish to take serious action. The Venetian senate had informed him of the calamity in a letter dated 29 September, and he sent the news around the Italian powers battling for a successor to the Duke of Milan, begging them to make peace at once so that they could present a united front against the barbarian danger. The appeal hit the spot. Although there might have been reason to think that the fall of Constantinople would do the worst damage to Venice (although for years Venice had protected herself against such an eventuality by cultivating a good relationship with the sultan), now people were beginning to wonder anxiously whether the whole of Europe might not be endangered. The kingdom of Naples seemed particularly vulnerable, not only to attack by the Turks but also to attack by the Emir of Tunis, Abu Omar Othman, who, evidently encouraged by the

---

[1]   E. S. Piccolomini, quoted in J. Delumeau, *La paura in Occidente (secoli XIV–XVIII)*. Italian translation (Turin, 1978), p. 405.

fact that the Turks had captured Constantinople, was busy raiding settlements on the Christian coastline, taking prisoners to turn into slaves and planning an assault on the island of Sicily.

Reactions to these threats were not exactly as Nicholas had expected. Genoa, for example, was not too displeased to see the Tunisians causing problems for the Aragonese, and even encouraged Genoese corsairs to do their best to aggravate these problems. In Constantinople the main preoccupation of the Genoese was to save as much as could be saved. The sultan was requested to deal leniently with the area in which the Genoese resided in Galata, and the sultan's possessions on the Black Sea were surrendered to the Bank of St George. The Genoese ruler of Lesbos, Giovanni Giustiniani Longo, joined wholeheartedly in the defence, bringing his own men and equipment. Venice abandoned its policy of territorial expansion instigated by Foscari and turned its attention to maritime affairs, meanwhile seeking an agreement with the sultan. In Milan the new duke, Francesco Sforza, had at first been quite pleased by the fall of Constantinople which caused such trouble to Venice. Nothing was made explicit, of course, but some of his declarations were revealing: 'of all these ills Venetians are the cause, and may God punish them for it'.[1] Obviously, therefore, the peace hastily brokered between Milan and Venice was not based on anxiety about the future activities of the Ottomans; now that the Hundred Years, War was over, there was fear that the French king might lay claim to the Duchy of Milan because of the close ties between the two families, Visconti and Orleans. The fall of Constantinople and the end of the war between the French and the English combined (although not in equal measure) to bring about the peace of Lodi and the so-called 'balance of power' which dominated the political scene in Italy for the subsequent forty years. In the treaties drawn up by the Italian League, the Venetians and the Florentines unanimously evaded the Ottoman problem, but the King of Naples insisted that the League should consider itself duty bound to cooperate in future in any action aimed at liberating Italy and Christianity from the Turkish threat. It is interesting that 'whilst the crusade as an ultimate aim does not appear in the original deeds of the Italian League, drawn up between the secular states, it is referred to in the document proclaiming the League's loyalty to the Pope'.[2]

The Pope himself was determined to put the crusade into effect. He was strongly encouraged in this by Emperor Frederick III's chancellor

---

[1]   G. Pistarino, *La politica sforzesca nel Mediterraneo orientale*, in *Gli Sforza a Milano e in Lombardia e i loro rapporti con gli Stati italiani ed europei (1450–1535)* (Milan, 1982), p. 343.

[2]   Fubini, *Italia quattrocentesca*, p. 197.

Enea Silvio Piccolomini, Bishop of Siena, who impressed on him just how astonished and upset the emperor had been at the news of the sack of the New Rome, and that he was willing to take on political and military responsibility for the planned expedition. The Archbishop of Mytilene, Leonard of Chios, who (with Isidore of Kiev) had been an eyewitness to the fall of Constantinople and had been wounded and imprisoned, wrote a famous description of the event for the Pope, *De urbis Constantinopoleos iactura captivitateque*. In this document, responsibility for the incident is apportioned and the part played by various protagonists in the city's collapse is emphasized: the seditious anti-unionist Greeks, the weak and hypocritical Western Christians, whose only thought was how best to avoid danger and to save their own skins, and Giustiniani Longo, appointed by the Republic of Genoa to defend the city.

Nicholas V enacted his bull, *Etsi Ecclesia Christi*, on 30 September 1453. It provides disturbing evidence of the reigning atmosphere of anxiety. Again the Ottoman prince was described as a prefiguration of the Antichrist, the red dragon of the Apocalypse; this led naturally to the usual directions on the subject of indulgences, on the tithes to be raised all over Christendom, and on the threat of excommunication and inter-dict to anyone favouring the Turks in any way.

The Pope's call to arms appeared to be very well received. The emperor gave signs of persisting in his intent; the Duke of Burgundy made a solemn vow to join the crusade during the *Voeux du Faisan*, a festival celebrated in Lille in the chivalric tradition; Alfonso the Magnani-mous seemed to be of the same mind, heaping praise and honour on Iskander Beg, whom he appointed his captain general. There was encouraging news from the Balkans as well: it appeared that the Ser-bians, the Hungarians and the Albanians were presenting a united front against the Ottoman advance. Meanwhile the Pope, reviving a custom which had been characteristic of the papacy since Gregory X and the Council of Lyon in 1274, was requesting treatises and historical records that would help to familiarize people with the Turks, and also permit study of their customs in order that the imminent and definitive crusade could be organized in the most effective way possible.

What in fact was happening was that the Christian princes were keeping well away from one another – they had no intention of joining a crusade that might favour some at the expense of others. The policy being pursued by the King of Naples towards the Balkans and his friend-ship with Iskander Beg were causing great anxiety in Venice, where, in order to counteract the disadvantage at which this placed them – the Strait of Otranto and free access to the Adriatic were at stake – the Venetians were drawing closer and closer (with all the appropriate safeguards) to the sultan. Meanwhile, the immediate danger was over, as was the first flush of enthusiasm. Crusading fervour was beginning to cool, and feathers were being ruffled by the heavy-handed methods used by the Church for collecting tithes. In April 1454 the emperor convened the diet of Ratisbon, inviting the Duke of Burgundy and all the Italian States. Only the Duke showed his face. The Italians made various excuses for not attending a meeting which they feared would end in their being allotted unwanted tasks. Furthermore, Frederick III was not convinced that this was the best time to put himself on public view. He did not appear in Ratisbon, leaving Piccolomini to conduct the meeting. Even Philip of Burgundy, whose commitment to the crusade was in no doubt, since he feared a French coup now that the threat from England had been removed, felt less inclined to be involved than he had previously. Piccolomini soon realized that he was hitting his head against a solid wall constructed partly of indifference and partly of premeditated obstructionism. The letters he wrote at this period, particularly a celebrated letter of 5 July, are brimming with pessimism. A second diet, convened in Frankfurt for 29 September (the feast of the Archangel Michael, patron saint of crusaders), resulted in failure yet again; the emperor did not appear at this meeting either, using Piccolomini as his delegate. A third diet, held in Wiener Neustadt in February the following year, began with a series of irrelevant preambles but broke up when the news of the death of Nicholas V reached the delegates.

Tommaso Parentucelli was unenthusiastic about the crusade before the fall of Constantinople, but became a convinced, if belated, supporter after the tragedy. He ended his days in the sad realization that the realities of politics, diplomacy and economics made a coherent and sustained effort by Christendom against a feared enemy impossible, but that they could be deployed very effectively, either explicitly or implicitly, in the games played within the European political structure. This was a lesson which the Christian powers would have done well to bear in mind over the subsequent three centuries.

The *Testamentum* of Nicholas, included in Giannozzo Manetti's *De vita et moribus Nicolai V summi pontificis*, is apologetic on the subject of the defence of Constantinople: 'in hac ipsa obiectarum rerum confutatione'.[1] The Pope, wounded by the reproaches levelled against him, rejoined with a denunciation of the princes and Christian states, whose collaboration had been so half-hearted. He also criticized (rightly or wrongly) the shameful haste with which the besieged Christians surrendered. In fact there was little else they could have done. Nor, in all likelihood, could the Pope have done any differently.

---

[1]  See *La caduta di Costantinopoli. L'eco nel mondo* (Rome/Milan, 1976), pp. 142–9.

# 9

# Renaissance Europe
# and the Turks

## Longitudinal Symmetries

The new Pope, Calixtus III Borgia, had no intention of allowing the enterprise set up by his predecessor to fail. He intensified efforts to construct a fleet with which to oppose Turkish supremacy. Under the command of Ludovico Scarampo, some of the ships did in fact manage to relieve Rhodes, which had been in Turkish hands since 1455, and to drive the Ottoman garrisons out of Naxos, Samothrace and Lemnos.

In the Balkans, the Ottoman advance was under way again. Novo Brdo, the big Serbian mining town south-east of the plain of Kosovo, was occupied in 1455. Only the miners, who were for the most part Saxon, were allowed to remain. The Turks lacked the technology and skills that were needed (early evidence of one of the Achilles' heels of the Ottoman Empire) and would not otherwise have been able to continue to exploit the veins of gold and silver in the area. The loss of Novo Brdo was a cause for further anxiety because it was clear that the sultan was aiming for Belgrade. To oppose the sultan the cardinal legate Juan de Carvaja had only a hastily assembled army, led by the old but trusted Janos Hunyadi and spurred on by the exhortations of an elderly cleric, the Minorite John of Capestrano.

The Turks did not, however, gain the upper hand. In the second half of June 1456, the sultan, who had previously been conquered in a naval battle on the Danube, then in an encounter on dry land, suspended the siege of Belgrade and withdrew his decimated troops, his splendid and terrifying Janissaries, his fabulous cannons and the huge crowd of intellectuals, technicians, engineers, foundrymen and Christian gunners who, whether for money or for adventure, had joined his ranks from Germany, Bosnia, Hungary, Dalmatia and Italy.

Belgrade seemed to have redeemed Constantinople. Following the agony of the fall of the city on the Bosphorus, a moment of peace, enjoyed by the whole of Europe, ensued. It became clear that the fate of Christian Europe was being decided on its further shores in the Balkan Peninsula.

Nevertheless, these were dangerous times. The sultan was loose in the Morea, whose despots had refused to pay him tribute. In early August he received the keys of Corinth, which had surrendered. At the end of the month he marched into vanquished Athens, filling with grief the hearts of humanists who regarded the Attic city as their spiritual home. The Venetian island of Negroponte welcomed the sultan as their guest and friend, and the Republic of Ragusa sent him tributes and assurances of loyalty. Only the second son of Hunyadi, Matthias Corvinus, who was still in his teens, dared defy the sultan openly, competing with him for possession of Serbia.

Enea Silvio Piccolomini, the humanist who became Pope in 1458 as Pius II, called a meeting of the Christian powers in Mantua in 1459. During this meeting prospects for a new general crusade were discussed. Events were moving quickly, however. The sultan had snatched the empire of Trebizond and the entire southern coastline of the Black Sea from the Comnenus dynasty. In Italy it was rumoured that the lord of Rimini, Sigismondo Pandolfo Malatesta, who was hostile to the Pope, wanted to invite the sultan to Italy and offer him his services as a military leader. The rumour may indeed have been true; at any rate, there was an exchange of correspondence between the two. Both were interested in the arts and in machinery. When Lesbos fell to the Turks in 1461 the Florentines of Galata joined in the rejoicing in the city that had become Istanbul, and lit bonfires in celebration.

Pius II, meanwhile, was working on a thesis whose consequences were unforeseen, either by him or by his contemporaries. Europe was the seat (*patria* and *domus*) of Christianity. It was identifiable with the *christiana religio* and therefore any European could be held to be a Christian: 'Europaei, aut qui nomine christiano censentur', as Enea Silvio had already written in his preface to the *Historia de Europa*.

The duplicity and reticence of the Christian princes offended him. At the end of October 1461, in bitter mood, the Pope published his highly controversial *Epistola ad Mahometem*, in which he declared that the sultan was immeasurably greater than the Christian monarchs and could therefore aspire to be the successor of the Emperors of Rome. If this new Constantine would accept baptism, the Pope (the new Sylvester) would place the crown of the world on his head. There are polemical elements in this letter in which old prejudices regarding Islam are reiterated; these make it obvious that the letter was in fact never sent to Mohammed II, although the sultan was probably able to read it as various printed editions were circulated after 1469. It could be regarded as a variant of the *epistolae excitatoriae* which, from the eleventh century onwards, were circulated throughout Europe in an attempt to encourage people to join the crusade. Pius II's *excitatoria* was sharp and critical: in it the Christian princes were reproached for being mean and treacherous. The 'scandalous' invitation sent by Pius II to the sultan after the failure of the diet of Mantua (convened to plan a general crusade) acquired dramatic notoriety as a symbol: if the sultan would convert to Christianity, Europe would be his and he would be Europe's new Constantine. This was a terrible insult to those ruling in the name of Christ, and an indelible stain on their dignity.

Even the humanist's most biting irony, made more acerbic by pontifical disdain and the scorn of an old Christian warrior, was not enough to mobilize Christianity. The Pope devised a new move, this time verging on madness, or at least on moral blackmail, which he divulged to a few trusted cardinals, in secret, in March 1462. The world would have been astonished to learn that he, the aging Pope, was willing to do what Gregory VII and Urban II were both thought to have wished to do: he was willing personally to take part in a crusade. Christian Europe would not have allowed him to go alone; it would have had to take up arms itself and follow him.

On 18 June 1464, having taken up the cross, Pope Pius set out for Ancona where he was to meet the entire Christian fleet. What he found was the usual motley collection of mercenaries. A vicious epidemic had broken out between July and August, decimating populations in the cities and killing would-be crusaders. The Doge of Venice had promised to put in a personal appearance, but arrived only in early August. Sailing slowly round the coast the doge arrived in Ancona on the twelfth, only just in time to give the Pope, who died three days later, a glimpse of his ships.

Pius' successors, Paul II and Sixtus IV, both appeared eager to carry on his works, but the Ottoman advance continued unchecked. In 1469 there were Ottoman incursions into Styria, Carinthia and Carniola, and in 1470 Negroponte was occupied. News of the island's collapse caused another wave of alarm in Christendom. The heavens were troubled; in 1473 a comet appeared in the sky, and the humanist Francesco da Meleto began feverishly to consult the Hebrew sages. Lorenzo Bonincontri, in his poem *De rebus coelestibus* published between 1472 and 1475, pondered the conjunction of Jupiter with Saturn.

The Turks, who were by now ruling the southern Balkans where Islam was beginning to take root (in Bosnia, for example, from the 1460s onwards), were continuing to make inroads. They landed in Friuli in 1472, and again between 1477 and 1479. The occupation of Cyprus by the Venetians in December 1474 did not seem to worry the sultan unduly. Duke Galeazzo Maria of Milan, who maintained good relations with Istanbul, as we learn from the diary of Cicco Simonetta, abandoned the question of Genoese rights to the island – to begin with, he had seemed set to support Genoese claims. On 6 June 1475 Kaffa fell into Turkish hands – another unexpected blow for Genoa, Milan and the whole West. St Mark was certainly weeping, but St George was not exactly smiling. Genoa found consolation in North Africa by regaining the same ground (in commercial terms) as had been lost in the East. Relations with the emirate of Tunis, guaranteed by the diplomatic and political support of Ludovico the Moor, continued to flourish in spite of the numerous (and unavoidable) outbreaks of violence.

The peace of 1479 between the sultan and Venice had almost no effect on relations between the Western Christians and the Muslims in general. The Republic of Venice sent the doge's official painter, Gentile Bellini, to the Bosphorus to paint the sultan, whose religion, in theory, prohibited any reproduction of the human form. The sultan rewarded the artist handsomely. The celebrated portrait, bearing the date 25 November 1485 (the sultan at that time had already been dead for four and a half years) is now in the National Gallery, London.

The year 1480 was equally full of alarms. In Genoa in March the Dominican Annius of Viterbo (his real name was Giovanni Nanni) preached on the Apocalypse, and his book *De futuris christianorum triumphis in saracenos*, better known as the *Glosa super Apocalypsim*, discussed the Antichrist in relation to certain conjunctions of the planets and the Turkish advance. In the *Glosa*, published in December 1480 under the name of the Carmelite Battista Canale (rather than under Annius' own name), the Antichrist was firmly identified with Mohammed and the final collapse of the Turkish Empire was predicted.

Another book on a similar subject to appear in 1480 was the prediction *De eversione Europae*, addressed by Antonio Arquato to Matthias Corvinus. In May 1480 the Turks launched another attack on the island of Rhodes. Between July and August a Muslim fleet besieged Otranto in Apulia, subduing and ransacking the city and massacring part of the population, after having offered them a choice between conversion to Islam or death. This was the last straw, leaving Italy reeling in shock. A league was rapidly created which comprised, as well as the Pope and the King of Naples, the ruler of Hungary and Florence; Florence was reconciled with the Pope on this occasion, thus closing the rift opened by the

Pazzi conspiracy and the war that ensued. Italy was in a state of alarm and turmoil. In 1482 and 1484 two apparitions of the Virgin in Tuscany, one at Bibbona in the Maremma, the other at Prato, near Florence, aroused strong popular feeling. It has also been claimed that certain scenes used in painting, such as the 'Massacre of the Innocents', featured much more frequently after 1480, inspired by the news of events in Otranto. Finally, in 1484, a fateful year in astrological terms, a mysterious cavalcade rode through the streets of Rome; this was the cavalcade of Mercurio da Coreggio, which was staged to promote general penitence and to announce a *Renovatio* in the future.

The 'events of Otranto' are still shrouded in mystery. What were the real roles of Florence and Venice, one city keen to cause trouble to the Pope, the other to the King of Naples? Was it not strange that a city which belonged to the Venetians' historic enemies should be besieged by Turks the year after a peace treaty had been drawn up between the Serenissima and the Sublime Porte? Was the siege of Otranto a 'siege on commission', or was it really an act of extreme bravado on the part of Ahmed Pasha, the admiral of the fleet? Otranto might have become the hub of an enclave in Apulia which, if it had survived, would have meant Ottoman control of the channel between the Adriatic and the Ionian Seas. Whilst they held on to Otranto, the Turks made raids on Brindisi, Taranto and Lecce. We know that Andrea Gritti, Venice's 'sheriff' in Constantinople, was charged with letting the sultan know that his government felt entitled to the ownership of Apulia, an area which had once belonged to the Byzantine Empire – of which the sultan was now overlord. This is one of the earliest pieces of evidence of a theme that was to develop in the succeeding century; having occupied territories in the Eastern Roman Empire, the sultan could be considered as, and could consider himself as, their legitimate heir.

The death of Mohammed II in May 1481, and the dispute for succession between his sons Djem and Bajazet, slackened the pressure for a while. Otranto was liberated and Venice, with the peace of 7 August 1481, returned the occupied Apulian towns to King Ferdinand of Naples. The peace did not prevent Venetian propaganda, which always presented the Republic as the champion of the crusade, from being turned almost completely on its head in Southern Italy. For the scholars and writers of the kingdom, Venice (particularly after the events of Otranto) was the Turks' deceitful accomplice and might have brought about the Ottoman occupation of the entire Italian Peninsula.

In 1484 great astrological upheavals were expected. Nevertheless, the Turkish advance about which such anxiety prevailed made no new progress. Bajazet's activities were focused on the struggle to succeed his father. He made haste to cultivate diplomatic relations with the

Knights of Rhodes to make sure that they were keeping his brother Djem securely under lock and key on the island, where Djem had escaped after a defeat in battle. The hapless Ottoman prince made a series of journeys through France and Italy, passing from the custody of the Knights of Rhodes to that of Pope Innocent VIII and finally to that of Charles VIII of France. Charles VIII marched across Italy in 1494, preceded and accompanied by a cloud of prophecies, having unfurled the crusading flag once more. Djem's illustrious custodians naturally demanded generous payment from the sultan for their hospitality to his brother, who died in Naples in mysterious circumstances. A portrait of him by Pinturicchio shows an isolated, melancholy figure decked in royal finery. He stimulated the imagination of his contemporaries, as did the diplomatic and commercial circumstances surrounding his case. Interest in Turkish dress began to lead Western aesthetics towards exoticism.

The death of Djem liberated the sultan from the need for circumspection. His relationships with the Venetians deteriorated at once, partly because in 1489 the Republic had managed to succeed the last Queen of Cyprus, Caterina Cornaro, and was also now in control of Naxos. From the Venetian point of view the occupation of Cyprus was an essential step which (for the time being, at least) resolved a risky game of puss in the corner. Queen Cornaro, the widow of James II of Lusignan, was on the verge of marrying one of the sons of the King of Naples. If this had happened the island would have been transferred into the Catalan-Aragonese 'Mediterranean Empire', which would thus have been extended to the Eastern Mediterranean, with very detrimental consequences for Venice's possessions and her maritime interests. On the other hand Istanbul, the Sublime Porte, also had its eye on Cyprus. The Sultan of Egypt, who needed the trade with the Levantine Venetians of Damietta and Alexandria (although faking a scowl at the Venetian flag fluttering on the island so close to its coastline), in reality far preferred the infidel republic as a neighbour than his Ottoman colleague and co-religionist. The diplomatic mission to Cairo of the sixty-year-old expert Pietro Diedo, and the renewal of the annual tithe of 8,000 ducats which the Lusignans were already paying to the sultan for Cyprus, smoothed out any remaining difficulties.

A few years later, in 1499, a rapid Ottoman campaign dislodged the Venetians from the Peloponnese, and there were Turkish raids along the coast between Trieste and Lubljana; in September the Turks reached Vicenza. In fact, Turkish attacks were never random. The Turks used precise, carefully judged intimidation rather than outbursts of animal ferocity. As Senator Domenico Malipiero makes clear in his *Annali veneti*, the aim of their attacks was never carnage or destruction. They were always attempting to confirm political hypotheses or test tactics. In this case they hoped to intimidate the Venetians and wear down their patience, at the same time exploiting the rivalries between Christian groups. A timid new call to arms fell on deaf ears; in any case the sultan was doing business with the Poles, who were on the point of going to war with Venice. With their raids the Turks were following an age-old tradition, used centuries earlier in almost identical fashion, by the Goths, the Lombards and the Hungarians. They would file through the narrow passes in the mountains of Gorizia, Carso and Cividale and then simply fan out over the plain of Friuli. In the end the Turks obtained what they wanted: the peace treaty of 1502–3 allowed Venice to retain the Ionian islands of Zákinthos and Cephalonia, but in exchange they had to abandon claims to Durrës and the ports of the Peloponnese.

Venice had other problems to worry about at this time. The discovery of the New World and the opening up of the Portuguese route to India and the East were combining to impoverish Venice by shifting the trade routes it controlled. It had a fellow-sufferer in the Sultan of Egypt: the spices flowing into Europe from the Portuguese markets cost far less than the spices coming from Alexandria and Damietta.

Whilst the Ottomans were enjoying huge successes in the Balkans and the Aegean, the last act of the drama of al-Andalus was being played out.

The Iberian Peninsula was still feeling the effects of the social, eco-nomic, spiritual and religious crisis of the mid-fourteenth century. An endless succession of dynastic wars, betrayals, surprise attacks and turmoil had induced a state of battle fatigue in the Iberian Christian kingdoms, resolved only by the marriage between Isabella of Castile and Ferdinand of Aragon on 19 October 1469 and, during the decade that followed, by the couple's accession to their respective thrones, which, for the time being, remained separate.

Although the conditions looked favourable for a return to lasting peace in the Iberian Peninsula, the state of cohabitation that existed between the followers of the three religions born of Abraham's seed continued to deteriorate. During the course of the fourteenth century relations between Christians, Muslims and Jews had already begun to show signs of strain. The Iberian Peninsula at that period was still regarded as a safe haven for communities of Jews expelled from France and England; the Kings of Castile had refused to comply with the decree, passed by the Lateran Council of 1215, which established the yellow *rota* as the identification mark for Jews. The refugees flooding in from the Pyrenees and the Mediterranean ports went under the blanket name of *francos*; their alleged crimes were lending money at exorbitant rates, poisoning wells in order to spread leprosy or the plague, massacring Christian children, mixing their blood into the unleavened bread eaten at Easter, and stealing and desecrating the consecrated host. Cohabitation made open discussion possible – as, for example, in 1263 when a debate between Christians and Jews was held in Barcelona in the presence of King James I of Aragon. When the debate ended the sovereign rewarded the rabbis for having defended their cause with such spirit, and on the following Saturday he attended a religious service in the synagogue.

The arrival of Jews in such large numbers to settle in Spain and Portugal sadly led to persecution there as well. The yellow badge was gradually introduced and massacres began to take place, beginning with the *navarrería* in Pamplona in 1277. The civil war made matters worse. Over the twenty years straddling the fourteenth and fifteenth centuries a terrible series of atrocities coincided with sermonizing campaigns whose 'hero', the Dominican Vincent Ferrer, was celebrated in so many other respects. In Castile, a royal edict in 1412 prohibited Jews and Muslims from living in separate districts, and the edict was repeated in Aragon in 1415. At this time the problem of *conversos* and *cristianos nuevos* raised its head. These new Christians were becoming ever more numerous because Muslims and Jews found it difficult to resist the dual pressure of persecution and preaching campaigns, but they were regarded with disdain by the *cristianos viejos*, who were proud of the purity of their blood.

The Iberian Muslims or *mudéjares* (the word denotes a Muslim who is a 'resident-subject' in a Christian country) were treated marginally better than the Jews. They were left in peace to ply their trades as carpenters, masons, gardeners or tailors (they produced the Moorish clothes that were fashionable in fifteenth-century Spain). They were less wealthy, less influential and less entrepreneurial than the Jews, which was one of the reasons why they suffered less from persecution, but in spite of this, they too began to grow impatient at an early date. In 1276, after a Muslim uprising in Valencia, James I expelled them by decree and confiscated their possessions. Anger and revolt increased in the two centuries that followed. In parallel with this, the outward signs of Muslim Spain's booming agricultural technology began gradually to disappear. Spain's new landowners, the warlike Christian aristocracy, wanted the quick returns guaranteed by cattle-and sheep-farming, and in the space of a few years most of the Iberian Peninsula was turned into a desert.

In 1480 the Catholic kings introduced the Inquisition tribunal into Spain and the Pope gave them permission to choose their own judges. The aim of Spanish society now seemed to be to purge the country of non-Christians and to ennoble those Christians who could boast the longest lineage, which relieved them of the need to earn a living.

Landowning, high office in the Church, government administration and the military were now the only occupations worthy of those with pure blood and the correct religious convictions. The _cruzada_, an ideal as well as a form of fiscal pressure, was the ethical backbone of sixteenth-century Spain.

In 1502 all the Spanish _mudéjares_ chose to be converted _en masse_. The haughty Iberian Christians never trusted these _moriscos_, accusing them of remaining Muslims at heart, as the _marranos_ had remained Jews. The Muslims and Jews who wanted to retain their religion did not wait to be expelled before sailing for North Africa or various parts of the Ottoman Empire. Many of the Jews, called 'Sephardim', left their beloved Sefarad (Spain) for Italy. To all the countries to which they emigrated they took the incomparable gift of their culture, their intelligence and their business acumen. In expelling her Jewish population, Spain lost a valuable heritage and impoverished herself permanently. The economic decline of the Iberian Peninsula stems from this period, before the arrival of silver from the New World caused a devastating 'price revolution'.

Thus did al-Andalus languish and die. After the splendid reign of Emir Mohammed I, founder of the Nasrid dynasty of Granada and the Alhambra Palace, the history of Nasrid rule was a lengthy succession of insurrections, _coups d'état_ and sedition. In Almeria and Malaga, separatist emirates supported by Castile or the Moroccans undermined the security of the Emir of Granada. In Granada the Nasrid dynasty was overthrown in 1453 by the adventurer Mulay Saad, who was deposed by his son Mulay Abu'l Hasan. In 1481, when the last of a number of truces with the Castilian–Aragonese axis expired, Mulay Abu'l Hasan began another phase of hostilities. The Moors conquered Zahara, the Christians Alhama: this was the beginning of the so-called 'war of Granada'. The ruling clan was divided, however. On one side were Abu'l Hasan and his brother Zaghal, on the other the rebel Abu Abdullah Mohammed ('Boabdil' in the Christian chronicles), the eldest son of Abu'l Hasan and in revolt against his father. The conflict was as fierce as it was chaotic as the Moors fought amongst themselves for possession of their spectacular capital city. Zaghal was bravely keeping even the Christians at bay.

Ferdinand decided to put a stop to the troubles. A young military commander who was beginning to make a name for himself for bravery was Consalvo de Córdoba, _el Gran Capitán_. Sixtus IV had sent the King of Aragon a large silver cross, used as an emblem by the crusaders, as a token of victory. After the last strongholds, including Malaga, had fallen, Zaghal laid down his arms and in early 1490 dismissed his troops. Boabdil promised to give up Granada to the Christians as soon as his uncle surrendered; in fact, when the time came, he refused to yield and instead took over control of the extremist wing of the Muslim resistance.

The Castilians and Aragonese fielded an army below the walls of Granada which has been estimated as numbering 80,000 soldiers. Isabella, Ferdinand and Consalvo led the siege. The Christians were quartered in a vast tented encampment which they named Santa Fe. Succumbing more to hunger during that harsh winter in the snows of the Sierra than to the superior strength of the Christian forces, the Moors surrendered on 2 January 1492, following negotiations conducted by Consalvo in Arabic, a language in which he was fluent. The Catholic Monarchs waited until Epiphany before entering the walled city. Later, feasting and celebrations, processions and spectacles were held all over Europe to celebrate the event.

The capture of Granada produced an extraordinary effect throughout the Christian world and was viewed as a fitting revenge for the fall of Constantinople thirty-nine years earlier. In March 1494, at Castello Capuano in Naples, during a party given by Alfonso, Duke of Calabria, a poem by Sannazzaro entitled *La presa di Granada* was recited.

The extreme south-west edge of the crusade belonged to the Portuguese, who sacked Ceuta in 1415. In 1471, following Henry the Navigator's defeat of the same city, they apparently conquered Tangiers during a crusade undertaken with the blessing of Eugenius IV. Crusading was by now deeply rooted in Portuguese culture. In 1420, Henry (later called 'the Navigator') became Grand Master of the Order of Christ, which (as written in the bull appointing him Master by Martin V) 'was established by the Kings of Portugal with the aim of waging war against and persecuting the Saracens, the enemies of the cross of Christ and other infidels, and of defending Christians from their assaults'.[1]

The Portuguese might have proceeded with the conquest of Morocco if they had not been distracted by a strong urge to pursue naval exploration along the west coast of Africa: the Cape of Good Hope was first rounded in 1488. The alliance with the 'Prester John of Africa', in other words the Negus of Ethiopia who, it was said, controlled the cataracts on the Nile and could cause flood or drought in Egypt, was the motivation for a new crusade against the Sultan of Cairo. The Aegean and the Balkans were a long way from Lisbon and the Algarve; the Portuguese had not yet fully understood that the Muslim threat was no longer simply a Mameluke threat. They continued to dream of ways of attacking the Nile sultanate, although it had been many decades since this had posed any kind of threat to Christianity – if, in fact, it had ever done so.

[1] *La caduta di Costantinopoli. L'eco nel mondo* (Rome/Milan, 1976), p. 99; see also P.E. Russell, *Portugal, Spain and the African Atlantic 1343–1490. Chivalry and Crusade from John of Gaunt to Henry the Navigator* (Aldershot, 1995).

## Teucrians and Turks

The last wars against the Moors in Spain were conducted under the ensign of the *cruzada* rather than that of the crusade, the latter having by now become a European defence against Ottoman expansion. The *cruzada* bore echoes of the chivalrous engagements that had taken place from the Iberian Peninsula to Syria in the Middle Ages. Spanish chivalric romance breathes the same atmosphere: the enemy infidel acts generously and magnanimously towards the Christian hero and friendship and respect are the outcomes of the war. Psychological and aesthetic admiration for the Moors, which was to be one of the components of exoticism and romanticism in the future, had features and dimensions that distinguished it from the general crusading problem of the period. The 'Turk', the 'Infidel' and the 'Saracen' were becoming established roles in courtly and popular entertainments in Renaissance Europe, and were thus entering folklore. With his highly coloured costumes and horrible appearance, the Moor was the antagonist in scores of *pas d'armes, pasos honrosos* and tournaments, all of which had now become genuine theatrical performances in which armed conflict was the pivotal scene. In pamphlets, too, the 'Saracen' was the target for jibes and taunts from his opponents. Enemies of the Cross, now considered to be the enemies of Europe, were natural candidates for the role of metaphysical enemies as well as enemies in jest. The Saracen had become a familiar (though still threatening) figure in the collective imagination.

On the other hand, however, although the 'Moors' and 'Saracens' were familiar figures to the Europeans, and even the Tartars and Mamelukes conveyed quite a clear image, the Turks remained enigmatic. Their name had been around since the end of the eleventh century, when vague rumours about the Seljuks reached Europe. As far as can be gathered from the scant information surviving from the Council of Clermont, Urban II referred to them (with a degree of accuracy) as a people from Persia. The anonymous Italo-Norman knight who wrote the chronicle known as the *Gesta Francorum* in the early twelfth century first discussed the extraordinary courage of the Turks in battle, then used this to put forward the theory that the Turks, Franks and Romans all had a common ancestry in the Trojans; they could thus be contrasted with the treacherous *graeculi* and the base, unreliable Byzantines. The anonymous knight concluded that it was only the Turks' status as infidels that stood in the way of their being a great people – a statement which anticipated that made by Pius II in his *Epistola ad Mahometem*.

Any possible link between the Turks and the people descended from 'pious Aeneas' was anathema to the humanists, on the other hand. They considered such comparisons with the barbarous infidels as unacceptable because the infidels were opposed to the Byzantine Greeks and were therefore the enemies of Hellenic culture. The plunderers of Constantinople could not be likened to the brave, generous Trojans; they were closer to the Shiites with their barbarism, or the fierce raiders of the distant past, described in the ancient sources with fear and loathing. From the Shiites these erudite humanists moved on immediately and quite naturally to the most brutal people of all antiquity, the principal enemy of Greece and Rome – the Persians, referred to earlier by Urban II. In his canzone O *aspettata in ciel beata e bella*, Petrarch established a direct connection between the crusade of the day and the wars between the Ancient Greeks and the Persians. The conflict between the Christians and the infidel thus gained a further dimension, one which did not necessarily obliterate its religious significance; in fact, it enhanced it by linking it to earlier encounters of significance: the struggle between Europe and Asia, as interpreted by Herodotus or by Aeschylus in *The Persians*, as a contest between civilization and barbarians. In fact, Enea Silvio Piccolomini had even used a page from Herodotus in his efforts to demonstrate that the Turks were descended from the Shiites. An equation was being established between civilized Christian European values on one hand, and pagan Asian uncivilized values on the other. Part of the equation, of course, was anti-Muslim or anti-Koranic debate, as contemporary polemical literature demonstrates. The texts of the day, heavily indebted to Peter the Venerable and Ricoldo of Montecroce, include Nicholas of Cusa's *Cribratio Alchorani* and the *Contra principales errores perfidi Machometi* by Juan of Torquemada. These were written in 1460–1 and 1459, respectively, and both were used by Pius II.

Nikolaus Chrypffs, born in Kues on the Moselle in Alsace in 1401 and known to us as Nicholas of Cusa, was certainly neither pro-Muslim nor pro-Turk. While other humanists were swarming all over Europe, ransacking monasteries for the Greek and Latin manuscripts in their possession, Cusa was contending with a manuscript that contained Robert of Ketton's Latin version of the Koran, the product of the great translation carried out in Toledo nearly three centuries earlier. Later, as the papal legate in Constantinople just before the city fell to the Turks, he charged Dominican and Franciscan friars with the task of providing new translations of the Bible.

Cusa was created a cardinal in 1448 and Bishop of Bressanone in 1450. He was an impassioned preacher and supporter of the crusade that was planned to avenge Constantinople and recapture the city from the Ottomans; although the crusade was proclaimed several times, it never took place. Alongside the armed crusade, however, the cardinal expended much thought on a crusade of ideas in the shape of a version of the Koran that would give Christians a clearer idea of the mass of contradictions and absurdities (according to the far from impartial Western exegetists of the day) which characterized it. This seemed to him the best way of giving ideological support to the military endeavour. The study of Islam in the West was evaluative rather than cultural or religious, based on discussions and debate.

To serve his ends, the cardinal required someone whose character was above criticism rather than a scholar. He found this person in one of the most devout men of the day, the mystic Dionysius of Ryckel, better known as Dionysius the Carthusian (1402–71), whose visions of the threat were becoming obsessional.

Dionysius was the author of a treatise in dialogue form entitled *Contra Alchoranum et sectam machometicam*, which today is more useful as a means of understanding fifteenth-century Western prejudices against Islam than as a serious approach to Muslim culture. Basing his study on Robert of Ketton's translation of the Koran, Dionysius (who was doggedly loyal to the methods of Ricoldo of Montecroce, however questionable they were) made a systematic analysis of the passages in which Christianity and Islam appeared most closely connected.

From the material collected, Cusa was able to write another treatise, the *Cribratorio Alchora* ('Examination of the Koran'), which he intended to be used by those wishing to convert Muslims to Christianity. The treatise was dedicated to the Cardinal's great friend Enea Silvio Piccolomini, now Pope Pius II, to complement the enigmatic document written by him in 1461, the *Epistola ad Mahometem*.

### Islam and the Reformation

The Turks were thus still a threat. 'Lord, will the Turks invade Rome?' were the anxious words spoken by Dionysius the Carthusian during a mystical vision. Some years later, Machiavelli made one of the characters in his *Mandragola* ask: 'Do you think the Turk will make it to Italy this year?' The two questions, which express the prevailing anxiety in such different tones and circumstances, expose the Great Fear that gripped the heart of Europe between the second half of the fifteenth century and the early years of the sixteenth, but they also contain the key to its conquest or control through being tamed and losing its power to convince. To what extent, in fact, could the Turkish advance be seen as a sign of prosperity? What role should it have played within the economy of Divine Revelation? The answers can be found in a combination of politics, theology, prophecy and astrology, and the interaction between them.

In the same year in which Constantinople fell to the sultan, Nicholas of Cusa (previously an ardent supporter of the crusade) wrote one of his most compelling books, *De pace fidei*, in which Turks, infidels and the armies of the Antichrist appear as the gentiles, ripe for conversion.

Girolamo Savonarola's prophesying contained no negative role for the Turks. He did not propose crusades, nor did he think that infidels should be punished; he imagined that their conversion to Christianity in the future would coincide with the punishment of 'false Christians'. He was aware of the Muslim devotion to Christ, and welcomed the theory which held that justice flourished amongst the Turks. When Angelo of Vallombroso, his troublesome adversary, foretold bloody massacres of Muslims, Savonarola continued to emphasize conversion as the sign that would accompany the Church's renewal.

The need for agreement between the Christians as a precondition for fighting the infidel (and equally, the need to avoid further postponement of the struggle for which Christian unity was deemed indispensable) was something about which Leo X always felt strongly and supported wholeheartedly. It was the subject of the *Libellus*, published in Rome between May and August 1513 by two Camaldolese friars, Paolo Giustiniani and Pietro Quirini (two Observants from the hermitage of San Michele, Murano). They presented the Pope with reasons why the long-awaited *reformatio* could be postponed no longer, and demonstrated clearly how the rapid progress made by the Muslims over the past few decades in their conquest of Europe was due to internal strife amongst the Christian fraternity. No diplomatic protocol or official declaration issued by the Christian powers at this time failed to emphasize the need to put a stop to encroachment by the *immanissimi*, *truculentissimi* and *perfidi* Turks; this was particularly true if the powers were fighting against one another, as happened at Cambrai on 10 December 1508 when the empire, Spain, France and the Pope all joined forces against Venice. Of course, this may have been simply a way of transferring to the current adversary responsibility for choices presented as voluntary or objective acts of collaboration with the Turks.

The Turk played a useful if equivocal role in the anxious vigil preceding the Reformation. After all, who was to blame for Turkish success if not the Christians themselves, *peccatis exigentibus*? Was it the fault of the heretics or the ills of the Church, was it the defects of believers or the corruption of the papal Curia and the prelates which drew the wrath of God so forcibly down on Christianity's head? Should the infidel, undoubtedly the expression of this wrath, be considered as the herald of the Antichrist or the instrument of divine retribution? Was it necessary, useful or even legitimate to fight the infidel?

In his *Encomion Morias*, Erasmus of Rotterdam categorized all war, including war against the infidel, as folly. In his *Querela pacis*, published in 1517, when there was still some hope of avoiding a head-on collision between France and the Hapsburgs, Peace laments the misfortunes that man foolishly inflicts upon himself: was it not shameful that Christians murdered one another yet poured scorn on the Turks as the 'enemies of Christ', as if they, the Christians, behaved any better than the Turks? It was rumoured that the Turks made sacrifices to the devil; was not a Christian who murdered another Christian doing much the same thing? The Turk certainly represented danger, but this was further evidence of the foolishness of the Christians, who fought amongst themselves in spite of the dangers surrounding them. Yet agreements between the Christians and the Turks were often withered.

Erasmus never expressed absolute opposition to the crusades, but he regarded them as a minor evil compared with the war between Christians; the latter was even more blameworthy because it directly assisted the Turks.

In a letter written from Basel to Paul Volz on 18 August 1518, used as an introduction to the Basel edition of the *Enchiridion militis Christiani*, Erasmus argued that the only convincing preliminary to peace was peace; it was hopeless to prepare for peace by making war. Commenting on the proclamation by the Pope of the new crusade in 1517, Erasmus returned several times in letters written over the next couple of years to the idea that, for the Christians, the only way to combat the Turks was to follow Christ's teachings in the most coherent fashion possible. Erasmus condemned the vanity of the war against the infidel particularly vehemently in the most hard-hitting of his *Adagia* series, the *Dulce bellum inexpertis*, in which the reasons behind the war received a substantial degree of recognition. Surely, Erasmus observed, things were going badly for the Christians if their cause was dependent on preparations for war against the infidel. The Turks should be shown Christian virtue, not the weapons of Christianity. The violence of others should never be used as an excuse for violence. Not that Christians should refrain from defending themselves against the Muslims, should they attack; but one should not abdicate one's faith. Even in war, Christian values should prevail.

When the Reformation came, even the Western Christians were experiencing the dramatic feeling of repulsion which had progressively gripped the Greek Christians before the fall of Constantinople: better the Turkish turban than the mitre of Rome. The traditional accusation brought by the Inquisition was that heretics and schismatics were 'worse than the infidel'; to this the reformed party would reply that the Pope and his prelates were more vile and dangerous than the Turks.

Although for many years Catholics and Protestants insulted one another with accusations of being allied with the infidel, they realized all along that it would be better to be allied with the infidel than with the other Christian group. Luther inveighed against the Muslims, it is true; but it is also true that when the advocates of Reformation discussed the crusades they were not critical of the ultimate aim but were deeply opposed to the system of tithes, vows and indulgences on which the *negotium crucis* had been based at least since the thirteenth century, in fact since crusading law had been formulated by jurists such as Henry of Sousa or Sinibaldo Fieschi.

At the onset of the Reformation, the Pope deemed it necessary to postpone all plans to unite the Christians against the Turks. In May 1518 he wrote to the Elector of Saxony, Frederick the Wise, to inform him of this decision. Two years later he sent the Prince Elector a copy of the bull *Exsurge Domine*, laying particular emphasis on the notion that Luther's rebellion favoured the Ottomans. There were objective reasons, in fact, to lend plausibility to his claims. It was undoubtedly true that Luther, with reference to the principle of divine retribution, had several times identified the Turks as the instrument of divine punishment against the papists. Leo X had already denounced this claim in his bull of 1520, but Luther reiterated it in openly challenging terms, upholding the opinion that the West should neither march against the infidels nor make any financial contribution to a war against them, because they were patently more sensible than the Catholic hierarchy. When the diet of Spira in 1529 established that propaganda about the Reformation should be stamped out if possible, Luther replied a few months later, in September, by proclaiming the neutrality of those who supported his protest, even in such dramatic circumstances as the Turkish siege of Vienna. In his *Epistle to the brothers of Lower Germany*, Erasmus does in fact state that Lutheran soldiers used to cry out that the 'Unbaptized Turk' (the sultan) was better than the 'Baptized Turk' (the emperor), and that in the Low Countries flags had been seen bearing the crescent moon and the motto *Plutost Turcs que Papaux*.

Events such as these may explain why, in Catholic areas, the crisis gave rise to a new topic of discussion: the resemblance between Protestantism and Islam. The reformers turned the accusations back against the Catholics, reiterating an opinion first expressed by John Wyclif who, in about 1378–84, when the danger of Muslim invasion seemed to have been averted, had emphasized the immorality and vileness which, objectively (in his opinion), made the Church under the leadership of the Pope resemble Islam. This was why, the champions of the Reformation continued, the moral renewal of the Church was more urgent than the war against Islam, which would have been conquered without any recourse to arms if the Christians had improved sufficiently to make an example to the Muslims of their virtue. It was in this fashion, using these arguments, that the Reformation and the Counter-Reformation introduced new complications and subtle distinctions into crusading, as *defensio Europae* and *defensio Christianitatis*.

In the Lutheran camp, meanwhile, the exegesis of chapter 7 of the Prophet Daniel was being promoted supported by Justus Jonas and Melanchthon, according to which the 'little horn' of the Beast was identified with the Turkish Empire, although this interpretation would have been rejected by Calvin. Luther had had much to say about the subject. In response to Luther's *Von Kriege wider die Turken* of 1529, possibly at the indirect instigation of the emperor, Erasmus produced in the following year, at Freiburg im Breisgau, a small treatise entitled *Utilissima consultatio de bello Turcis inferendo*, the culmination of his long years of letter writing. For many years he had been appealing to the rulers of Europe to abandon hostilities and to present a united front to their common enemy.

Like everyone in Germany at the time, Luther was worried by the Turks, but not over worried: Saxony, where he lived, was situated a long way from possible invasion, and the Ottoman attack on ultra-Catholic Vienna had failed to upset him unduly, as has already been noted. His tendency to treat his adversaries indiscriminately, putting them all – Jews, Turks, Papists, followers of Zwingli and so on – more or less on the same level, is demonstrated on several occasions. He spoke quite frequently of the Turks in his celebrated *Tischreden*, or dinner-table speeches.

In 1531 Erasmus declared that if the Duke of Saxony were to march against the infidel, he would willingly follow him, sure in the knowledge that his martyrdom would persuade God to exterminate the Ottomans. In 1532, when it was known that Sultan Suleiman, who three years previously had been forced to withdraw from the siege of Vienna, was preparing another offensive, Erasmus was visibly anxious about the way the Germans were making themselves ready for the event. He declared that Ferdinand of Hapsburg was bound to be beaten and that the Pope's intention was to throw the Germans into conflict with one another, and the Turks over them all; the idea that the Turks and the Catholics were secret allies was behind these considerations. The Catholics, meanwhile, were letting it be known that the Turkish threat was the expression of God's wrath following the spread of Lutheran beliefs.

According to Luther, the Turks (that is, the Muslims) and the Catholics were also linked by resemblances between their two religions. Both, for example, held that God would assist only the pious, not the sinner. Comparing doctrine on justification through books strictly about Muslim law might seem strange; but the point is (Luther continued) that

Muslims, like the Pope, cannot approach God through Christ, the former because they do not recognize Christ's divine nature, the latter because he has betrayed God's word. In reality the great reformer had no very clear idea about Islam (treating it at times as a heretical sect, at others as a religion), and he showed no great interest in it. The Turks were one matter, and they represented a danger; their religion was quite another, and in Luther's eyes it was worthy only of contempt. Luther nevertheless remained a loyal subject of Charles V; in September 1532 he noted with satisfaction how Francis I of France had been humiliated in Pavia seven years earlier, in spite of relying on Turkish assistance. He certainly could not have been expecting the French and Lutheran princes to seek agreement with the Turks just a short while later.

Luther was in any case not impressed by the Turkish successes. He was well versed in Roman history and at Christmas 1537 he remarked that, in the space of about one hundred years, the Ottoman Empire had grown only about half as much as the Roman Empire had done in the same amount of time; the empires of Charles and Suleiman were, he added, mere semblances of empires compared with the Roman Empire.

The continuing discussion of the Turks and Islam inevitably led to a demand for scholarly texts on the subject, including general historical works such as *Fasciculus temporum* by Werner Rolenwick and *De inventoribus rerum* by Vergil Polydore. In these works the subject of Islam, based on the usual Byzantine and medieval sources, appeared more and more abundantly and frequently. From the errors scattered liberally throughout such texts there arose a series of misunderstandings which are difficult to describe, let alone disentangle. To give an example, in his *Consultatio de bello Turcis inferendo*, Erasmus developed an amusing misunderstanding found in Vergil Polydore, according to which the Prophet Mohammed was killed by the Turks who, having first been his followers during his military incursions, then rebelled against him.

The Turks were above all the subject of prophecy. From Lauterbach's *Diary*, it appears that in 1538 there was much talk of the Antichrist, of the 'greatness and power of the Turk', whose reign had been foretold by the prophet Daniel and the Apocalypse. As we have seen, Luther tended to identify Mohammed with the 'little horn' of Daniel's vision; he pointed out how certain prophecies could apply to both the Pope and the Turk, noting that the papacy and Islam both started to grow in the seventh and eighth centuries. Applying one of the more complex exegeses from Apocalypse 12.14, in which the reign of the Antichrist was reckoned as lasting 'three times and a half' ('a time' was interpreted as a period equivalent to Christ's age, thirty years according to Luther), the time attributed to the reign of the Antichrist was one hundred and five years. Since the capture of Constantinople in 1453, argued Luther in 1538, eighty-five years had passed; the Turks had only twenty years left in which to oppress the Christians. Everything was in God's hands, he concluded, and man could only pray and do penance.

For the record, twenty years after this prophecy, in 1558, almost nothing was happening in the Turkish camp. However, the war between the Ottoman Empire and Ferdinand of Hapsburg, begun in 1551, was in full swing; it ended in 1562 with the Turkish occupation of Hungary and a tribute to be paid by Vienna to the Sublime Porte. Whilst Christian Europe was being reduced to poverty by the conflict between Hapsburg and Valois, and between Catholics and Protestants, the shadow of the sickle was lengthening dangerously over the Balkans, the Danube Peninsula and the Mediterranean.

The Reformation produced one logical if unexpected result: a definite boost to the positive evaluation of Islam, and therefore to the birth and development of an often conventional and mannered pro-Islamic stance. Once Ottoman pressure on Europe had slackened, it bore generous fruit in overcoming the mind-set and militarism of crusading, and in fostering the nascent culture of Orientalism. The soil had already been prepared for this development in the Middle Ages, as is made clear by the chivalric legends featuring Saladin, or the frequent comments by scholars and polemicists (and also by merchants and Christian pilgrims) on the kindness and generosity of the infidel, compared with the miserliness and boorishness of their co-religionists. The Reformation generated more vehement and coherent arguments between Christians, the ultimate effect of which was to favour the Muslims. It became customary amongst Catholics and Protestants for each to censure the 'vices' of the other's religion and to emphasize that the infidel exemplified the corresponding 'virtue', which naturally would have been much better suited to the Christians. Postel praised Muslim alms-giving and the discretion with which it was performed. In his preface to the collection of Muslim texts printed and edited in 1543 by Bibliander, Luther made a distinction between reprehensible Islamic beliefs and the admirable way in which they were put into practice. In fact the arguments between Catholics and Protestants frequently led to a competition as to which of the two could hurt the adversary more by heaping praise upon the infidel.

With regard to the rest of the Muslim world – which, with the exception of the Holy Land, Egypt, North Africa and, to some extent, Persia, was outside the European purview – the Turks had one more claim to fame: their courage, valour and discipline in battle. In contrast to the dismal display of confusion and corruption provided by the armies and encampments in Europe in the sixteenth and seventeenth centuries, the sultan's armies were an admirable model of order, economy and moderation. They had a reputation for cruelty, but they had long dispensed with the violent fury that was so common amongst the European armies before the military reforms of the eighteenth century. The most varied voices now joined in praise of Muslim military manners: diplomats, merchants, travellers and clerics were all agreed that the Turks, who were so implacable in battle, so rigorous and pitiless in repression and the administration of justice, were at the same time loyal, honest, sincere, charitable, modest and hospitable in everyday life.

The huge literature which appeared on the problem of renegades managed to spread these ideas so comprehensively as to make them appear almost a justification for those abandoning Christianity for Islam. 'Becoming Turkish' out of desperation or disillusion, or in response to any of life's vicissitudes, was one of the recurrent themes of European and Mediterranean history between the sixteenth and the eighteenth centuries.

# 10

## Sultans, Pirates and Renegades

### The Magnificent Law-giver

Between 1516 and 1517, Selim I, who died in 1520, managed to subdue Mameluke Egypt and to extend his rule to the Holy City, meanwhile forming close relationships with the Muslim rulers of Tripoli, Tunis and Algiers. He was succeeded by his twenty-four-year-old son, who bore the same Biblical forename as he did (the name of King Solomon, the wisest of the Biblical kings). Solomon, or Suleiman, is known in the West as 'the Magnificent', but in Turkish and Muslim tradition he is celebrated under the even more glorious epithet of *al-Qanuni*, 'the Law-giver', a name which links him directly with Emperor Justinian and sustains the continuity between the Roman and Ottoman Empires.

Probably no Muslim dynasty has ever exercised so much influence over the destiny of Europe as did that of Suleiman the Magnificent. The presence of the Ottomans in Southeastern Europe during the Reformation exerted a powerful influence over the course of events, particularly in the most southerly part of Near-Eastern Europe. The sultan owed a large part of his success, especially in land battles, to the loyalty and effectiveness of his favourite crack infantry corps, the 'new guard' of the Janissaries. Having undergone selection by the *devshirme*, the obligatory conscription of Christian boys, the recruits were housed in purpose-built barracks and dressed in highly distinctive uniforms with white caps; they were submitted to iron discipline and a frugal way of life. Celibacy was enforced and they were all considered to be members of the same religious brotherhood (the *tariqa bektasshiyya*). The regiment was established by Sultan Murad I in the second half of the fourteenth century; when Suleiman acceded to the throne, the Janissaries numbered about five thousand, and by the time of his death their numbers had swollen to at least twelve thousand. Until the end of the eighteenth century they were both the scourge of Europe and the object of great admiration; heads of state and military leaders all over Europe attempted to imitate their organization and even their banners, weapons and uniforms.

The need to encourage the Janissaries as well as keeping them occupied was certainly partly responsible for Suleiman's intense offensive activity during the first ten years of his reign. He immediately unleashed a campaign in the Balkans which terminated in the conquest of Belgrade in 1521. Meanwhile, the Turks mobilized their navy and in 1522 conquered the island of Rhodes. Emperor Charles V provided the Knights of St John, formerly a powerful maritime Order, who were forced to leave the island where they had been based for more than two centuries, with a new base on the island of Malta. Between 1526 and 1533 the sultan took advantage of the divisions existing between European nations and of the wars that plagued Christendom to launch a fierce military campaign between the Balkans and the Danube, culminating in the siege of Vienna in September-October 1529. At this time the pirate Khair ad-Din was terrorizing Sicily and Southern Italy from his base in Tunis.

The main target of this powerful onslaught was Charles V, who was known as an implacable enemy of Islam. He inherited the task of implementing the wishes expressed in the testament of the Catholic Monarchs, 'to continue with the conquest of Africa and to fight the infidel in the name of religion'.[1]

The emperor did not regard himself as an uncompromising adversary of the Muslims. In time he came to recognize and tolerate them, guided by a simple political principle: the enemy of your enemy is potentially your friend. He opened negotiations with Shah Tahmasp of Persia, which led to a decision to attack Suleiman on two fronts, closing in on him in a pincer movement. The 'Grand Turk', as the sultan was known in the West, responded with an attack against the Persians. In doing so he aligned himself with the Ural-Altaic potentates of Transoxiana, heirs to Emperor Timur, who were of the same ethnic origin as the Turks and were also Sunni Muslims.

The wide-ranging Hapsburg offensive obliged Suleiman to take measures that were even more audacious. He entered negotiations with Francis I, King of France, who in his determination to avenge the defeat of Pavia and to remove the emperor from his powerful position had allied himself with Pope Clement VII through the 'League of Cognac'.

Meanwhile, renewed expectations and apocalyptic fears (which had never really been appeased) had to be taken into account. In 1527, Pope

---

[1]   Quoted in R. Menéndez Pidal, *Formación del fundamental pensamiento politico de Carlos V*, in *Charles et son temps* (Paris, 1958), p. 2.

Clement VII ordered the arrest of the 'prophet' Brandano, who claimed that in 1530 the Turks would capture the Pope, the emperor and the King of France and that only then would God save Christianity. Although objectively the prophecy may have appeared as a condemnation of all the rulers of Christendom, its primary aim may in fact have been to denounce the alliance between Clement VII and Francis I against Charles V, who appeared to be the bulwark of Christian opposition to the Muslims. It seems that, in order to counteract the gloomy forebodings of those who attributed any new Turkish political or military success to the political cynicism of the Pope, Clement VII was lending a respectful ear to the Jewish 'prophets', David Reubeni and Shelomò Molko, who held out the prospect of a combined Jewish–Christian front against the Ottoman Empire. Such a suggestion, a bold one to make at a period when *conversos* were such a prominent feature, may have had anti-Spanish undertones; this would not have entirely displeased the Medici Pope, at least before the treaty of Cambrai in 1529. To do battle against the infidel whilst isolating Spain and the empire might seem a noble undertaking and an interesting strategic and political goal; the problem, as always, was to translate such suggestions into reality.

Nevertheless, the Mediterranean crusading front was still developing, giving enormous importance to the manoeuvres being carried out by the papal court. The Venetians and the Germans, both traditional enemies of the Sublime Porte, were involved in military activities in the Balkans and around the Adriatic and the Aegean. The Serenissima, however, maintained a somewhat ambiguous stance. Andrea Gritti, the doge since 1523, had spent adventurous years in Istanbul and was a personal friend of Suleiman. He kept in regular contact with the sultan and would send him frequent marks of his esteem and admiration.

Meanwhile, the Mediterranean front was causing serious anxiety to Spain and the Order of St John. The entire coastline, from Gibraltar to the Straits of Sicily, was threatened, communications were unsafe, and there was a constant drain on men and merchandise caused by continuing harassment by pirates. In the fateful year 1529, when the Ottoman armies besieged Vienna, a renegade Greek who may have originated from Lesbos, Khair ad-Din (known later in the West as 'Barbarossa'), who already controlled the coast of Morocco, occupied Algiers in the name of the sultan.

The combination of the siege of Vienna and the problem of Algiers led the Pope and the emperor to terminate hostilities between themselves as quickly as possible and forced Francis I to fall in line with their wishes, although he did so with the utmost reluctance. In 1583 the Pope requested the empire, the Italian states and Hungary to organize a new crusade. Meanwhile, the Knights Hospitallers, who had been expelled from Rhodes, succeeded in establishing themselves in Tripoli. The Spaniards, having taken advantage of the lull in hostilities to besiege the stronghold of Algiers, were trying to strike a bargain with the sultan for peace in Hungary in exchange for their withdrawal from the fortress. Khair ad-Din had by this time been appointed Grand Admiral of the Fleet by the sultan. Having ransacked the Italian coastline as far north as the mouth of the Tiber, he then succeeded in capturing Tunis and expelling the emir, who was under Spain's protection. This created an enemy base in the immediate neighbourhood of the coast of Sicily, and made it almost impossible for Christian ships to pass through the Sicilian Channel.

By this stage the Mediterranean was dominated by Muslims, who were strengthened by their secret alliance with the King of France. For ethical reasons it was impossible for the king to denounce crusading ideals, but he remained convinced that any enemy of his enemy Charles V must be his friend.

In 1535 the emperor made preparations to attack Tunis with all his forces and to invest this campaign with the religious character of a crusade. He placed his trust in the 'Redeeming Cross', made a pilgrimage to the shrine of the Madonna of Monserrat, patron saint of Catalonian sailors, and made sure of the support of Pope Paul III, the Knights Hospitallers and the Portuguese. The imperial fleet, with seventy-four galleys and 330 ships, landed on the coast of Tunisia on 16 June. Less than one month later the fortress of La Goulette had been taken, the majority of the Turco-Berber fleet captured and 20,000 Christian prisoners liberated. Finally, on 21 July, Tunis itself was sacked. Charles V is said to have celebrated his triumph in Rome, bringing locks and bolts from the looted city. Whilst Khair ad-Din took refuge in Algiers, the Spaniards handed over Tunis to a Muslim governor (their subject) again, thus maintaining direct control over La Goulette.

The success of the imperial armies along the coast of North Africa had the effect of bringing the two great enemies of Charles V, namely Suleiman and Francis I, even closer to one another. A series of treaties followed (the 'Capitulations', ratified in 1569), which gave the French king permission to appear in Ottoman lands, above all in the Holy Land, as the defender of the Christian communities there. Diplomatic links brought with them reciprocal military commitments, some of them secret. A joint effort by the Turks and the French was, however, unsuccessful in enlisting Venice into their secret alliance; the policy of the Gritti doge, favourable as usual to his old friend in Istanbul, was overwhelmed by the strength of a powerful 'war party', which had been so heartened by the success of the imperial armies that it pressed for the resumption of maritime warfare. By way of retaliation against the

Venetians' change of course, the Turks blocked the Strait of Otranto and besieged Corfu.

Between 26 and 27 September 1538, in the Ionian Sea of Prevesa (now called Prêbésa), at the entrance to the Gulf of Arta, Khair ad-Din soundly defeated the armada raised by the papal-Venetian-Imperial alliance – ninety-five ships and nearly 60,000 men, plus 2,500 cannon. It has sometimes been claimed that the defeat was partly due to lack of enthusiasm on the part of the commander of the Christian fleet, Andrea Doria from Genoa, who was not excited by the idea of a Christian victory because it would mainly have benefited Venice. The defeat of Prevesa was in fact the prelude to the end of Venetian domination in the Morea. The old doge, who was to die before the year was out, had the bitter satisfaction of being able to reproach his adversaries for their imprudent militarism.

The Christian alliance now melted away like snow in sunshine. A couple of years later, the Serenissima signed a separate peace treaty with the Sublime Porte which involved the payment of crippling compensation and the return of the last remaining Venetian forts on the Greek mainland, such as Nauplia and Monemvasia. The emperor tried to take revenge in 1541 by besieging Algiers, the stronghold of Khair ad-Din, but this was another fiasco, partly because of a violent thunderstorm. The sultan's pirate admiral retaliated by unleashing a furious succession of raids which terrorized the coastline from Provence to the Ionian Sea. This was to be his swansong: he died a short while later, in 1546.

The Turkish fleet boasted a number of very brave admirals, most of them renegade Christians. One need only recall the Croatian Piyalè Pasha, or the Calabrian Luca (possibly Giovanni) Galieni, born in 1520 and kidnapped by Berbers when he was sixteen; he became Uluj-Ali Reis, known in Italy by the nickname 'Spectacles'. The death of Khair ad-Din shattered a myth, however. Charles V took advantage of the situation in 1550 with an attack on al-Mahdiyah in Tunisia, which was now the military base of Barbarossa's successor Turghud Ali, known in the West as Dragut. The city was captured on 8 September, but Dragut succeeded in escaping.

By this time the threat posed by Turkey and Barbary was beginning to worry the ecclesiastics who had assembled at the Council of Trent. Pope Julius III had no qualms about threatening Francis I's successor Henry II with the proclamation of a crusade directed against him if he continued to give support to the Turks and the Protestants.

Meanwhile, further disasters were taking place on the coast of North Africa. In August 1551 the Knights Hospitallers were forced to beat an ignominious retreat from Tripoli, which the sultan had assigned to Dragut. The Christians were showing signs of fatigue and loss of con-

fidence. Pope Paul IV, growing paranoid about the power of the Hapsburgs, gave the impression of accepting a kind of unwritten truce with
the Sublime Porte. He managed to make it known that he had secretly
offered to ally himself with the Turks against Spain. By this time corsair
attacks in the Mediterranean were endemic and reciprocal. However,
even *el rey prudente*, Philip II, who had succeeded his father to the
throne of Spain, was evidently of the opinion that when all was said
and done, the Turks were a distant threat while the heretics and rebels
living in the Iberian Peninsula were far more to be feared. Mediterranean
battles alternated with Balkan battles and sometimes there was interaction between the two theatres of war. Between 1560 and 1565 the
Christian navies received a rap on the knuckles near the port of Djerba,
whilst the Ottomans made an unsuccessful attempt on Malta, heroically
defended by the Knights. In exchange, the Ottomans conquered the
island of Chios and, in Hungary, the fortress of Sziget.

The great Suleiman died in 1566. The West breathed a sigh of relief,
and the sultan's death was celebrated in certain places, but the festivities
were dulled by a genuine sense of sadness. He had become a prominent
protagonist in the history of the century, a politician and ruler who
exerted a fascination over the West as well as the East. In the West he
was a constant subject of discussion; the pomp and opulence of his
entertainments and his magnificence were widely imitated, he was
admired personally and his portrait was painted more than once. Titian
painted him at least three times, basing his work on the pictures of the
sultan that were available to him and putting his own interpretation on
what he saw. Paolo Giovio praised Suleiman for his piety and magnanimity. It was mainly thanks to Suleiman and his reputation in the West,
fuelled by Montaigne, Bodin and Charon, that the Turkish Empire was
admired for its justice, order and for the power that it wielded; these
attributes went hand in hand, however, with a fearsome reputation in
war and some vicious customs. The many travellers to Turkey in the
sixteenth century were fulsome in their praise of the Grand Turk, who
ruled his subjects in a peaceful and just manner. The 'Turkish peace' he
imposed on his empire was honoured, evidently because it bore some
relation to the *pax romana*, but there were also plenty of criticisms of
Suleiman's tyrannical and violent method of government.

The imposing Ottoman war machine was on the move again. Having
put a provisional end to hostilities on the Balkan-Danube front in 1568
with the peace of Adrianopolis, the new sultan, Selim II (1566–74),
returned to lead an impassioned attack on the Mediterranean area,
from various quarters. A couple of years later the Christians had lost
Tunis (occupied in 1569 by Uluj-Ali, who succeeded the defunct Dragut
as governor of Algiers) and Cyprus, conquered by the infidel between

July 1570 and August the following year after the surrender of the Venetian stronghold of Famagusta. The continuing alliance with the French made the Turkish offensive even more successful.

Meanwhile, in the sultan's entourage, the political and diplomatic career of a man of genius was starting. Joseph Nasi was the influential spokesman of the Spanish Jewish exiles in Istanbul and in other cities of the Ottoman Empire. When the vizier Mehmet Sôqüllü insisted that the war with Spain for the control of North Africa be continued, and the war against the Hungarian Empire be resumed, Nasi warmly supported a war against Venice. He intensified his promotion of this war after 1566, when the Turkish ruler created him Duke of Naxos and of other islands in the Aegean. In the meantime he organized the creation of Jewish colonies around Tiberias, inviting the Jews expelled from Italy to settle there.

Although in his North African policy the sultan followed the advice of his vizier, the counsel of his Jewish friend was certainly not ignored. On 25 March 1570 Turkish demands relating to the restitution of Cyprus were received in Venice. The Serenissima – which, after Prevesa, had so far avoided compromising herself by entering into any explicit anti-Turkish alliance with Spain in order not to be dragged into their North African problems – now had to appeal for assistance to the only person who seemed disposed to stop the Ottomans in their tracks: Philip II. Christian Spain responded with enthusiasm. Andalusia had suffered a surprise attack from North Africa followed by a revolt of the *moriscos* in the region between 1565 and 1570. Cyprus, as we know, pursued its destiny: Nicosia fell on 9 February 1570 and Famagusta on 5 August 1571. Four days later the half-brother of the *rey prudente*, John of Austria, who had conquered the *moriscos* of Andalusia, landed in Naples. Just a month later a fleet comprising Spanish, Venetian and papal ships set sail from Messina.

The West was assailed by a flood of news from Cyprus, which produced the opposite effect from the one foreseen by the Turks, who as usual were spreading terror through cunningly displayed acts of cruelty. News of the atrocities perpetrated on the Venetian commandant of Famagusta, Marcantonio Bragadin, who bore his punishment with imperturbable stoicism, soon made the rounds of Christendom. This shortly produced what the wily grand vizier Mehmet Sôqüliü had been doing his utmost to avoid – an alliance between Spain and Venice.

On 7 October 1571, in the Gulf of Patras, an event took place which was hailed unanimously as a miracle by Christians, Catholics and reformed Christians alike.

The victory against the fearsome naval forces of Uluj-Ali at Lepanto was something quite spectacular. Of the 230 Turkish galleys (matched by only 208 belonging to the League, who also possessed six galleons), eighty were sunk and 130 captured: very few escaped being surrounded by the enemy. A flood of books, poems, pamphlets and other celebratory literature swept through the Christian world.

Nevertheless, the context of the Christian victory was a fragile one and events seemed to vindicate Emperor Maximilian II, who, in spite of the 'family pact' connecting him with his Hapsburg relations and allies in Spain, did not want to enter the fray. He stood by the promises to which he had signed his agreement and continued to pay tithes to the Turks – as had his father Ferdinand I. With well-calculated severity, the emperor declined invitations to alter this policy now that the sultan was in difficulty; he deemed it unworthy of a Christian prince to go back on his word, even to an infidel. Turkish pressure also obliged him to maintain and increase the concessions made to the Protestants: he was wise enough not to put himself in a position where he had to confront the consequences of such action, with the Turks now firmly established in Hungary. As the saying went in Germany at the time, *Der Türke ist der lutheranischen Glück* (the Turk spells good fortune for the Lutherans). It has been claimed, perhaps with some exaggeration, that without the Turks the reformed Christians of the sixteenth century might have met the same fate as had befallen the Cathars in the thirteenth century.

Meanwhile it was becoming increasingly clear that, because of a fundamental disagreement amongst the allies, the consequences of the battle of Lepanto had not been exploited to the full. On 10 February 1572 the Holy League was renewed; a few days later Pius V sent a letter to his flock in which the latest phase of the struggle against the Turk was unmistakably invested with the characteristics of a new crusade. Meanwhile, the sultan had rebuilt his fleet with incredible speed. Instead of attacking the sultan's ships in the Adriatic and then attempting to recapture Cyprus as the Venetians who were busy in the Morea would have wished, John of Austria recaptured Tunis in 1573 and occupied Bizerta. The Holy League broke up. Angry and exhausted, the Venetians abandoned their alliance with Spain and concluded a separate peace with Selim, which cost them the island of Cyprus, finally and permanently, and 300,000 ducats in compensation, while it allowed the sultan to concentrate his attention on the North African campaign. Without Venetian involvement in the League, the Turks were able to drive the Spanish from Tunis and Bizerta.

If the effects of the ephemeral encounter at Lepanto are examined in a different light, they look more durable. The battle was prepared in an intensely prophetic and apocalyptic climate, during which some of the old Jacobite ideas were resuscitated. The victory intensified this climate. 'And lo, there appeared in the sky a great sign; a woman dressed in the sun, with the moon beneath her feet and her head encircled by twelve stars'.[1] As we know, the *mulier* of Revelation became a basic canon in the exegesis and iconography of representations of the Virgin Mary. The apocalyptic image of the woman standing directly on the moon recalls a long series of divine personages connected with the night, the moon or womanhood: from Artemis/Diana to Isis to a succession of 'mother-gods' of micro-Asiatic and Semitic origin. The image was interpreted in typically anti-Islamic fashion, at least from the sixteenth century onwards. The Virgin is seen trampling the moon, itself a traditional symbol of Islam, but more specifically of the Ottoman Empire. The intercession of the Madonna of the Rosary in the victory of Lepanto was not fortuitous: 7 October, the day of the victory in 1571, became the feast of the Madonna of the Victories at the wish of Pius V and was finally established as the feast of Our Lady of the Rosary by Gregory XIII.

This observation is not intended to diminish the significance of the battle of Lepanto: its military outcome was considerable and its symbolic aftermath quite extraordinary. The fact remains, however, that Cyprus was still in Turkish hands and the Holy League, which had been formed with such enthusiasm to counteract the Ottoman threat, did not survive to see the final outcome of the conflict, which was in any case inconclusive. The game continued, without winners or losers. The impression, in Europe as well as in the Ottoman Empire, was that whether the victor or the vanquished in individual battles, the sultan was stronger in attack whilst the Christians remained timidly on the defensive. The ruler of the Bosphorus was still the Lord of Fear.

Nevertheless, the Christians were proud of their victories. Every sixteenth-or seventeenth-century painting of armoured troops has its lances bearing banners decorated with a crescent moon, or insignia snatched from the tails of Turkish horses. Contemporary monuments to governors and generals all show prisoners with shaven heads, long plaits and drooping moustaches sorrowfully following the victor's chariot in chains or languishing in shackles at his feet.

Although it was neither coherent nor unified, the crusading front covered a very wide area. Failure to recognize the fact that the theatre of war stretched from Gibraltar and the Maghreb to the Red Sea, the Black Sea, the Caspian and the Indian Ocean would be to misunderstand the significance of the military conflict between Christianity and Islam at the period. For example, Sultan Selim II (and others) gave military support to the revolt of the Andalusian *moriscos* between 1568 and 1570, and also advised the *moriscos* to attempt an alliance with the

---

[1] Revelation 12.1.

Lutherans; at the same time, he was studying the possibility of building a canal to join the Volga to the Don. If the Turkish fleet had been able to move from the Black Sea (and the Mediterranean) to the Caspian and vice versa, thus endangering the northern borders of the rival Persian Empire, the consequences for the history of the world could have been extraordinary.

The conflict was beginning to assume global proportions. Pius V, fully aware of what was happening, kept a constant eye on the situation in Portugal, inviting the Portuguese military Orders to take up their position on the North African border and insisting that no one could claim to belong to the Orders unless he had been a soldier for at least three years. Spain, meanwhile, showed no intention of becoming involved in the Mediterranean/Oriental conflict after the war with Cyprus, and an ever more vigilant eye was being kept on African affairs. In 1573 Spain organized another attack on Tunis, but it was short-lived and unsuccessful. Less than a year later, in July 1574, a Turkish armada 230 galleys strong and with 40,000 soldiers recaptured the city, this time permanently.

These events were followed with close attention by Sebastian, the nephew of Philip II of Spain, who had been King of Portugal since 1557. Sebastian was born in 1554 and had been king since he was only three years old, with a succession of regents ruling in his stead. His own character was a mass of dark and contradictory emotions, and he squandered the benefits of the crown while pursuing his own delusions of grandeur. Strictly educated by the Jesuits, his idol was the Infante, Henry the Navigator, who had established Portuguese maritime might one hundred years earlier. Henry dreamed of bringing Jesus Christ to India; Sebastian dreamed of taking Christ to Africa, beyond the great sweep of the Niger and fabled Timbuktu. He wanted to be master of the sea routes by which gold and ivory were imported into Europe, and to bring Christianity to the continent of Africa – a continent which was now revealed to be much larger than the early geographers had reported it to be.

In order to achieve this aim, however, it was necessary to control Morocco in the way that the Spaniards (using different methods) were attempting to control the area that is now Algeria and Tunisia: they were trying to withdraw the area from the Ottoman Empire and to regulate the activities of the Barbary corsairs.

In June 1578 Sebastian set out to conquer Morocco, setting sail from Lisbon with an army of about 10,000 Portuguese soldiers and 1,600 Spaniards, in addition to about 5,000 volunteers or mercenaries of various nationalities, including Germans, Italians and Moroccan followers of a sultan whom Sebastian wanted to place in control of the

Maghreb instead of the sultan (chosen by the Turks) in power at the time. The crusaders disembarked near Tangiers and set off towards the interior. A battle took place on 4 August at al-Kasr el-Kebir (Alcazar to the Europeans) and was later named the 'battle of the three kings', because there were three kings involved: Sebastian and the two rival sultans.

None of them survived. Sir Thomas Stukeley, who also lost his life, was an English Catholic who was in command of a papal contingent originally destined for Ireland but diverted to Morocco at the last minute – a detail which speaks volumes about the complexity of the crusading ideal at the time.

No trace was ever found of Sebastian – the sand and stones of Morocco failed to yield up his body. Instead, it was prophesied (the prophecy later being users by both Camoes in *Os Lusiades* and Fernando Pessoa as the subject of a poem) that the young king, known as *O Encoberto* ('the Hidden One'), would one day return from the sea, emerging from the Atlantic mists to inaugurate the 'Fifth Empire': after the Greek, Roman, Christian and British Empires, the hegemony of Portugal would finally be confirmed, and the true mystical vocation of Europe accomplished.

### Corsairs, Renegades and Prisoners

In 1580, two years after the death of Sebastian and in the year in which Philip II assumed control over Portugal, another warrior in the same romantic mould as Stukeley, the French Huguenot François de la Noue, wrote his *Discours*, one of the masterpieces of sixteenth-century political and military literature. At the time of writing it, de la Noue was languishing in jail in Limburg, where he had been cast by the Spanish for having taken part in defending the Calvinists in Flanders. He saw the new crusade, unencumbered by the Pope and undertaken collectively in order to liberate Europe from the Turkish menace, as one of the means by which Christianity could regain its unity.

The European powers at this time were studying ways of creating problems for the sultan and the eastern part of his empire. Legions of travellers, explorers, merchants and diplomats, or characters somewhere in between these categories, visited Persia in the sixteenth and seventeenth centuries, attempting to encourage the Safavid Shah of Persia to join them in a crusade against the ruler of Istanbul. In fact, the Persians were giving the Turks a very hard time: Tsar Ivan IV of Russia was at this period directing his energies against the Tartars of the Golden Horde, who were vassals of the Sublime Porte, and against a crucial area of

Central Asia, Astrakhan. If the Russians and the Persians had joined forces between the Caspian and Aral Seas, the Turks would have had to confront a new, compact continental front in the East. For this reason, the Sultan of Istanbul was eagerly pursuing a military alliance and friendly relations with the Turco-Mongol potentates who ruled the vast open spaces between Transoxiana, the Tien Shan and the Karakorum. The Western world was beginning to look towards Central Asia, too. From Florentine merchants such as Giovan Battista and Girolamo Vecchietti to the adventurous Roman polygrapher Pietro della Valle, these passionate, erudite travellers were all chasing the same dream, one which had first emerged in the thirteenth century: that of an allied Central Asian force that would grip Mediterranean Islam in a stranglehold and liberate Christian Europe from the evil Muslim threat.

The Turks did not represent an evil threat to everyone, however. It has already been shown how, from France to England to Protestant Germany, many people regarded the Turks as potential allies (although some of them kept it a secret): the 'enemy of an enemy'. In addition there were some people, particularly on the shores of the Mediterranean, who realized that they were exposed to the Turkish threat or that of their subject allies, the Barbary corsairs, but who regarded this state of affairs as a minor evil, or even as a possible opportunity. The poor, the weak, the landless, who were without money or resources in the rigidly hierarchical political and institutional structure of Christianity, looked at the Muslim world with hope and envy: there, even if you were born a Calabrian fisherman or an Albanian mountain-dweller, you could become a king or an admiral. Some – heretics, perhaps, or resentful losers, dreamers or the disinherited – even went so far as to hope for a Muslim victory over their thankless, unjust Christian homeland. In Europe anyone who showed too much freedom of spirit in matters of religion ended at the stake. The cruel Turk, on the other hand, who flayed and impaled his enemies, left his followers free to worship the God of Abraham if they wished in exchange for a simple act of submission and payment of a modest tax. A Muslim captured by the ships of Malta or St Stephen during a raid by Christian corsairs on the coast of the *dar al-Islam* ended up at the oars of an enemy galley, or languishing in a dungeon in Livorno or Toulon. A Christian captured from a ship waging war against the crescent moon, if he was young and handsome, or enterprising, or lucky enough to meet up with a sympathetic and influential master, could soon start to make his way up a steep career ladder, even arriving at the Sublime Porte or at the feet of the Great Sultan.

Capture and imprisonment by Muslims was a constant threat to coastal dwellers, merchants and pilgrims, or those honouring their crusading vows. Special Christian Orders such as the Trinitarians or the

Mercedarians were set up to deliver their brothers in Christ from slavery. There are many stories of boys and girls, or men and women, being captured in the Mediterranean by Turks or Barbary corsairs. Although many incidents are known to us, there were many others that we shall never know about. The stories are frequently tragic, but there are also tales of adventure with a happy ending. At times fact is more striking than fiction. Written memoirs and diaries may be fictionalized as far as specific events are concerned, but they are based on eye-witness accounts. This is so in the case of Andrés Laguna, a doctor from Segovia, who is well known for his scientific work and is also presumed to be the author of a *Viaje de Turquía* published in 1557. In pseudo-autobiographical style, it tells the story of Pedro de Urdimalas, captured in August 1552 off the coast of the island of Ponza and subjected to hard labour first as a galley slave, then as a slave in Constantinople. With the help of some medical books, he was able to free himself by posing as a doctor, first curing the illness of the pasha, his slave master, and then restoring the sultana herself to health.

If a fictional story could be taken as evidence of adventures that were more astounding than the literature which engendered them, the reverse could also happen: a literary narration could conceal a genuine experience. The most famous slave was Miguel de Cervantes, who was captured by Barbary pirates during a journey from Naples to Spain in 1575 and was taken in chains to Algiers. He tried unsuccessfully to escape several times; finally, a ransom was paid for him and he was liberated in 1580. He has left a vivid account of his experiences in chapters 39–41 of *Don Quixote*, in the story of the *cautivo*. The most extraordinary aspect of the adventures of Miguel de Cervantes the *cautivo*, who was later obliged to defend himself against accusations of being compromised by the Muslims and being on the verge of conversion to Islam, was his relationship with the Bey of Algiers, Hassan Pasha. Not only did the bey not punish Cervantes for his attempts to escape, he kept him by his side while he was captive.

There was frequently a kind of continuity, almost an affinity, between the position of a Christian prisoner and that of a renegade. Four centuries of silence separate us from the mysterious relationship existing between Miguel and Hassan, and it can never be broken. Cervantes' knowledge of the Muslim world went well beyond the horizons of Andalusia or North Africa – usually the outer limits of knowledge for cultivated Spaniards. The latter were familiar with Ottoman history and civilization. This forms the background to the play *El otomano famoso*, written at the end of the sixteenth century and the beginning of the seventeenth by Lope de Vega and dedicated to Othman, founder of the Ottoman dynasty.

Cervantes' friend, the Bey of Algiers, was a renegade from Dalmatia, whose predecessors as governors of Algiers had also 'become Turkish', from Barbarossa himself to the Sardinian Hassan Aga, the 'Corsican' Hassan and, finally, the Calabrian Uluj-Ali. Many renegades ended up as commanders of the fleet or as *caid*, governors of inland territories. In Algiers the most successful renegades were the Genoese and the Venetians, but there were also Calabrians, Sicilians, Neapolitans, Albanians, Greeks, French and a few Jews. Still famous today are the Ligurian Osta Morato, who became the Bey of Tunis in 1637 and founded his own dynasty – the Muradites – which remained in power until the early eighteenth century, and Ali 'Piccinino', who was of Venetian origin and who was virtually in sole charge of Algiers between 1638 and 1645. It was not until the second half of the eighteenth century that the fortunes of renegades of Mediterranean origin began to wane; they were partly succeeded by other renegades, particularly of English and Flemish origin, who were called 'Ponentines'.

The decline of the empire brought with it a progressive diminution of the role of the renegades. There were some exceptions, nevertheless, including the aristocratic Frenchman Count Claude-Alexandre de Bonneval, who deserves a mention here. Born in 1675 into a large family which was connected with the writer Fénelon, he became a colonel in the French army. In 1706 he deserted and was condemned to death by the French but he transferred to the Imperial army and obtained the rank of lieutenant general. He collaborated with Eugene of Savoy until they quarrelled, at which point he was accused of high treason and imprisoned in the Spielberg, from which he managed to escape. By now disillusioned with Christian society, he finally sought refuge in Istanbul where, as head of the sultan's army, he took part in the military reforms introduced by Sultan Mahmoud I under the name of Ahmad Bonneval Pasha. He maintained links with his own country through his friendship with the Marquis de Villeneuve, Louis XV's envoy in Istanbul.

Many of these Mediterranean adventurers are worth a brief description. Orazio Paternò Castello, from the Catanian family of the marquis of San Giuliano, became a fugitive in 1783 after murdering his wife. Captured by corsairs from Tripoli, he converted to Islam and assumed the name of Hamad before becoming a dragoman (or interpreter). He told his story to a Miss Tully, the sister of the British consul in Tripoli. Another Sicilian aristocrat, Prince Giovan Luigi Moncada, was intercepted by Tunisians (who may have been colluding with the ship's captain) while sailing from Palermo to Naples in July 1797. He regained his liberty a few months later, but only after promising to pay a sizeable ransom. Once he had returned to Sicily, however, the prince refused to keep his word and a long lawsuit ensued. The Bey of Tunis appealed to the royal tribunal and the case dragged on for several decades.

Naturally, after a time, many renegades – who had been circumcised, unless they managed to avoid the ritual – returned to their native land and after doing penance were readmitted into the Church. It is difficult to estimate how sincere their conversions were and, in individual cases, how genuine their return to their ancestral faith. For each case that we know about, there is silence over the countless others which have been swallowed up by the past.

By the end of the seventeenth century, the piracy wars which appeared to be so necessary to the pressure groups of renegades who formed the upper echelons of Ottoman society, and to the whole system of prisoners and slaves on both sides, were gradually beginning to decline. Nevertheless, a century later, in Sicily and Sardinia, people continued to feel threatened. In 1798, during a Tunisian raid on the island of San Pietro, near the coast of Sardinia, nearly a thousand islanders were taken prisoner. There was a recrudescence of Muslim piracy in 1815–16 which continued for several years, affecting Southern Italy, Tuscany and the two large Tyrrhenian islands. The Barnabite priest Felice Caronni was imprisoned in North Africa in June 1804; he was captured by Barbary pirates and taken to Tunis but was able to return home after a few months. The prospects for prisoners in a Muslim country had improved by the end of the eighteenth century: Mozart's *Die Entführung aus dem Serail*, or Rossini's *Italiana in Algeri* would not have been written as they were if the conditions experienced by Christian prisoners had not changed for the better. On the other hand, neither opera would have been written if the danger of being captured had not for years represented a grave threat to Christianity.

The reduction in Turkish and North African piracy produced a corresponding contraction in the seafaring and pirate activities of the Knights of Malta and of Santo Stefano, and also of independent Christian corsairs in the Mediterranean. These groups were particularly active in the thirty years between 1580 and 1610. In addition to the need to respond to Muslim attacks with equivalent strength, slave labour was required to row the galleys and to build coastal fortifications. Prisons all over the Levant and the Maghreb were raided, the most renowned examples being the sack of Hamamet in August 1602, when the galleys of the Knights of St Stephen captured between four and seven hundred men, and the sack of Annaba in September, which yielded about one thousand five hundred slaves and which was celebrated in an exceptionally tedious poem, *Bona espugnata*, written at the end of the century by Vicenzo Piazza. Between 1708 and 1715, Christian pirates (for example, pirates from Livorno protected by letters patent from the Grand Duke of

Tuscany) raided the coast of Palestine, causing problems for the French consular authorities on whom the sultan relied to 'protect' Westerners in the area. Pirate ships often passed themselves off as innocent boats taking groups of pilgrims directly to the Holy Land. Members of the local Christian community were scapegoats in these cases and were attacked by enraged Muslims by way of retaliation.

The fate of Muslim prisoners in Christian countries was on the whole less happy and less varied than that of their Christian counterparts in Muslim countries. There were very few 'renegades', converts from Islam to Christianity; this may have been because Islam was a more solid faith than Christianity, or because little pressure was put on the prisoners to convert. Conversion would have been uneconomic, since a slave who became a Christian had to be freed. The fact that the few cases of conversion which did take place were greeted as great occasions confirms how rare it was. It was an advantage to have some slaves in reserve so that prisoners could eventually be exchanged. In 1543, Pope Paul III established a College of Neophytes in Rome to accommodate Christian converts of Jewish or Muslim origin, but it was never well attended. Christian sources, occasionally endorsed by information from the Muslim side, speak of the covert sympathy felt by some Muslims for Christianity. The fact that in the *dar al-Islam* apostasy was a capital offence meant, however, that such feelings (if and when they occurred) remained a closely guarded secret.

The 'liquid continent', as the Mediterranean was known, provided innumerable opportunities for peaceful encounters and cultural exchanges. It was a border area as well as being one where trade was carried out and where in some respects there was integration. Many of the sanctuaries in the region were used by both Christians and Muslims. The two religions met and their paths crossed (without merging) in places such as the Church of the Assumption in Jerusalem, the 'Grotto of the Milk' in Bethlehem, St George of Lydda in Palestine, St Catherine's, Sinai, the Marian sanctuary of Mataryya near Cairo (where the famous balm came from), Our Lady of Good Council at Scutari in Albania and the cave of the Madonna in Lampedusa. These encounters were based on the recognition that Christianity and Islam had common origins in Abraham; although the Muslims bore a touching devotion to Our Lady, there was no real hint of syncretism.

## The Birth of Islamic Studies

The art of Gutenberg was soon playing its part in the diffusion of Muslim culture. Islamic texts were not published immediately, however.

Texts began to appear on the subject of Islam, but in general they were very poor – either because they presented an inaccurate picture of Islam or because they covered it in contumely. In the fifteenth to sixteenth centuries the existing 'balance of culture' (similar to the 'balance of trade') was being turned on its head. Until this time Islam knew more about Christianity than Christianity knew about Islam. However, the interest aroused by the Turkish advance into Europe, plus the fact that European merchants and travellers were travelling to Islamic lands in ever increasing numbers, was beginning to reverse the balance. Muslim scholars showed little interest in learning more about Christianity, whereas the reverse was happening amongst the Christians.

A literature which could almost be defined as 'Islamistic' had been in existence since the early sixteenth century. Although on one hand it still promulgated the old errors of medieval debate, on the other it focused attention on a phenomenon that was rapidly growing in strength. In 1511 the theologist Jacques Lefebure of Etaples printed a French version of Ricoldo da Montecroce's ancient treatise, thereby restoring it to fame as well as reiterating its errors. Not only did it invalidate much of the available information, it also helped it to spread. The wheat and tares which grew together were for the moment impossible to separate.

In the fifteenth century, encouraged by Cardinal Cusa, the Carthusian Dionysius of Ryckel painstakingly compiled his treatise-dialogue *Contra Alchoranum*. It was printed posthumously in 1533, about eighty years after it was written, at a time when Christians and Turks were confronting each other on the plains of Hungary. A proportion of the Magyar nobility had elected to defy the Hapsburgs and adopt the reformed religion, thus allying themselves with the Ottomans. The work of Dionysius of Ryckel was dedicated to Charles V's brother Ferdinand, who was King of Hungary and Bohemia at the time and who would be elected emperor some twenty years later.

In 1543, some ten years later, the Latin translation of the Koran prepared in the mid-twelfth century by Robert of Ketton was printed in Basel, at the famous Oporino press. Despite being four hundred years old, it wore its years lightly. This edition was edited by Theodore Buchmann, a theologian from Zurich who was known in the academic world by the Latinized name Bibliander. Saddled with the lengthy title of *Machumetis saracenorum principis vita ac doctrina omnis, quae et Ismaehelitarum lex et Alchoranum dicitur*, the volume also comprised an *Apologia* written by Bibliander, a *Praemonitio* by Luther and a series of other texts, including the editions of Ricoldo da Montecroce and Nicholas of Cusa. Finally everything was gathered into one enormous volume, a genuine monument to the birth of Islamic studies: the *Sylloge scriptorum adversus mahomedanos*, published in Basel between 1543 and 1550. The only problem with it was that it could not be used in Catholic areas: Luther's torrent of abuse against the Holy Roman Church led Pope Alexander VII to ban its circulation in countries which had remained faithful to Rome.

In the Protestant world affairs were conducted differently, and it was suggested that the Latin texts provided by Bibliander should be translated into German in Basel in order to make them accessible to a wider public. However, the influential theologian Bonifaz Amerback advised against it, on the grounds that it was better not to give inexperienced readers access to a 'profane' and 'heretical' religion, since it might interest them, or (worse) influence them.

The medieval texts reworked by Bibliander certainly helped to distribute erroneous and tendentious information about Islam and quotations from the Koran that were misinterpreted and misunderstood. The growing interest in the Muslim world, however, and the desire for more accurate information (engendered by Suleiman's success and by the ever increasing importance that merchandise from the Turkish Empire was assuming in the Western economy) led to the development of promotional and descriptive literature of a much higher quality. Evidence of this can be found, for example, in the space reserved for Islam in general, and the Ottoman Empire in particular, in an extraordinary volume published in 1544 by Guillaume Postel, *De orbis terrae concordia*.

Postel returned to France from his forays in the Middle East with a large collection of valuable Arabic, Syriac and Armenian manuscripts. He was a professor at the Collège de France and, briefly, a member of the Society of Jesus (he was soon expelled). Amongst other things, he published a treatise on comparative linguistics and an Arabic grammar, with the intention of using this knowledge to promote a utopian ideal, the foundation of a universal civilization and religion.

Although he had complete access to Bibliander's texts, Postel rejected their outlook completely, thereby bringing about a genuine revolution in methodology. Whereas the controversialists had emphasized the differences existing between Christianity and Islam, dissimulating if not actually concealing any similarities or points of contact, Postel's approach was the direct opposite. This inevitably led him to question the Latin translations of the Koran which, with his exceptional linguistic knowledge, he could check at first hand. As a result, comprehension of the text improved, but some extraordinary exegetical complications arose, posing a constant challenge to Postel's results on the linguistic front.

Not surprisingly, Postel attracted censure and criticism from all sides; he was described by the learned Henri Estienne as a *monstre exécrable* on account of his 'sympathy' for Islam. In addition, his comparisons between the Muslim faith and the reformed Christian Church turned into a series of arguments which tended to favour the law of the Prophet. At times he seems deliberately confrontational. He pursues his suggestion of a parallel between Islam and Protestantism to the limit, proposing the existence of a *calvinoturcismus*, meanwhile claiming to be in search of a universal harmony which to some seemed to be inspired by Cusa's *De pace fidei*, to others to be a precursor of the work of later philosophers such as Rousseau and Kant. While all this was taking place, the Council of Trent was expected to proclaim a new crusading counter-offensive against the Ottoman Turks; onlookers wondered if the Council would roundly condemn the reformed Church, or whether it would decide to become reconciled with it.

Postel's forward leap met a world that was perhaps not ready to receive impartial opinions on the *inimicus crucis*. Or perhaps his extraordinary erudition, which had something obsessional about it, made his work unacceptable. It may have been nothing of the sort, of course. The feeling one gets if one analyses the context in which *De orbis terrae concordia* was produced is that Europe was ready to take a decisive step forward in the quality of its objective understanding of Islam. Postel returned several times to the subject of the Turks, for instance in his treatise *De la République des Turcs*, published in 1560.

In Spain, where ideological opposition to Islam was only one facet of the repression of the Muslims converted against their will, the *moriscos*, Cardinal Francisco Ximenes de Cisneros, Archbishop of Toledo and Grand Inquisitor of Spain, tirelessly hunted down Arabic manuscripts of every description and had them burnt in a colossal *auto da fé* in the main square of Toledo. Evidently such measures were insufficient – anti-Muslim pamphlets were being circulated in increasing numbers. An operetta, *Confusion*, was composed in Seville in 1540 by one Juan Andreas, who billed himself as a Muslim ex-lawyer, but who in fact was using this label to legitimize the traditional arguments of Christian controversy. The insistence with which such calumnies were disseminated proves that their credibility was under duress, thanks to the increase in circulation of much more convincing information which proved them wrong.

In fact the first vernacular version (in Italian) of the Koran was published in 1547 in Venice, a city that was more accessible to contacts with the Turkish world than any other. As usual, it was based on the Latin translation by Robert of Ketton, much compressed, although it claimed to have been taken directly from the original. The editor of the Italian version, Andrea Arrivabene, dedicated it to Gabriel Puetz, Baron d'Aramon, France's new ambassador to the sultan, who at the request of his sovereign was pursuing a policy of alliance with the Sublime Porte. Arrivabene's letter of dedication to Baron d'Aramon is accompanied by the usual potted history of Arabia, the life of the Prophet and the Islamic religion.

The arsenal was familiar – Islam was a Christian heresy, a doctrine that licensed sexual excess, a maze of contradictions – and the same old misunderstandings and prejudice abounded. However, the increase in publications devoted to Islam was a sure indication that things must, in the long run, improve.

The conflict between Catholic and Protestant passions was now expressed (as further crusades were discussed) in mutual accusations of pro-Islamic tendencies. Throughout the sixteenth and seventeenth centuries, however, the conflict was accompanied by the development of increasingly well-informed studies in Arabism, Turcology and Islam. By the following century these studies were thoroughly systematized. Postel made an important contribution in his book *Histoire et considération de l'origine, loy et costume des Tartares, Persiens, Arabes, Turcs*, published in Paris in 1560.

Confusion and error (which may not have been accidental) were certainly to be found in the pages of illustrious historical writers such as Grotius, Boterus and Baronius; it was no easy matter to abandon the deeply entrenched controversialist tradition, and there were very few authors who could deal with Islam without at the same time trying to refute its doctrines. Tenacious areas of incomprehension and lack of information still persisted in the work of such authors as Blaise Pascal who, on the subject of Mohammed, wondered if the Scriptures contained any predictions about his arrival on earth. Evidently Pascal knew nothing of the arguments surrounding the famous "little horn" prediction in the Book of Daniel. Pascal also wondered what moral principles Mohammed followed and if he had ever performed miracles: he should at least have learned from Postel that the Koran states categorically that the Prophet had nothing to do with the dimension in which miracles take place.

Meanwhile, the number of genuine specialists was increasing. Erpenius, or Thomas van Erpen, professor of oriental languages at Leyden, published an Arabic grammar in 1613; in 1639 Edward Pocock, a professor at Oxford, produced a *Specimen historiae Arabum*; the Arabist Johan Hottinger, a lecturer first at Zurich, subsequently at Heidelberg, wrote grammar books and lexicons and produced anthologies of source material; Jibrail es-Saynni ('Gabriel the Syonite') was an Arabist in Rome; Yusuf Simaan es-Simaani ('l'Assemani'), who was Syrian, was prefect of the Vatican Library under Pope Clement XII and compiler of a *Biblioteca Orientalis*; Ibrahim al-Ekleni ('Abraham Echellensis'), the historian and philosopher, was the author of a *Synopsis propositorum* published in 1641. Some of the more educated travellers and diarists made invaluable contributions to the early history of oriental studies, including for example the Roman Pietro della Valle. The study of oriental history, in particular the study of the Ottoman world, was gradually developing, as can be observed in the work on the sultans by Giovanni Sagredo, *Memorie istoriche de'monarchi ottomani*, published in Venice in 1677.

The defeat of the Turks beneath the walls of Vienna in 1683 marked the culmination of the *Türkenfurcht*, the Muslim nightmare that haunted the West, and the beginning of its end. Now Islam and the history of the Ottoman Empire could be approached more objectively. There were still some emotional repercussions, certainly: many people were of the opinion that the victory of the Christian armies was a sign of divine favour, and pamphlets on the conversion of the infidel proliferated now that it was considered easier to bring about, since God had punished them for their overweening pride. This was the claim made by Tirso Gonzalez de Santalla in his *Manuduction ad conversionem mahumetanorum*, published in Madrid four years after the grim events in Vienna. The withdrawal of fear and the gradual diminution of the arguments which had for centuries fuelled controversialist literature helped produce, at the end of the seventeenth century, the monumental *oeuvre* of Ludovico Marracci, a monk from Lucca. He made a faithful and complete translation of the Koran into Latin and provided a non-judgemental commentary: the *Alcorani textus universus* and the *Refutatio Alcorani*, both published in Padua in 1691 and 1698, respectively.

Two years after the death of its author, Barthélemy d'Herbelot, the *Bibliothèque orientale* was published in Paris in 1697, with a *Discours* by Antoine Galland. This marks the beginning of systematic Islamic studies.

Turcology, which should have proceeded hand in hand with Arabic and Islamic studies, came to maturity rather more slowly. Nevertheless it progressed, and in the course of the eighteenth century produced the admirable study published in Rome in 1794 entitled *Principii della grammatica turca ad uso dei missionari apostolici a Costantinopoli* by Cosimo de Carbognano, who was dragoman to the legation of the kingdom of Naples in Constantinople. Soon after this, Persian studies took off through the efforts of Abraham Hyacinthe Anquetil du Perron, and Kurdology through the Dominican priest Maurizio Garzoni.

# 11
# The Age of Iron and the Enlightenment

### Eclipse of the Sickle Moon

In the early seventeenth century the collapse of the Ottoman Empire seemed only a distant and remote possibility: Istanbul was still the capital of a large and threatening country. The West, however, had begun to make progress owing to its superiority in technology, and the Ottoman world was thus inevitably placed in the position of passive client. The many economic, financial and trade concessions accorded by the empire to the French, Dutch and English (in particular) caused its irreversible descent into the condition of 'dominated economy'. The sultan's coffers may have been swollen by the proceeds of these concessions, but there was no sign of any indigenous middle class developing. Turkish society was increasingly characterized by the distance between the military aristocracy and landed gentry, who were rich, and an urban and rural population growing progressively more impoverished. The very restricted middle class of small farmers, modest local merchants with no credit facilities, shopkeepers and artisans was not sufficient to produce an economy that could compete with Europe.

Under ever more aggressive European pressure, the Turkish government first reacted by trying to master the techniques that would provide an adequate response to its needs; It succeeded in developing neither an economy nor the technology to meet its requirements, and therefore had to place its trust in Western merchants, financiers and engineers. Turkish bureaucracy extended right across the vast empire but was increasingly inefficient and greedy: a blind, monolithic financial system, largely inherited from Byzantine tradition, stifled all initiative and used corruption as the sole cure for theft.

For a brief period between the sixteenth and seventeenth centuries, the Porte seems to have collaborated quite efficiently with the European powers. A durable peace was concluded with Spain in 1580, and in 1606 a new war in the Balkans against the Holy Roman Empire concluded with the transfer of Transylvania to the Turks, in exchange for their renunciation of the taxes levied from the entire country of Hungary. The sultan who had raised such hopes, young Murad IV, died suddenly in 1640, very soon after defeating Shah Abbas, his Persian rival in the East, and thereby becoming lord of Azerbaijan and Georgia.

Murad's involvement in the East would have been an embarrassment if the West had tried a new offensive at this point. It appeared, in fact, that something was about to occur, something originating in the kingdom of France. During the 1620s Cardinal Richelieu and his secretary and adviser, the Capuchin priest Père Joseph, nicknamed the *Eminence Grise*, lent his support to a crusade planned by Charles Gonzaga, Duke of Nevers, as well as to the Holy See. The Duke was related through his father to a princess of the Palaeologus family, who provided the last *basileus* of Constantinople, and was planning an undertaking which he hoped would return him to the throne of his ancestors. The Greeks of the Morea sent a diplomatic mission to the descendant of their Christian *despotai*, declaring their readiness for rebellion; Venice might have lent them her support. Crusading glory was needed to consolidate the new Bourbon dynasty and to obliterate the memory of its Huguenot origins: in 1611 the Calvinist Jacques Bongars had dedicated to the young King Louis XIII a valuable printed anthology of the earliest crusading chronicles, the two volumes of the *Gesta Dei per Francos*.

Père Joseph wrote a poem of 4,637 lines entitled the *Turchiade* to accompany the new expedition and began renewing diplomatic relations between the pontifical court, the court of Savoy and the Hapsburg/Spanish court. The beginning of the Thirty Years' War sabotaged all his efforts, however: Although for the Sublime Porte, who were busy fighting the Persians, the European conflict represented salvation, the Turco-Persian conflict was also fortunate for the Europeans because they might otherwise have been subject to attack by the Turks. It also prevented the European factions now at war from striking a bargain with the sultan, either publicly or in secret, as had happened on so many occasions in the previous century.

From the European point of view, no Catholic or Mediterranean power (matters were different for the others) could escape its duty to take sides against the Turks and the threat from North Africa, at least in theory and at an official level. The Pope, the emperor, the rulers of Spain and France, and Venice all found this an obstacle to their freedom to deploy all their political and diplomatic resources, but it also provided a useful pretext for obstructing their adversaries.

In practice, however, areas of agreement and compromise tended to be sought. The last great 'prophetic' voice to be heard loudly and clearly speaking in favour of crusading, war against the Turks and the urgent need for world renewal was that of Tommaso Campanella, first in his *De monarchia Hispanica* written in 1600 in the prison of Castel Nuovo in Naples, then in 1638 in his *Eclogue* written to celebrate the birth of His Most Serene Highness, the Dauphin of France, hailed by Campanella as *orbis christiani Summa Spes* (the Dauphin later acquired an epithet that would surely have pleased the Calabrian friar: the Sun King). One should not be misled, however, by the strictly realistic tone and the convincing air of strategic skill to be found in Campanella's instructions for the conduct of the war against the Ottoman Empire. Fra Tommaso paid no attention whatsoever to the true political and historical conditions prevailing at the time at which he was writing: his proposals were based on the *renovatio saeculi*.

The long period of relative peace in the Mediterranean, which began with the truce between the Turks and Venice in 1573 and the Turks and Spain in 1580, ended suddenly in 1645, when the Ottomans mounted an attack on the island of Crete, Venice's Candia. Venice put up a strong resistance and trounced the sultan's armies on several occasions, but this provoked a revolt by the Janissaries who murdered Sultan Ibrahim I and replaced him on the throne with Mohammed IV, a ten-year-old boy and a pawn who was at the mercy of all the power struggles and intrigues at court. This was the right moment to strike at Ottoman power, particularly as the Thirty Years' War was over and the pacts signed at this time in Westphalia allowed all nations a voice, with the sole exception of Turkey. It was as if to say that renewed hostilities against the Ottomans would have the effect of strengthening the European peace. The idea of *pax inter christianos* had been a precondition of any crusade since the Middle Ages; now the assumption of *mutua inter christianos tolerantia* was taking root.

In 1656, Venice's fleet scored a memorable victory in the Dardanelles and for a while it was thought that the Ottoman Empire was over. However, the new Grand Vizier, the Albanian Mehmet Kôprülü, was able to restore matters by cleansing the court of pockets of conspiracy and corruption, imposing order on the insubordinate Janissaries, adopting a strict policy of fiscal reform and harmonizing the situation with Venice by recapturing the islands of Lemnos and Tenedos. The vizier's son Ahmed, who succeeded his father, continued to implement these reforms.

Meanwhile, the Turkish government declared its vassal George III Rakoczy, Prince of Transylvania, unfit to govern and replaced him with a person of its own choosing. Rakoczy's refusal to withdraw brought the Pasha of Buda to the scene, at which point the Hungarians turned for help to the court of Vienna, from whom they expected assistance and support in matters connected with Transylvania. In 1661, Emperor Leopold I sent an army into the region; few soldiers survived the onslaught. The Turkish counter-offensive overwhelmed the Imperial armies and forced them back into northwestern Hungary. In September 1663, when the Ottomans had nearly reached Pressburg, Vienna began to feel threatened and the emperor called for assistance from the Christian world.

This time not even Louis XIV, who while proclaiming France's glorious achievement in the crusades had relentlessly been pursuing a pro-Turkish policy, could remain uninvolved. The Imperial army included a substantial French expeditionary force. The entire Christian army was under the command of Imperial field marshal Raymond, Count of Montecuccoli, who defeated the armies of the Grand Vizier on 1 August 1664 at the battle of St Gotthard an der Raab. This great victory was partly nullified by the subsequent truce of Vasvar, which permitted the Turks to remain in control of the fortresses they had conquered after 1660. They were also free to continue their war with Crete with renewed energy, until the fall of Candia in 1669.

Candia seemed to cancel out St Gotthard. In the endless round of confrontations between the Balkans and the Eastern Mediterranean, diplomacy and propaganda rather than shows of strength appeared to be keeping the balance. Perhaps the emperor had been too obliging to the Ottomans (for which he was severely censured), and the war of the Spanish succession was looming on the horizon. In any case, the idyll with the Sun King, overshadowed by the banner of the crusades and the glory of St Gotthard, was not set to survive much longer.

## The Last Great Fear

A new crisis, provoked this time by a Turkish military campaign against Poland, reawakened hostilities. Between July and September 1683 the troops of the Grand Vizier Kara Mustapha laid siege to Vienna. The Sun King at this time, on the recommendation of his 'Chambres de Réunion', annexed the regions of Alsace and Lorraine, the Saar and Luxembourg to France and invaded the Spanish Low Countries. In spite of impassioned pleading by the Pope, he refused any assistance to the city of Vienna, which was surrounded by Muslim troops.

Sultan Mohammed IV would have preferred to avoid a siege, and the Khan of the Crimean Tartars and the Pasha of Buda advised against it. The Hapsburg capital of Austria was a target which could unleash reprisals from the whole of Christendom. Kara Mustapha foolishly gave way to pressure and advice from pro-Turkish Hungarian aristocrats – and also undoubtedly to the prospect of a speedy capitulation and rich pickings. Although Charles of Lorraine, the Imperial commander in chief, had at his disposal an army of 50,000 men, he despaired of confronting the enemy without the auxiliary troops he was expecting from Germany and Poland.

The courage of the besieged inhabitants of Vienna, the splendid example of their commanding officer, Rüdiger von Stahremberg, and the fierce encouragement of the Capuchin friar Marco d'Aviano allowed the Duke of Lorraine and the King of Poland, Jan Sobietzki, to march through the Vienna Woods with their army of Poles, Saxons and Bavarians and defeat the enemy at the battle of Kahlenberg on 12 September.

Sobietzki's 'hussars', with the great wings fixed to the top of their helmets, must have seemed like liberating (or avenging) angels. *Fuit homo missus a Deo cui nomen erat Johannes*: with these words, from the Gospel according to St John, the King of Poland was hailed in the *Te Deum* sung in his praise in churches throughout Latin Christendom.

The victory was remarkable and total. The vizier abandoned his camp at once, leaving the victors to the enjoyment of their prize. Shortly afterwards the vizier was strangled by Janissaries in his encampment near Belgrade; the silken chord used to strangle him was sent for that express purpose by the sultan.

After the unexpected success in Vienna, enthusiastically welcomed all over the Christian world, an offensive was planned and implemented which brought about the abdication of Mohammed IV. The new sultan, Suleiman II, was forced to retreat on all fronts, from the Sea of Azov to the Balkans and the Aegean, pursued by the Imperial, Russian and Venetian armies. This was the occasion when, in September 1687, the Parthenon in Athens, which was being used as a gunpowder magazine by the Turks, was blown up by a Venetian bomb. Only the renewal of hostilities between Louis XIV of France and the empire prevented the Ottomans being brought to their knees, this time perhaps permanently. The sultan realized that he could delay no longer the negotiation of a twenty-five-year truce; for him it meant surrender. The Karlowitz agreement signed on 26 January 1699 gave the whole of Hungary (except for the banat of Temesvár), Transylvania, Croatia and Slavonia to the Holy Roman Empire; the Morea and most of Dalmatia to Venice and Podolia to Poland.

History had reached a crossroads. On the European–Asian stage three great empires (the two Muslim empires, Istanbul and Isfahan, and the Christian empire of Vienna) now had to face a fourth: the Muscovite empire of the Romanovs, which nursed ambitions that were plain to see. It was interested in the area between the Black Sea, the Caucasus and the Caspian as well as in Central Asia; it also had its eye on the Mediterranean, to which it hoped to gain access by two different routes, the maritime route through the Dardanelles and the land route via the Balkans. The Russian powers were active on various fronts. To the Slavs they presented themselves as champions of the Slav peoples against the Turkish menace and German supremacy. To the Orthodox Christians they posed as the heirs to the Byzantine Empire and the patrons of oriental spirituality against Ottoman tyranny and papist hegemony. Their position was fortified by a strong interest in Jerusalem and the Holy Land, where the Tsar of all the Russias was gradually making it understood that he wished the sultan to consider him as the genuine heir to the *basileus* of Constantinople and therefore protector of the Orthodox Christian *millet* led by Greek prelates (subjects of the Sublime Porte) and mainly composed of Arab-speaking believers. All this activated a complex network of allegiances based on triangles of opposition: Austrians, Russians and Turks in the Balkans; Turks, Russians and Persians in the Caucasus; and French, Russians and Turks in Istanbul and Jerusalem, where the newly arrived Tsarists were disrupting the traditional habit of considering the French as sole protectors of Christians in the East.

Tsar Peter the Great refused to be included in the Karlowitz agreements; it was not until 1700 that recognition of the ownership of Azov persuaded him to put away for the time being the sword he wielded as defender of the Orthodox Church in the Balkans. A few years later, however, following a succession of intersecting provocations, the war began again. On one side was the tsar, ceaselessly fomenting rebellion amongst the Balkan Orthodox Christians; on the other, the sultan was being urged to react against the Russian menace by the tsar's sworn enemy, Charles XII of Sweden, who, having suffered defeat at the hands of the Russians in the battle of Poltava in 1709, had taken refuge with the Turks and was contemplating revenge. The old lord of Versailles was stirring the fire from a distance, as usual. The military campaign turned into a disaster for Peter the Great. He found himself encircled on the river Prut and was forced to agree to a humiliating peace, pay a heavy ransom for his freedom and relinquish the fortress of Azov.

Victory over the Russians gave the Ottomans renewed confidence. The result was a fresh war against Venice. The Turks directed their attention towards Corfu, an island with formidable fortifications (*ingens opus Corcyrae*) which was considered by Venice to be the key to the Adriatic. Corfu's system of defence meant that it represented the Republic to the entire Levant. The conflict led instead to the Turkish conquest of Corinth and, after 1669, of the strongholds held by Venice on the island of Crete. A century later Byron dedicated a rambling poem, *The Siege of Corinth*, to this battle.

The entry of the empire into the fray changed the fortunes of the conflict. On 15 August 1716, at Peterwardein, Prince Eugene of Savoy defeated the numerically superior Ottoman army in a battle destined to remain a milestone in the history of Warfare through the centuries. The route through Belgrade was open once more, while the city fell into the hands of the Imperial armies the following year. These victories were ratified in the treaty of Passarowitz. Although the Lion of St Mark was forced to withdraw its venerable old claws from the Morea and from the Greek archipelago, in exchange the two-headed eagle annexed the Banat of Temesvár, a part of Old Serbia, with its historic capital city, and Lesser Walachia.

The game was not yet over, however. The Porte realized that the Christian powers fighting it out on the Adriatic–Balkan chessboard would eventually collide, and that there was much to be gained by exploiting the conflicting rivalries of the Austrians, the Russians and the Venetians. Meanwhile, Russia was eyeing the conflict in the Caucasus with great interest, which brought it into confrontation with another traditional enemy of the sultan, the Shah of Persia. The Russians had already tested the Caucasus area in 1722–3, with an expedition designed to inflame the hearts of the Armenians in the mountainous regions of Karabagh and Siwnik and to incite them to rebellion under the guidance of Dawit Bek. Their attempt, however, was cruelly repressed. Between 1725 and 1727 a military and diplomatic agreement between Russia and Turkey almost resulted in Turkish subjugation of Transcaucasia, but the Persians succeeded in confounding their ambitions three years later.

The year 1730 saw yet another rebellion by the Janissaries, who, on the eve of a new campaign against Persia, were irritated by a delay in payment of their wages. This revolt brought Sultan Mahmoud I (1730–54) to the throne. He naturally paid his troops promptly throughout his reign, but this was not the extent of his reforms. He pursued a systematic defence policy around the borders of the empire, built fortresses and established permanent surveillance garrisons, putting his trust in the skill and good humour of Count de Bonneval, known as Ahmad Bonneval Pasha, who in 1734 established a school for engineers in Istanbul which aimed to teach modern artillery techniques so that the empire would no longer find it necessary to hire foreigners and Western renegades to perform these functions on its behalf. Five years earlier, in 1729, a printing press installed in the capital produced the first printed book in the Turkish language. The seeds were sown, but the time was not quite ripe; neither the printing press nor the artillery school was able to withstand the reaction of the traditionalists for long. At first this reaction consisted simply of an edict forbidding the press from producing a printed version of the Koran and allowing only secular works to be published. Soon, however, the forces of reaction succeeded in having both innovatory institutions closed. In addition, the usual hostility of the Janissaries prevented Bonneval Pasha from proceeding further with his military reforms and extending them to the sultan's entire army. Nevertheless, the friendship between Bonneval and the French ambassador Villeneuve encouraged diplomatic and military relations between Turkey and France to develop considerably. The *lale devri*, 'the age of tulips', was gradually coming to an end in opulent Istanbul. Successive painful attempts at renewal and revival were being made and a period of peace was required. The 'perpetual' peace treaty signed in 1733 was intended to meet this requirement.

France's collusion with Turkey had no effect on the renewed outbreak of hostilities between Russia, Austria and Turkey. The Turks were anxious about Russian policy in Poland with regard to the war of succession to the Polish throne, whilst the Russians had their sights fixed on Azov and the Crimea once again. An agreement entered into in 1726 obliged Emperor Charles VI (who had suffered a series of military reversals in Germany and Italy) to side with the Russians. Bonneval Pasha's reforms evidently bore fruit: the Austro-Russian alliance was repeatedly vanquished between 1737 and 1739 and was compelled to sign the treaty of Belgrade, restoring the city of Belgrade to the Turks and returning the situation in the Balkans to now it had been before Passarowitz, with the exception of the Banat of Temesvár. The Russians were permitted to retain Azov but had to dismantle their defences; they were forbidden to sail any type of ship in the Black Sea, including merchant ships.

During peace negotiations, the sultan enjoyed the constant support of the French government and the assistance of that very exceptional diplomat, Villeneuve. As a reward for his good offices, the Sublime Porte granted in 1740 a renewal of the Capitulations relating to Jerusalem: these were no longer to be considered temporary. In the name of his successors, and on their behalf, Sultan Mahmoud I committed himself to what, from a diplomatic point of view, looked like a genuine treaty. In particular it ensured that the 'Frankish' members of religious Orders who were settled inside and outside the Holy City would no longer be disturbed and that the right to repair the sanctuaries would be granted them by the Porte without difficulty, on condition that this was done at the behest of the French ambassador.

However, the great diplomatic success of Belgrade marked the Indian summer of Imperial power. The modernization programme was soon halted, partly as a result of rigorous questioning carried out by Muslim jurists and theologians. Meanwhile, the evolution of policies in Central Europe provided a new alibi for the powers interested in launching a fresh attack on the Turkish Empire.

In 1768 a violent uprising against Russian interference in neighbouring Poland caused Catherine II to send her armies to invade the country. Encouraged by the French, many of the insurgents fled to safety in Turkey where, as devout Catholics, they were protected by the King of France. The Russians, however, did not hesitate to follow them.

Although this situation may not have been deliberately provoked by the government in St Petersburg, it was the *casus belli*. As usual, France was adding fuel to the flames of wounded Turkish pride. A war broke out which confirmed how little effect the admirable reforms of Bonneval Pasha had had on the Turkish Empire. In spite of possessing a redoubtable army numbering 60,000 soldiers, augmented by Tartar auxiliaries, the Turks were humiliated and their navy was destroyed in the Black Sea. While the Russian armies swept through Moldavia and Walachia, welcomed as heroes by the Orthodox Christians (but not by the boyars, who were vassals of the Porte), the empress's agents were criss-crossing Greece, inciting Christians to rebel. The war continued in spite of Frederick II of Prussia's offers of mediation – Frederick, alarmed by the great success being enjoyed by the Russians, organized the first division of Poland in 1772 – and it was only Catherine II's anxiety about Pugachov's revolt which finally brought it to an end.

The treaty of Kuchuk Kainarji on 21 July 1774 ratified the Russian victory. The empress agreed to withdraw from Moldavia, Walachia and Bessarabia, but she obtained Azov on a permanent basis as well as all the territory between the Dnieper and Bug. Her rights to navigation in the Black Sea and the Mediterranean were recognized and autonomy from the Sublime Porte was accorded to the Crimean Tartars and the Romanian princes, the first step for both towards domination by Russia. There was more: in political and institutional circles in the vanquished country the Russian triumph was acknowledged and the sultan's promises of modernization and Westernization were wrested from him.

In addition, the Russians were given permission to build an Orthodox church near Istanbul, in the suburb of Galata, and the empress was recognized forthwith as the protector of the Christian *millet* throughout the entire empire – a title that had belonged traditionally to the King of France since the sixteenth century.

The religious and institutional aspects of this treaty were much more important than they seemed at first. The empress was perfectly aware of the importance of the prestige of France's position in the Holy Land; she aimed to fulfil the same function for the Orthodox Christians in the Sublime Porte as the King of France had fulfilled for the Catholics. The treaty meant the she had the right to 'speak up for' the Greek Orthodox Christians in the Aegean islands, and for the Orthodox Christians of Moldavia and Walachia. Another feature of the treaty (although somewhat obscurely expressed) was that it gave Russia the same prerogatives as the Capitulations had given France and England, and sanctioned the great empress's role as protector of Orthodox Christians throughout the Levant. Under the pretext of protecting Christians in the Holy Land, the duel between France and Russia (or between the Catholic and Orthodox Churches) for pre-eminence over the Christian communities in a depressed, depopulated and partly demolished Jerusalem had begun. The Turco-Russian protocols obviously ran counter to other agreements made with other countries by the sultan and his predecessors, particularly with France. The 'error' was intentional, it seems, and was committed by both signatories, with different aims in mind. The Russians were eager to break a monopoly; the Turks wanted to do everything in their power to provoke hostility, even possibly war, amongst the Europeans.

The dream of Catherine II was beginning to take shape in all its aspects, from the political to the military and religious. Her empire now stretched from the Baltic to the Mediterranean, from Greece to the Caspian. This made it necessary to enter into a truce, albeit a temporary one with Russia's partners and rivals in the area of expansion in the Balkans and Austria and to tackle the problems of Slav unity and Orthodox freedom. In 1780 the empress met her Imperial colleague, the Holy Roman Emperor Joseph II. The outcome of their meeting was the treaty of 1781, which was in essence a plan for the division of the Turkish Empire on a far bigger scale than the plan for the division of Poland. Having annexed the Crimea and the lands north of the Danube, Russia would form an independent Dacia (the borders of which remained somewhat ill-defined), ruled over by the queen's favourite, Prince Potemkin. Austria would take Bosnia, Serbia and part of Dalmatia, while Venice would take back Cyprus and the Morea. If the sultan were then hounded out of Istanbul the city would revert to being the New Rome, Constantinople; the ruler of this new Byzantine Empire would a nephew of the empress of the Third Rome, Prince Constantine (*nomen omen*, indeed). Meanwhile, in order to pave the way for a new offensive, the Russians were plotting with the Tartars of the Crimea and attempting to strengthen their position in Georgia.

Catherine's plan was by no means foolish. If it had succeeded (and it could have done so), it would have caused an upheaval in the balance of power of the entire continent and might have altered relationships permanently. But in this case the imponderable was Sultan Abdul Hamid I, who in 1787 launched an unexpected preventive campaign against Russia, catching the empress on the wrong foot and her armies unprepared. After the disastrous treaty of Kuchuk Kainarji, the Turkish Empire experienced a crisis of confidence. The knowledge that the backward state of its technology and manufacturing industry compared with Europe was responsible for the inadequacy of its resources renewed the attempts at modernization that had been rejected by the adversaries of Bonneval Pasha and the traditionalists during the 1740s. Paradoxically enough, these Russian-induced efforts at modernizing Turkish institutions and customs – hateful at the time to the Turks because the process was imposed by foreigners and infidels, under a treaty that was far from generous – had the effect of laying the foundations for a dramatic recovery. A symptom, almost a symbol, of this recovery was the reopening in 1784 of the printing works where books were published in Turkish. The sultan, who was in favour of these reforms, also reopened Bonneval's artillery school under Baron de Tott; new guns were acquired from France, while the navy was reconstituted and modernized through the efforts of French engineers Le Roy and Duirest.

The new Turkish fleet, and bad weather, jointly conspired to destroy the Russian army on the Black Sea, while Emperor Joseph, who had honoured the treaty of 1781 by bringing his army down to support the empress, was beaten in Serbia. The Banat of Temesvár was invaded and after years of painful and inconclusive campaigns the new emperor, Leopold II, was forced to accept a separate peace in 1791. Left on their own, the Russians signed the peace of Jassy a few months later, which allowed them to annex Bessarabia, the area of Moldavia situated east of the Dniester. The *philosophes* who had pronounced the end of Ottoman despotism (and the consequent destruction of Muslim fanaticism) as inevitable in the near future were proved wrong. France and England were in any case opposed to the disappearance of the empire on the Bosphorus: its replacement by a superpower in control of the Straits and the Mediterranean Middle East, dominating the entire Orthodox world and turning to its own advantage economic and commercial activity in the Black Sea, the Balkans and the islands ruled by Venice, was certainly not to be welcomed.

The populace and the different religions were excluded from all these plots and complex diplomatic, political and military manoeuvres. Between the Danube and the Crimea the inhabitants were subjected to continual boundary changes during which they were treated as chattels.

Orthodox Christians, whether they knew it or not, were regarded as a pretext for Russian imperialist manoeuvres; the Muslims were treated as if they did not exist by the Europeans, who considered them as followers of a fanatical religion that would soon be totally eclipsed by the ineluctable march of progress and reason.

This is how things appeared to be. The reality was somewhat different.

### Turqueries

'Do you think the Turk will make it to Italy this year?' The remark comes from Niccolò Machiavelli's *La Mandragola*. In 1814 Gioacchino Rossini composed a comic opera, *Il Turco in Italia* ('The Turk in Italy'), whose title seems to have been borrowed directly from Machiavelli. Between the first and the second 'Turk in Italy', however, lay three centuries, the sixteenth to the eighteenth – and what centuries they were. Throughout the three centuries fear of the Turks, *Türkenfurcht*, and the Turkish problem, *Türkenfrage*, were characteristic features of European Mediterranean life that was lived under the anxiety-provoking shadow of the crescent moon to which the many lookout towers scattered around the coastline of Europe, from Spain to the Aegean islands, bear witness. The coasts of Africa and the Near East are also dotted with lookout towers, from Thrace to Morocco, evidence that the Europeans countered Turkish and North African aggression head on. The unfortunate circumcised males languishing in the dungeons of Livorno were suffering similar torments to those endured by the baptized Christians languishing in the dungeons of Algiers.

Between the Middle Ages and the modern period it was generally agreed that Turkish and Barbary coast Muslims were ferocious in attack, and Christians in defence. What, in that case, can have projected the Turk, with his turbans and frogging, from tragedy to European comic opera from the time of Mozart? Mozart created the Moor Monostatos in the *Magic Flute* and the moustaches, 'the triumph of man, the plumes of love', of the pseudo-Turkish lovers in *Così fan tutte*. The most characteristically 'Levantine' figure in literary cliché, however, is 'Raguseo' in Riccardo Bacchelli's *Mulino del Po*, who claims, ambiguously, to be 'a complete Turk in my own home'.

It is not easy to decide whether what we refer to as Orientalism runs parallel to the broader stream of exoticism: does Orientalism merge into exoticism, or does it derive from it?

As we have seen, the medieval world displayed an interest in things Muslim. The first manifestation of this is the *Legend of Mohammed*;

next came translations of the Koran and fantasies about the world of the 'infidel', imagined as 'pagans' and linked with the marvels and magic of secret Asia; and finally there were the journals, often replete with precise, very realistic details, that were produced by merchants, diplomats and pilgrims from the late Middle Ages onwards. Even the slaves and manufactured products that reached Europe from the Orient helped foster an interest which increasingly demonstrated familiarity and manifest sympathy. Deep in the recesses of the Western imagination lay submerged Islam, irrecoverable apart from a few clues: the Moorish and Tartar slaves and servants populating the Mediterranean cities of Europe between the thirteenth and sixteenth centuries; the Tartars scattered all over Russia and Poland between the sixteenth and nineteenth centuries; the Indians and Indonesians so often to be found in England and Holland, often with babies and young children; they all told stories and painted word pictures. The dreams of European dreamers were filled with magic carpets and Aladdin's lamps (albeit heavily disguised) long before Galland adapted the *Thousand and One Nights* to suit ears more accustomed to the *Contes* of Perrault, and before Irving and Doré translated the courtyards, gardens and fountains of Granada into words and images that could be grasped by Western minds.

Medieval Islam was composed of 'Arabs' and 'Moors' and Africans; from the thirteenth to the fifteenth centuries these figures (with the addition of Tartars) appeared more and more frequently in Western art, particularly in scenes such as the journey of the Magi to Bethlehem, a typically exotic parade in the 'autumn' of the Middle Ages.

In the fifteenth century, such scenes frequently included Turks in huge turbans, flowing robes or the tall white headdresses of the alarming Janissaries, particularly in the painting of Northeastern Italy, for example the work of Mantegna and Carpaccio. There are also many important examples in late Gothic painting and illumination in France, Spain, Germany and Southern Italy.

With ever increasing frequency, 'Oriental' ambassadors (whether genuine or fake) would arrive at the courts of Europe, and from the courts they would transfer to the public square. During the Council of Florence in 1439, and also during the pontificate of Pius II, performances became popular and helped to develop a taste for the exotic in fifteenth-century Italian society, which, like Spanish society (although for different reasons), could already boast remarkable familiarity with the Asian and North African world. These Oriental visitors were often impostors who managed to extort small sums of money from the Pope or the reigning monarch, or to scrounge hospitality and gifts, after which they would vanish into thin air with their pickings. The taste for such spectacle is reflected in scores of Renaissance dramas and in the painting of the period.

In these early images, Muslim costume and architecture were depicted as inaccurately as the customs and habits of mind of the Muslim world were described in writings by merchants, pilgrims, preachers and proselytizers, in spite of the fact that, as we have seen, there was no shortage of information circulating on the subject. It was logical that those Christian societies most exposed to the 'infidel' should provide the most accurate information (although this was not always the most readily acceptable); in the Middle Ages this meant Spain, Sicily and the coastal cities of Italy, and Venice from the fifteenth to the seventeenth centuries, particularly for information about the Turks (by this time the Arab world had been partially eclipsed and Persia still seemed too remote).

Venice especially enjoyed frequent and profound contacts, first with the Egyptian and Syrian Arabs, then for a long time with the Turks and the Persians. Between the fifteenth and the seventeenth centuries it was quite usual for the sea ports of the Levant to provide education in finance and economics (as well as politics and languages) to the offspring of the Venetian ruling classes.

Although merchants from the West were able to travel freely in the *dar al-Islam*, Muslim merchants were not allowed into the *dar al-Haib* until the sixteenth century, and even then their movements were restricted. This was not only because there was little to be gained by their going there. In a Latin poem written in the eleventh century and dedicated to Matilda, Countess of Canossa, the monk Donizone reported the presence of dark-skinned Africans in the port of Pisa. We do not know, however, to what extent this information (which he added by way of recrimination, to show just what bad Christians the Pisans were) describes something that was unusual or episodic. At any rate, Muslim embassies to Europe – in the time of Charlemagne embassies from Baghdad and Spain were famous – were few and far between, the exception rather than the rule. It was not until the early sixteenth century that it became an accepted fact that the Ottoman Empire had permanently replaced the old Byzantine Empire, and that Turkey had become an inalienable trading partner – and might also engage in diplomatic relations. Now Persian and Turkish ambassadors were received more frequently in the courts of Europe and became the object of great curiosity amongst certain sections of Western society.

Turkish merchants were not seen in Venice before 1514; later, after the peace treaty of 1573, the first warehouse-dwelling built 'for the Turkish nation' was opened, the genuine Fondaco dei Turchi. The establishment of a mercantile residence for the infidel, who thereby became trading partner and honoured guest of the Venetians in their own home, while remaining the 'historical enemy', was not achieved without difficulty and debate. It was partly as a result of this that, up to the seventeenth and early eighteenth centuries, Venice played an ambivalent role as the place from which all information about the European powers was transmitted to the sultan. The government of Venice seems on several occasions to have become involved in spying, to have encouraged it then to have contaminated it, and sometimes to have treated spying as just another of the many commodities that were imported into and exported from the city. In 1621, the Fondaco dei Turchi by the Rialto had become too small and a plan was approved for another large habitation that would house Muslim merchants from many different countries, including Persians and, in separate quarters, even Armenians.

It follows that, in fifteenth-century Venice, familiarity with Islam took perceptible steps forward. Donato da Lezze, who was related to the house of Zen which conducted so much business with Istanbul, had already edited a *Historia Turchesca* covering the fourteenth and fifteenth centuries. Marc'Antonio Sabellico, the historian of the Republic, showed a particular interest in Ottoman affairs; considering the political situation, this might also have been expected. A short while later, in 1516, Giovan Battista Egnazio returned to the subject of the Turks in his *De Caesaribus*, and Giovio printed his *Commentario delle cose de'turchi* in 1531. Andrea Cambini's *Origine de' turchi e imperio delli ottomani* was published in several editions between 1528 and 1541, and there was also Benedetto Ramberto's *Cose de' turchi*. Finally, Nicolò Zen, in his *Dell' arabico*, took up the discussion of Islamic religion and culture in a deliberately systematic way, which won him the consideration of Francesco Sansovino in his *Storia dell' origine e impero de' turchi*. This is the background against which the translation of the Koran by Andrea Arrivabene, published in Venice in 1547, should be viewed; it was only four years after Bibliander had completed the great feat of organization culminating in the appearance of his treatise on Islam in Basel in 1543.

The accelerating frequency with which genuine ambassadors, particularly Turkish ones, were appearing on the scene had the effect of increasing general curiosity about Muslims as well as sympathy towards them. Of course it was said that the ambassadors had come 'to spy'; the despatches, or *faretname*, sent by Turkish diplomats to the Sublime Porte soon became famous because of the jumble of acute observations, prejudice and misunderstanding they contained. Nevertheless, the sultan's representatives were entertained in style: the city was decorated, the diplomats were guided around the most impressive sights and accorded maximum attention and interest. There were still causes for concern, however; in 1594 a repressive team of Avogadori de Comun (local law-enforcers) inflicted severe punishment on anyone who molested these honoured guests.

Then came the period of the great embassies. In 1665, Kara Mehmed Pasha made a visit to Vienna with a retinue of one hundred and fifty persons, while at the end of 1669, Louis XIV received Suleiman Agha. The visit ended in humiliation for the king, however. Suleiman, who enjoyed extraordinary success in aristocratic *salons*, did not deign to inform the king about the current state of friction existing between Istanbul and Versailles (the French ambassador had recently been imprisoned and then expelled). In his *Mémoires*, the knight d'Arvieux, who was well informed about Turkish affairs, relates that the sovereign ordered him to collaborate with Molière and Lully in a piece for the theatre that would in some way contain the costumes and the customs of the new guests. The result was *Le Bourgeois gentilhomme*, a comedy-ballot presented successfully at Chambord on 14 October 1670. The play contained, among other things, a hilarious scene in which Jourdain, the *bourgeois*, is invested with the noble title and (imaginary) Turkish rank of *mamamusa* amidst a welter of Muftis, whirling dervishes and a torrent of a *lingua franca* based on Italian: '*Mahametta per Giurdina – me pregar sera e mattina – voler fare un Paladina – con galera e brigantina – per deffender Palestina – . . . dara, dara, dara . . . bastonara bastonara*' ('Mohammed is all for Jourdain – pray to me night and morning – aim to make a Paladin – with galley and brigantine – for the defence of Palestine – tara, tara, tara, . . . boom boom boom'). One hundred and forty-three years later, in *L'Italiana in Algeri*, first performed in 1813 – itself an important date, coinciding as it did with the resumption of the Barbary wars – Gioacchino Rossini had his Mustapha Bey invested with the rank of *pappataci*, his equivalent of the Turks in Molière's play.

Many other more solemn voices were raised in defence of the Turks and the Muslims and in support of their fascination, mystery and dignity. In Corneille's *Le Cid*, written in 1636 and inspired by the *Mocedades del Cid* published less than twenty years earlier by Guillen de Castro, the Moors are depicted as magnanimous and loyal enemies. In 1637, Dalibray produced a tragi-comedy called *Soliman* and Mairet staged the terrible death of Mustapha, the second son of Suleiman the Magnificent, who was killed by his father at the request of the sultana, Roxelane. In 1672 the great Racine, whose plays had hitherto always taken their subjects from classical antiquity, presented a story which he himself described as daring and modern: the tragic and violent tale of an event which occurred in the sultan's seraglio in Istanbul in 1635, which Racine had come across in the despatches of Count de Cézy, the French ambassador to the Sublime Porte. It dealt with the murder by Murad IV of his brother Bajazet, in compliance with the inexorable Islamic laws of succession, complicated in this case by a story of thwarted love, violated honour and betrayal. After Racine, the Western image of the seraglio was never the same again. The harem as the scene of pleasure and death began with *Bajazet*, which took part of its inspiration from the age-old topos of the Muslim East as a turbulent, cruel, sensual world.

There were other components of this image that were far from romantic – quite the reverse, in fact – including some highly practical steps being taken to bring Europe closer to the East. Jean-Baptiste Colbert, who in the 1660s warmly supported the creation of the Compagnie Française de la Chine, des Indes et du Levant, was energetic in his promotion of the teaching and study of Oriental languages at the Collège Royale as a buttress to French colonial and mercantile policy. In the 1670s Colbert sent a trusted colleague, the Marquis de Nointel, to the Levant charged with accomplishing a series of complex tasks, ranging from renewal of the Capitulations with Turkey to commercial relations and the purchase and collection of objects and manuscripts. After Nointel came Antoine Galland, a young man, *savant en langues orientales*, who travelled frequently and widely in the Levant between 1670 and 1688 and who picked up the trio of Islamic languages, Arabic, Persian and Turkish, to which he added demotic Greek. After producing an impressive body of translations, he entered the Collège Royal in 1709 as professor of Arabic.

Before taking up his professorial chair in Paris, Galland had in 1704 already translated and published the first volume of the *Thousand and One Nights*, which immediately became (for better or for worse) a milestone in the Western image of the Orient. Even earlier than this, in 1697, a posthumous work appeared by another professor at the Collège Royal, Barthélemy d'Herbelot de Molainville: the *Bibliothèque orientale*, subtitled the *Dictionnaire universel contenant généralement tout ce qui regarde la connaissance des peuples de l'Orient*. From the French presses at this time there also came a flood of tales by travellers who were also explorers, diplomats, merchants, archaeologists, collectors, spies or missionaries, from Jean Thévenot to François Bernier, from Jean-Baptiste Tavernier to Jean Chardin. With Galland and d'Herbelot a definite structure for Oriental studies as a scientific system had been reached; there was by now a methodically organized body of knowledge which included a variety of disciplines. Orientalism as it affected taste had become a basic and prevalent component of what has been defined as exoticism.

The *Encyclopédie* was later at pains to distinguish the 'Orient', that part of Asia lying to the east of the Euphrates, from the 'Levant', to be understood as the cluster of Asiatic countries lying to the west of the great river. Many features of the Levant were to reach distant parts of the world without losing any of their glamour and became accepted features of everyday modern life.

Such was the case with coffee, for example, which, with its rival beverage tea, was to share the dubious fate of representing the 'conquest of the conquered', a sort of cultural vendetta waged by the militarily or technologically weaker side against the greedier, stronger side as, in spite of its defeat, it manages to impose something of itself on the victor. From Ethiopia and Arabia the dusky beverage spread to Egypt and Turkey, then, by way of Germany, Italy and France, invaded Europe; its cultivation was also profoundly to alter the agriculture of South America. Tea spread from India to conquer England, and from China and Central Asia to Russia and Poland, both assailed simultaneously from the south-west across the Turkic-Mongol khanates beyond the Caspian, and from the south across Persia and the Caucasus. In the seventeenth and eighteenth centuries coffee and tea saved Europe from alcoholism and exerted a profound influence over daily life and manners as well as personal relationships.

At the outset, the fate of coffee in Europe was not easy. The plant spread across the continent during the last twenty years of the sixteenth century but was as yet confined to botanical gardens. It began to arouse curiosity because diplomats such as the Venetian Gianfrancesco Morosini and travellers such as Pietro della Valle from Rome described the strange Turkish habit of drinking the thick, dark brew. Controversy broke out as some people maintained that coffee was beneficial to the respiratory tract and the digestion, while others were convinced that it was harmful to the internal organs and caused impotence. Francesco Redi, head physician to the Grand Duke of Tuscany, admitted to a strong preference for wine over the 'bitter and sinful coffee'. When the great statesman Colbert died in 1683, it was rumoured that a post mortem revealed his stomach to have been burned up by the black poison.

During an otherwise unsuccessful visit to Louis XIV, Suleiman Agha introduced the fashion for coffee, and it soon spread from Paris all over France. In Venice and Marseille in the early 1670s, grocers cornered the market for the by now very expensive beans, causing high anxiety to wine producers and wine merchants. William Harvey and his disciple Ramsey claimed that coffee could be invaluable against alcoholism, which was already a terrible social scourge in England. Coffee was given its final accolade immediately after the siege of Vienna in 1683. A very durable legend claims that sacks of coffee beans were brought back from the encampment of Kara Mustapha by an obscure soldier, Franz Georg Kolschitzky, who opened the first coffee shop in the West; the subsequent use of milk and honey as a sweetener would have horrified any good Muslim. It is also claimed that, in the euphoria following the liberation of Vienna, the *Kipfel* or *croissant* was invented, a sweet roll whose crescent shape echoed the symbol of defeated Islam. Since this time it has always accompanied morning coffee.

A few residual adversaries of the fashionable new beverage still remained. Princess Elector Charlotte of Bavaria, for example, wife of the Regent of France Philippe d'Orléans, never lost an opportunity to make public her aversion to coffee, tea, chocolate and all the other new drinks, out of loyalty to good old German beer. Although the Dutch and later the French in the late seventeenth and early eighteenth centuries tried to acclimatize the coffee bush to other locations, from Java to the West Indies, the idea of coffee was still closely linked with the Muslim Middle East from whence it originated: when Madame Du Barry posed for her portrait in the costume of a sultana, she was painted sipping the contents of a delicate little cup. In Venice, still the gateway to the East, Turkish merchants with their large white turbans and cherry-red robes filled the Caffè Pignatta in St Mark's Square. In Paris the Café Procope became the favourite haunt of the *philosophes*; as had happened in Mecca a couple of centuries earlier, intellectuals sat up all night imbibing the stimulating drink and discussing ways of changing the world. In Montesquieu's *Lettres persanes*, coffee received its crowning literary accolade.

The *Lettres* were first published anonymously in Cologne in 1721. A few years later Johann Sebastian Bach paid musical tribute to the beverage from Arabia in the Coffee Cantata, no. 211, *Schweigert stille*, which was dedicated to the women of Leipzig and their passion for coffee.

Montesquieu's *Lettres persanes* demonstrate that the Orient was now in a position to be promoted as a metaphorical place, an imaginary state of mind 'above and beyond' reality, which was better for collating and criticizing the vagaries and follies of one's own civilization and the way of life shared between the two. The Turkish menace was receding; fear of the Turks, which had held Europe in its grip for three centuries, was disappearing so fast that it was by now nothing more than a bad memory. It was natural for France to set the pace in matters of ethics and aesthetics as well as in dress, and soon the whole of Europe was imitating its example. This was the time of *turqueries*, when dressing, building and furnishing '*à la turque*' were in vogue and when Turkey's favourite beverage became all the rage in Europe (the English and the Russians continued to prefer the drink favoured by the Indians, the Persians and the Chinese). It was at this time that Voltaire proclaimed his admiration for the wisdom and good nature of the people of the Bosphorus, the mild, sweet-tempered cultivators of gardens and roses.

He praised the wisdom, moderation and *savoir vivre* of the Chinese in similar terms. Turks, Persians, Chinese, Indians and 'noble savages' populated the century of the *Encyclopédie*. Unlike the other people who had been revisited and reinvented, however, the Turks had something pathetic and slightly ridiculous about them and were still in the grip of a terrible (and, for the *philosophes*, unendurable) tyrannical form of government – a fate which they shared with the Muscovites and the Japanese. According to Montesquieu's *Esprit des lois*, the relationship between despotism founded on fatalism and a disposition to accept power passively was typical of Islam. In Christianity the spirit of liberty had taken the religion's followers in a diametrically opposite direction. Meanwhile, the great gallery of stereotypes upon which to base a cultural model continued to be put forward: the Persians retained the secret of their distant origins, which were shrouded in obscurity; the Arabs carried with them the mystery of the desert and the cruel customs of its nomads and tribespeople; Northwestern India, land of the Moguls, now occupying the colonial limelight following France and England's duel during the Seven Years, War, had the soft colours of its snowy peaks dissolving into the mist, between the Karakorum and the Hindu Kush; Central Asia had its caravanserais from Bukhara, Khiva and Samarkand and its fierce, opulent khanates – the Kirghiz, the Uigurs, the Turkomen – heirs to the distant memory of Timur; while in the South, beyond Andalusia with its Moorish past, beyond the Barbary fishing boats which infested the Mediterranean, were ancient cities built of baked bricks and painted tiles, of dried mud and scented wood, and camel caravan halts between the Atlas and the Sahara through which Sudanese gold arrived from Timbuktu and the mouth of the Niger, together with white gold (ivory) and black gold (slaves) from darkest Africa. Islam was the amalgam which bound together all these different populations, these enigmatic peoples in their thousand different costumes, with their thousand languages, who prayed at identical hours of the day and night, all facing the same spot and reciting the same prayers in the same language – even though the differences of pronunciation and infection were legion. While Enlightenment Europe strained to define Reason, Nature and Happiness, the Muslim world appeared as a shadow filled with flashes of light and mysterious silence: their religion was lunar and anti-rational (although it gave rise to some of the world's greatest philosophers), and their creed was violent and intolerant (although it produced courtesy, compassion and hospitality). Now that the noise of the armed struggle was dying away, it was time humbly to acknowledge these paradoxes and to listen carefully to what they said. Not all Enlightenment thinkers were willing to suspend their judgement.

In Europe the threat posed by Islam for so long was not easily forgotten. In the new climate of peace and tolerance, believers in Koranic law were pressed into the role that historically seemed to befit them: deluded dreamers, servants of vanished or vanishing empires, figures of fun, often fools. In addition, France had not forgotten her conflict with Turkey amidst the power struggle of the *Grand Siècle*.

Between 1685 and 1686 John Locke, exiled from his native England to Holland, wrote his *Epistula de Tolerantia*. It was composed on the basis of his *Essay concerning Tolerance*, written in 1667 for an England that was exhausted by civil war and bloodshed and for a Europe that had recently emerged from the Thirty Years' War. After its victory over the Turks in Vienna in 1683, Europe had heaved a sigh of relief and looked forward to a long spell of peace. Locke's great essay underpinned the *mutua inter christianos tolerantia* which, combined with the gradual process of secularization, dominated the ethical life of the West over the succeeding three centuries. Although he was mainly preoccupied with tolerance between Christian countries and peoples, in the *post scriptum* to the *Epistula* Locke lingered over the different concepts of heresy and schism with regard to apostasy and *infidelitas*. If different religions justified different laws, and therefore different value systems and types of behaviour amongst their respective believers, what justification could there be for conflict aimed at determining which side in the conflict was correct?

The question had been asked, although it was a long way from being answered. Was tolerance a matter for Christians only, or was it a universal requirement? Voltaire was to return to this subject several times, ever since, as a young man of only thirty, he had become fascinated by it during the time he spent in England between 1726 and 1729. It was here that he learned to appreciate the works of Locke and Newton, becoming their tireless promoter. The years 1763 and 1764 were inspired for Voltaire, when he produced his *Traité sur la Tolérance* and his *Dictionnaire philosophique*. Both works, and in particular certain passages in the latter – for example the dialogue between Tuctan, Pasha of Samos, and the gardener Karpos in the *Catéchisme du jardinier* – emanate a message of comprehension and sympathy for the Muslim world, the same message that inspired the strongest invective against the crusades in the *Essai sur les moeurs et l'esprit des nations*. These passages were gathered into a separate volume as a riposte to the strange apologia composed by the scholars of the court of Louis XIV, the *Gesta Dei per Francos*, in the previous century.

Could Islam seriously pretend to tolerance when it was being presented as the historical (and contemporary) breeding ground of intrigue, lust and fanaticism? We learn from the letter of introduction to Voltaire's *Zadig* (inspired by the Persian poet Sa'adi's *Gulistan*) that Madame de Pompadour was habitually known as 'Sultana' (and made no objection to the epithet). Gotthold Ephraim Lessing provided a reply in 1778–80, when he wrote and published his *Nathan der Weise*, a work which has to be read in the context of two other works by Lessing is the same period, his essay on the education of the human race and his dialogues on freemasonry. *Nathan* is the Enlightenment's real manifesto on tolerance, and it is symptomatic that Lessing uses two terms of comparison as source and scenario for his work: Saladin's Muslim Orient and the crusading Middle Ages. It is a precursor of the Romanticism that was just round the corner.

Lessing's choices are revealing. Saladin, though noble and generous, represents the tyranny which fuelled the Islamic power machine. In addition, according to a scheme that was tried out in the Middle Ages and never completely abandoned, the negative nature of Islam was due entirely to the more inauspicious aspects of its founder. In his tragedy *Mahomet, ou le fanatisme*, Voltaire, who had frequently represented the Muslims as understanding and tolerant, and Islam as positive in comparison with Christianity, concentrates the characteristics of violence, hypocrisy, deceit, tyranny and intolerance in the figure of the Prophet. In August 1745 he sent a copy of his tragedy to Benedict XIV, accompanied by an unusually flattering letter, in Italian, in which he recommended to 'the leader of the true religion this work directed against the founder of a false and barbarous sect'.

A different story is told in *La Vie de Mahomet* by Henri de Boulain-villiers, in which the Prophet is a great, wise and honest law-giver who founded a rational and genuine religion that was later betrayed by Muslim jurists and theologians. Once again this is a discourse on Oriental matters that needs to be read bearing Western metaphor, and arguments against the early Christian Churches, particularly the Catholic Church, firmly in mind. Nevertheless, it opened the gates to a flood of praise for Islam and its founder – written from a theistic, rationalistic or genuinely atheistic point of view.

The Orient, meanwhile, was invading the arts of music and poetry. In Mozart's *Magic Flute* the Egypto–Zoroastrian (and gnostic-solar) wisdom of Sarastro is juxtaposed with the treachery of the Moorish slave Monostatos, the embodiment of the intellectual decadence of an Orient ruled by Saracen bigotry. Christoph Willibald Gluck's *Armide*, first produced in the Palais Royal in Paris in September 1777 and inspired by Tasso, seems to kill dead the serenely rationalist view of Islam promoted by the enlightened, encouraging Voltaire, in the manner of Ariosto.

The Orient as a seductive, mystical, magical environment informs the poem *Oberon*, by Christoph Martin Wieland, a friend of Goethe and von Kleist; the poem was published as a *romantisches Heldengedicht* in the *Teutsche Merkur* in 1780, and in it the chivalrous Christian West was contrasted with the magical Muslim East. A few years later *Oberon* was set to music by Carl Maria von Weber; by that time Islam and the Middle Ages were becoming a magic mirror of the 'elsewhere' of Romantic literature. As we know, the Latin for 'elsewhere' is *alibi*.

Mozart and Rossini enjoyed a joke, and it was easy to raise a laugh with Janissaries and eunuchs, harems and minarets, in the eighteenth and early nineteenth centuries. It was a relief to laugh, perhaps, now that the threat of imprisonment or impalement by the Turks was gone, and barbarous raids and massacres were a thing of the past. Now the turban and the scimitar could retire to the stage, and harems and mosques to the backcloths of plays and comic operas.

# 12

## From the 'Sickness' of the Ottoman Empire to the Third Wave of Islam

### New Pilgrims, New 'Crusades'

General Bonaparte set sail from Toulon in May 1798. He landed in Egypt on 1 July and captured Alexandria the following day, remaining in the Middle East until July 1799. Between February and May 1799 he fought in Palestine and Syria; he massacred three thousand prisoners and their families in cold blood in Jaffa, but confronted the plague with great courage. He never saw Jerusalem.

The young general had grandiose ambitions. On 2 July he sent a proclamation to the Egyptians in which the words Liberté, Egalité, Fraternité were mixed with exhortations in the name of 'the true Islam'. He dreamed of ruling the Orient from Alexandria, of rousing Persia and India against Russia and England, and of imposing the principles of the French Revolution while laying claim to the glory of the *Gesta Dei per Francos*. He knew little about Islam, but had chosen excellent collaborators and possessed an extraordinary talent for dealing with the situations in which he found himself.

Modern crusading studies and Egyptology both date from Napoleon's campaigns in Egypt and the Middle East. Chateaubriand, Michaud and Doré would never have made pilgrimages to the Holy Land, nor would they have discovered and fallen in love with the crusading epic without the example of Napoleon's exploits in the East.

Sultan Selim III could not rely on his English, Russian and Austrian 'protectors': the three countries were undoubtedly drawn together by their common interest in preventing revolutionary France from taking over the whole Mediterranean. They were also determined to find a place at the Orient's richly laden table, with or without the French, and to enjoy the leftovers of an empire whose borders until a few decades earlier had extended from the Danube to the Tigris and from the Volga to the Upper Nile. The great sultan experienced no difficulty in accepting the peace of Amiens in 1802, on the basis of an agreement with France in which the Capitulations were renewed in their entirety.

The policy towards the Sublime Porte adopted by the man who became Emperor of France on 2 December 1804 was richly ambiguous, but was inspired by a certain sympathy with Islam. While still a young man, Napoleon dabbled in what is today called 'Orientalism': he read François Augier de Marigny's *Histoire des arabes* and enjoyed both the *Voyage en Egypte et en Syrie* and the *Considérations sur la guerre actuelle des turcs* by Constantin-François de Chasseboeuf, Count of Volney, published between 1787 and 1788. He is known to have discussed Voltaire's *Mahomet* with Goethe, and to have defended Islam and the Prophet. His interest in the East was accompanied by a strong sympathy with the crusades (he took the opposite view to Voltaire); imperial propaganda was aimed at bolstering French supremacy, from Louis IX to Louis XIV, and claimed to be a continuation of it.

Napoleon came and went like a meteor. As well as the Code Napoléon and liberalism, his bequest to Europe included Egyptology, the fruit of his expedition to the Nile. To the Egyptians he bequeathed the idea that revolutionary ideals and Islam were in some way compatible; another of his legacies was the beginning of freemasonry. The crusade and its revival can be viewed from many different angles, of which a few shall be described here.

The first is embodied (as so often) by Chateaubriand. In 1811, when the empire was still in the ascendancy, he set off for the Holy Land, in the footsteps of the eighteenth-century travellers as well as on a traditional Christian pilgrimage; his description of the experience, in the *Itinéraire de Paris à Jérusalem*, is famous. During the journey he passed through Tunis. Ten years later, after he had embarked on a career in politics (he paid the restored monarchy for the cost of a pamphlet against Bonaparte), *Chateaubriand* recalled his journey in a speech to the parliament of the day in order to draw attention to the revival of piracy on the Barbary coast and to request, in the name of French tradition, the proclamation of a new crusade. His words were echoed three years later in 1819 by Pierre Deval, the French consul in Algiers. In 1822, in a small book by Gianpietro Vieusseux, published in Geneva, the

European powers were enjoined to gather under a single banner to make the Barbary corsairs listen to 'the voice of justice and reason'.[1]

This was the backcloth to the French conquest of Algiers; it was also the Bourbon King Charles X's final attempt at regaining popularity by stemming the wave of aversion which finally ousted him. His kinsman and successor, the 'July monarch' Louis-Philippe, proceeded along the same route of colonial expansion, using the crusades and the desire for progress and civilization as his alibi. At the request of Louis-Philippe, a liberal and constitutional monarch, five rooms in the palace of Versailles were decorated with frescoes devoted to the crusades. Napoleon III welcomed this trend and helped to further it, and he also encouraged the work of the scholars of the Société de l'Orient Latin, who published a 'Recueil des Historiens des Croisades'. As might have been expected, the preaching of the crusade was a somewhat muted affair; the expansion of colonial interests and the 'mission' to bring political liberty and civil, social and technological progress to non-European peoples competed (in differing ratios) to justify military expeditions to Asia and Africa. A crusading ship could occasionally be glimpsed amongst these expeditions, but it was generally there for propaganda purposes only. The same could be said for the French expedition to Tunisia in 1881–3; of General Gordon's campaign against the Mahdi Mohammed Ahmed in 1884–5; of the Italian occupation of Tripolitania in 1911–12; of the Spanish campaign in Rif between 1921 and 1926, when the young Galician soldier Francisco Franco distinguished himself (he was later to be the *caudillo* of another *cruzada*); and finally of the two Italian wars against Ethiopia – a deeply Christian country and former ally, which had been part of the Genoese and Portuguese projects in the fifteenth and sixteenth centuries.

## Far Pavilions

'You smile upon the land you plunder.' With these words Gabriele d'Annunzio addressed the Vittoria Italica in 1911, at the time of the conquest of Tripolitania. For many centuries, but with particular intensity in the late eighteenth and early nineteenth centuries, Europeans from Voltaire to Kipling had smiled upon the lands they were in the act of plundering. And they fell in love, as apparently kidnappers and jailers often fall genuinely in love with their victims; they in turn apparently

---

[1]  J. E. Humbert and G. Vieusseux, *Les barbaresques et les chrétiens* (followed by G. Vieusseux, *Extrait d'une lettre du Lazareth de Livourne*), edited by L. Neppi Modona (Florence, 1983).

reciprocate the feeling, or pretend to reciprocate it. While Lord Byron went to the assistance of the Greeks, sorely oppressed by the Turks, and died of malaria in Missolonghi in 1824, his compatriots and other Europeans were filling their museums and their private collections with objects and archaeological finds from the Orient, and their bank accounts with the fruits of their plunder.

Their love may have been obfuscated by aesthetic excitement, but it was genuine. Between 1826 and 1829, Washington Irving visited a dusty, decaying Granada and was able to revive its former glory (like Chateaubriand in *Les Aventures du dernier Abencérage*); in so doing he created a taste throughout the West for splendid Spanish ruins. Gérard de Nerval spent 1842 and 1843 in the Orient and produced a long fanciful traveller's tale which haunted the minds of his successors Gautier, Flaubert, Hugo and Loti as well the Orientalist painters.

Nineteenth-century Europe abounded in palaces and pavilions in the Turkish, Moorish or Mogul style, and was covered in neo-Gothic churches, railways stations and even factories. The fake Orient and the fake Middle Ages were the embodiment of an Elsewhere which ran parallel to reality, the object of fascination and desire, the objective of profound revulsion but even more powerful attraction.

To the world of Islam, Europe represented something quite different. In 1785 in Istanbul the reforming prime minister Halil Hamid was assassinated, along with other 'admirers of the West', and was thrown into the Bosphorus with a placard round his neck naming him as an enemy of *shari'a* and the empire. Nevertheless Sultan Selim III, who ascended the throne in the fateful year 1789, continued to send young people of good family to study in the West. He opened embassies throughout Europe and began to implement a series of (cautious) reforms aimed at laying the foundations of a modern state – modern in the Western sense: a disciplined army, an honest and efficient administrative system, an orderly financial system and an economy regulated by clearly laid down standards. If these reforms were not implemented, the Ottoman Empire would be strangled by the West and would not survive. The French Revolution and the restoration of the monarchy taught the Ottomans that although in Europe regimes might change their political colour, finance, the economy and technology continued to move in the same direction.

The victory of the Holy Alliance over Napoleon and the two Russian–Turkish wars of 1803–12 and 1828–9 seemed to place Turkey in the control of the tsar. This meant that the Russian fleet now controlled the Black Sea and could make a triumphal entrance, via the Straits, into the Mediterranean. This state of affairs persuaded the French and the English to join forces against Russia, but it also encouraged the Greeks to rebel against the Turks, thereby supporting Mehmet Ali's experiment. Mehmet Ali was an Ottoman official of Albanian origin who, on becoming viceroy of Egypt in 1805, swept away what remained of the Mamelukes in a most vicious and treacherous massacre in Cairo in 1811 before energetically setting about modernizing the country. His son Ibrahim (1789–1848) continued his father's work – he was heir to his father but predeceased him – winning splendid victories with his army organized in Europe. He brought shame on the Wahabite sect of Arabia by placing the whole western side of the Arabian Peninsula, the Hejaz, under Egyptian rule; he was behind the Turkish repression of Greek insurgents; and, finally, when his father openly rebelled against the Porte with the aim of making Egypt independent, he conducted a brilliant campaign in Syria. After the capture of Acre in 1832, he began to set his sights on the realization of a bold dream – the conquest of the Turkish Empire. He invited Western countries to flock to the Holy Land (the British opened a consulate there in 1838) and removed all entrance fees to the holy places, which for centuries had enriched the Ottoman rulers and aggravated pilgrims.

Ibrahim aroused great hopes and strong feelings: his actions were watched by an Arab world that was gradually reawakening and showing signs of wishing to shake off the Ottoman yoke. In spite of the fact that he was responsible for the demise of Greek liberty, Western liberals had high hopes of Ibrahim and were convinced that they were dealing with a liberator and modernizer. It required the full strength of the Russian army to stop his march on Istanbul.

After Ibrahim, however, the way was open. Following the English example, France, Prussia, Austria and Spain opened consulates in the Holy Land; Russia sent in an observer. Since an important factor in discouraging Westerners from reviving the practice of pilgrimage was the poor sanitary conditions to be found in Jerusalem, interested countries began to carry out public works in the city and to open hospitals.

Encouraged by this eagerness for renewal, even diaspora Jews began gradually to return to the land of their origins. Many established themselves there, even buying small properties, so keen were they to put down roots in *Eretz Israel*. The sultan's government approved of their return, as did the Arab population and the Western consulates. The Israelis had never forgotten the Promised Land and never ceased to live there. The Jewish community in Jerusalem won the sultan's favour and prospered in the city from the late fifteenth century onwards. The greatest scholar of the kabbala, Isaac Luria (1534–72), was born in Jerusalem. In 1700 Rabbi Jehuda He-Hassid emigrated from Poland to Jerusalem with one thousand Ashkenazi Jews, who were immediately subjected to persecution and repression of all kinds (their Sephardic brethren, who were better integrated, generally experienced no such problems). In 1720, being unable to pay the heavy taxes imposed on them, they were forced to witness the destruction of a synagogue that they had built with great sacrifice in the southwestern part of the city. It was not until a century later that they were able to rebuild the venerable temple, which was completed in 1864 and named *Hurva* (Hebrew for 'ruin') after the destruction.

Meanwhile the rule whereby events in the Holy Land mirrored events in the outside world continued to operate, with all the often dramatic consequences that that implied.

In the Grotto of the Nativity in Bethlehem, located since the fourth century in the crypt of the splendid Basilica of Constantine, which even the Persians had not dared to desecrate, a silver star decorated with an inscription in Latin marked the exact spot where, according to tradition, Christ was born. One day this symbol, which with its Latin inscription testified all too obviously to the rights of the Latin Christians, was stolen from inside this very basilica belonging to Orthodox Christians. The theft provoked a diplomatic incident involving both Catholic and Orthodox communities. The tsar intervened with characteristic force in favour of the Orthodox Christians, sending a strong ultimatum to the Sublime Porte. France and England drew up their forces in defence of the sultan – with some embarrassment, since for decades liberal romantic propaganda had successfully depicted the Ottoman government as a decadent and corrupt regime, fierce and vicious. More was at stake this time than the star of Bethlehem or the romantic dreams of literature or 'Orientalist' painting. The real problem, of which the star and the ultimatum were symbols, was control of the Straits and of the Russian fleet's access to the Mediterranean.

The outcome was the Crimean war, fought between 1854 and 1856 and brought to an end by a session of the Congress of Paris on 25 March 1856 during which the principle of reform in favour of Christian minorities in the Ottoman Empire was sanctioned and the tsarist government was forced to abandon its claims to exclusive protection of these minorities. By now the situation of the Christian communities in the Holy Land and the holy places had become part of a much larger picture, the so-called 'Oriental question'. France and Russia seemed, to all intents and purposes and in spite of events, to be the two main interlocutors in matters relating to the handling of Christians in the Holy Land. Meanwhile, 1869 saw the opening of the Suez Canal, presented in Europe as the route by which civilization, freedom and progress would speedily reach Asia.

The canal project coincided with a dream that had been cherished by the Sultans of Turkey since the sixteenth century; if it had been realized then, the history of the world would have been very different. In 1833 a group of enthusiastic admirers of Saint-Simon arrived in Egypt, strongly of the opinion that digging a canal would favour their 'crusade' for progress. Mehmet Ali put obstacles in the way of their plans for fear of the international complications that might have been caused by putting them into effect. In 1854 the concession to build the canal was awarded to a Frenchman, Ferdinand de Lesseps, and in 1858 the Suez Canal Company was set up with assets of 200 million francs. Work began the following year. England energetically opposed the plan, fearing that the Ottoman navy would be revived and that the influence of Bonapartist France would be strengthened in the Near East; a further cause for anxiety was that the French would compete on the route to India. The canal was opened on 17 November 1869, in the presence of Empress Eugénie of France and Emperor Franz-Joseph of Austria (who spent time in Jerusalem in the same year, humbly accepting the simple hospitality of the Franciscan Friars of the Holy Sepulchre, who had no proper guest quarters). Although Austria had been conquered three years earlier by Prussia, a diplomatic project dear to Empress Eugénie's heart was still perhaps being considered: a political and military alliance between the Catholic countries of Europe. The situation regarding the canal was soon reversed with the defeat of Napoleon III in the war against the Prussians the following year, the widespread penetration of the English into Egypt (with the conquest of the Upper Nile by Samuel Baker between 1870 and 1873 and the appointment of Charles George Gordon as governor of the Sudan in the following year) and, finally, the transfer by the khedive (who was in financial difficulties) of his shares in the canal (equivalent to 100 million francs, the major shareholding) to the British government. A new era was beginning for the Mediterranean: marginalized by navigation since the sixteenth century, it was now returning to the centre of the world. The Suez Canal under British control also gave the Rock of Gibraltar an entirely new role. Now Her Britannic Majesty's gunboats and merchant and passenger ships sailing towards India no longer had to stop at Alexandria (under military occupation since 1807) to unload, nor did they have to sail right round the continent of Africa.

Faced with such comprehensive diplomatic and economic penetration by Europe, Russia had no option but to respond by turning to the question of religion. In 1877 the tsar declared war on Turkey, his pretext being that he could no longer tolerate the abject state of the Orthodox Christians who were the sultan's subjects there, particularly in the Balkan Peninsula. The Russian army arrived in Istanbul and was stopped in its tracks by the 'peace of San Stefano' (3 March 1878). The Turkish Empire by this time was beginning to collapse; the prerogatives it now had to concede to the tsar dealt a final blow to its prestige and independence. At this point Western Europe began to grow anxious again, particularly England, who feared Russian control of Turkey (which would have meant Russian ships in the Mediterranean and intensive use of the Suez Canal by the Russians, with a strong concomitant risk to British control of the sea), and Austria, who were anxious about the balance of power in the Balkans. Anglo-Russian conflict was averted by the Congress of Berlin and the agreement brokered by Bismarck, the 'honest broker'.

Another complex contest had begun, meanwhile, beyond the Caspian: a chess game for two, with crowds of interested observers behind each player perfectly willing to change sides. The English called it the 'Great Game' and the Russians 'jousting with shadows'. The ruthless contest between Russia and England to gain as much land as possible between the Caspian and the Hindu Kush was played in the second half of the nineteenth century across the entire area between the Syr Darya and the Tien Shan; the Turco-Mongol nomads of Central Asia, who were Muslims, could expect precious little assistance from their 'caliph', the Sultan of Istanbul, now brought to his knees by the European powers.

Central Asia had for years been the scene of turbulence, but also of the odd tremor presaging revival. The rejects of a demoralized Europe were attracted to it like iron filings to a magnet. Consider, for example, the case of Paolo Avitabile, born in Agerola in 1791, who fought in Murad's army in the Punjab and became governor of Peshawar, as well as a hanger and flogger and proprietor of a harem; as an old man Paolo returned to his native Campania, where he was honoured by King Ferdinand II and died in 1850. Soldiers of fortune met with a different fate, however.

The Russians and the English did not only use soldiers. They had at their disposal a whole army of spies disguised as geographers, ethnologists and merchants who swarmed over the deserts and the steep slopes of the world's highest mountains. Their numbers included some admirable mercenaries and genuine scholars, such as the explorer Nikolai Mikhailovich Przhevalsky, a general and zoologist of international renown. Or Shoqan Ualikhanov, nephew of a Kazakh khan, a military cadet at Orenburg and later a secret agent for the tsar in Kazakhstan and Kirghistan, who was a botanist, geographer, painter, friend of the exiled Dostoevsky and a liberal democratic thinker. He died in 1865 at the age of only thirty.

When Timur's empire broke up, Central Asia became a mosaic of khanates and emirates in fierce conflict with one another; alliance with these small groupings was hotly contested between the Turkish, Persian and Chinese Empires. Russia and Great Britain forced their way unscrupulously into this uneasy balancing act. Frustrated by their unsuccessful attempt to break through to the Mediterranean in the Crimean war, the Russians hurled themselves hungrily at the land then generically known as Turkestan. In 1865, against the tsar's orders, General Mikhail Grigorevich Chernyayev conquered Tashkent, receiving for his pains a sword studded with diamonds and orders from the tsar to resign; however, the deed had been done. In 1868 the city of Samarkand surrendered to General Konstantin Kaufman. In 1881 the conquest of Central Asia was completed by General Skobolev, and the Russian railway was extended from Astrakhan to the Amu Darya.

The Turco-Mongol khans tried to withstand attack. In 1863 the Khan of Kokand sent an official of Tajik nationality to Kashgar, beyond the Tien Shan, where the Uigurs and 'Dungans' (Chinese Muslims) had rebelled against the imperial Manchu government. Yakub Beg, an official, soon took over present-day Xinjiang and from 1867 began ruling in a way that aimed to manoeuvre skilfully between Turkey, England and Russia. Yakub Beg's ambitious project foundered, however, because of rivalry between the Russians and the English, both contending for the favour of the Emperor of China, from whom the Tajik had snatched Xinjiang. When Yakub died in mysterious circumstances in 1877, his kingdom did not survive; only the Sultan of Istanbul, recognized by the Turco-Mongol Sunnis as their leader, could have sustained it, but there were other matters to be considered on the Bosphorus at the time.

The nomads of Central Asia never ceased to look towards the Ottomans, since the religion they shared was linked with both ethnic and linguistic affinity. Nationalism, the buzzword of the late nineteenth century, and pan-Turkism – based on the model of pan-Germanism – were already rife in Turkey, particularly amongst the urban middle classes and the military.

In India, a chapter seemed to close when, in August 1858, the British parliament transferred government of the subcontinent from the East India Company to the crown. In Central Asia, however, it was clear that the by now collapsing Persian and Chinese Empires could entertain no hope of power; they had previously only played a supporting role either to Her Britannic Majesty and Empress of India or the Tsar of all the Russias. Although the two European powers appeared to have taken up positions along the watershed of the lofty Tien Shan and the Karakorum, this had not really happened.

The culminating chapter of this fascinating tale was written between 1918 and 1925 by two extraordinary personalities, Enver Pasha and Mikhail Frunze.

Enver was born in 1881 and took part in the revolution of the Young Turks in 1908. A great admirer of pan-Germanism, he was a volunteer in the Libyan campaign against the Italians in 1911. He became Turkey's Minister of War in 1914 but was exiled in 1917, first to Berlin, then to Moscow, where he became Lenin's great collaborator over the problems of Central Asia. He was sent to Turkestan in 1921, when he tore off his mask. He had always dreamt of founding a Turkish Empire between the Caspian and the Tien Shan, with Bukhara as its capital, which would be joined to the new Turkey of Mustapha Kemal Atatürk. The new empire would be upheld by the marvellous Turkish and Tajik warriors, whom the infuriated Russians named 'Bashmaks' (assassin-bandits), worthy adversaries of the newborn Red Army.

The Soviets had also found a Central Asian hero of their own. It is a great shame that so little is now remembered of Mikhail Vasilievich Frunze, the formidable Bolshevik Napoleon born in Bishkek, capital of present-day Kirghistan. A bronze statue of Frunze on horseback still stands in the city, there is a small museum devoted to his memory. Frunze gave one of his sons the fateful name of Timur, the same as the great Turanian hero. In their own way, Enver and Frunze were very much alike.

The Turkish revolutionary was only forty when he challenged the Red Army, turning to the Emir of Afghanistan for assistance and giving himself the title 'Commander in Chief of the armies of Islam, kinsman of the Caliph and envoy of the Prophet'. His *jihad* inflamed the Muslims of Central Asia. By the spring of 1922 he had conquered a large part of the emirate of Bukhara, but he died too soon, on 4 August of the same year, allegedly leading a suicidal cavalry charge against Soviet machine guns. The Bashmaks continued their resistance until the 1930s, in spite of being hunted and brutally suppressed in a manner that was only marginally less vicious than the lies and calumny later directed against their heroism.

Three years after Enver's death, his opponent Frunze, the creator of the Red Army, died in equally ambiguous circumstances. The leaders of the Supreme Soviet in Moscow learned that he was suffering from a gastric ulcer; inevitably, the operation to which he was subjected went badly. The Central Committee entrusted the education of Frunze's children to Voroshilov, one of his few real friends. Boris Pil'njak's story, *The Assassination of a Commandant*, is almost the only remaining witness to a despicable crime, committed by a revolution which devoured its own, especially the best of their kind.

## An Open Dialogue

Returning to Western Asia, the Franco-Prussian war of 1870 left the French humiliated, which inevitably had repercussions for the prestige and prerogatives the French had gained over nearly three centuries of tutelage of Catholic communities and residents in the Near East. The era of Francis I and Villeneuve was long past. In 1870, in the Hall of Mirrors in the palace of Versailles, the Federal German Empire was proclaimed. Its chancellor, Prince Bismarck, was famously opposed to the Catholic Church, in spite of the fact that a large majority of the new empire's subjects belonged to the Catholic religion. The pastoral care of German Catholics could not be left to the Emperor of Austria; too many Germans were looking mournfully in his direction, since until 1866 the moral guidance of the German Confederation had been his responsibility. In 1875, although in the midst of intense cultural warfare, the German consul-general in Egypt formally declared that his government was not disposed to permit any single European government to have exclusive rights over the representation and protection of Catholic settlements in the Orient and claimed the German government's right to defend any German subjects to be found in such settlements.

In June–July 1878, Bismarck held a Congress in Berlin at which it was proposed that a disinterested mediator be appointed who would end the conflict between Turkey and Russia and conclude a lasting agreement between Russia, Austria, England, France and Turkey; Italy was to participate, too, thereby gaining a measure of international prestige, its reward for constantly giving way to German demands. The readjustment of the Balkans was the ostensible subject of the Congress: in fact, steps were taken towards the dismemberment of the Ottoman Empire and the distribution of the dismembered parts. England obtained the right to occupy Cyprus, while France was to take possession of Tunis (which it did in 1881); Italy, which had also hoped for Tunis (a possible outcome in geographical and historical terms), was held at bay with vague promises of Albania as compensation. To save face, the Western powers imposed some 'liberal' reforms on the sultan, which allowed the Congress of Berlin to present itself (in accustomed fashion) as a dazzling step along the road of civilization and progress rather than what it actually was, another act of colonialist brigandage.

In return for its participation in the Congress, France explicitly requested that questions about Egypt, Syria and the holy places should remain outside the discussion; nevertheless, the famous status quo which almost single-handedly provoked the Crimean war was confirmed, at France's insistence since its rights were thereby recognized. On the other hand, Berlin made it clear that in future if clerics and Christian pilgrims had problems in the Holy Land, they should apply to their own consular officials and thence to their own governments. The sultan's authority was completely marginalized by the exercise of prerogatives of this kind with respect to Western people and possessions, even though the holy places were still part of the territory ruled by him.

Continual foreign interference in matters concerning the Ottoman Empire finally began to foster nationalistic feelings amongst the ruling class, even though such feelings were foreign to Islamic culture. They seem to have arrived as an accompaniment to modernization. After the revolution of 1909, Turkey requested at several international gatherings that the Capitulations should be abolished; by the beginning of the Great War it had denounced them unilaterally. On 2 November 1914 Russia declared war against Turkey, thereby dragging it into the conflict with the countries of the *entente cordiale*. As was rightly said, it was the pro-German policy of the 'Young Turks' and the secret agreements entered into on 2 August that bound Turkey to Germany; it was also the result of decades of humiliation and bullying at the hands of imperialist powers – the Russians, who had undermined Turkish security and prestige in the Black Sea, the Straits and the Balkans, and the French and English, who divided up what was left of the Ottoman Empire from Tunisia to Egypt.

The Franco-British response to Turkey's entry into the war appealed to the nascent patriotic spirit of a united Arab world; the creation of a 'great Arab nation' was promised, a single kingdom governed by a local ruling dynasty which would unite all Arab peoples from Syria and Mesopotamia to the Arabian Peninsula and Egypt. For this to take place the Arabs had to be freed from the Turks, no easy matter when Muslim *pietas* shrank from the idea of taking up arms against the sultan, who was invested with the dignity of a caliph. The Muslim mind could grasp the idea of *umma*, the community of believers, but had the greatest difficulty in understanding the Western concepts of 'fatherland' and 'nation'. For the French and English, therefore, it was expedient to their immediate political and military interests that Arabs should be incited against the Turks. By supporting the Islam of the Arabs, they made an important contribution to its Westernization and moderniza-tion. The means of liberating the Arabs from the Turkish yoke were encouraged. In order to convince the Arabs to rebel against the sultan-caliph without causing them problems with their religious conscience, they promised the throne of the new Arab nation to the custodian of the holy shrine in Mecca, Sharif Hussein of the Hashemite dynasty.

The contribution made by the Arabs to the liberation of Syria and Palestine from Turkish military occupation during the First World War was considerable, possibly even crucial; diplomatic events however, deprived it of importance. The Sykes–Picot agreement (named after the two diplomats who signed it) took no account of the promise made to Sharif Hussein, establishing the division of the Middle East at the end of the war into two zones of influence: France would retain Syria and Lebanon, according to well-established cultural tradition, while England would take Palestine, Transjordania and Mesopotamia. Apart from a few minor emirates along the coast which Britain wanted to keep within its sphere of influence in order to protect its interests in the Indian Ocean and the Persian Gulf, Arabia would be a monarchy ruled by the Saudi Wahabite family. The agreement was kept secret, but the Russian government of course knew about it. After the revolution that transformed Russia into the Soviet Union, the substance of the agreement was revealed. Turks and Germans did their utmost to persuade the Arabs that the promises made to Hussein by the Allies were only a hoax and that 'Greater Arabia' would never exist. Meanwhile, the Allies had marched into Baghdad, Damascus and Jerusalem. The British kept the throne of Iraq for Hussein's son Faisal; the French prevented the British from adding Syria to the package – Syria belonged to them and they planned a republic under their control. Faisal's brother Abdullah was created King of Transjordania. The Sykes–Picot agreement was confirmed by the treaty of San Remo in 1920 and the Capitulations were abolished, thereby setting in train a series of complex diplomatic manoeuvres as a result of which the Council of the League of Nations gave temporary control of Palestine to a British mandate.

By now a new element had been introduced into this complex game. In 1862, Rabbi Zevi Hirsch Kalischer suggested that the Messiah would not reappear miraculously, as the Jewish people hoped, but that humanity would have to cooperate in his second coming. The re-establishment of the Jews in the Holy Land, in *Eretz Israel*, would be the pledge and sign of readiness for the event. The Ottoman government had allowed the Jews a chief rabbi in Palestine, based in Jerusalem, since 1841. After Rabbi Hirsch Kalischer's initiative the Universal Alliance of Jews established a school of agriculture, *Mikve Israel*, in Palestine.

The worsening conditions experienced by Oriental Jews, especially in Russia, encouraged a tremendous exodus in the late nineteenth century. Many chose the United States, others moved to Europe, particularly to France; from about 1882 onwards, about 30,000 opted for Palestine. Between 1889 and 1895 an association named *Chowewei Zion* ('the Friends of Zion') collected large sums of money for the establishment of Jewish colonies in Palestine, much of it coming from wealthy philanthropists such as Baron Edmond de Rothschild. In 1896 the journalist Theodor Herzl wrote, in a few weeks, a book entitled *Der Judenstaat*, now considered the real manifesto of Zionism: Herzl was officially received in Jerusalem by Kaiser Wilhelm in 1898. In 1902 a religious type of Zionism made its appearance, which was quite different from the secular, nationalist Zionism promoted by Herzl, who was simply looking for 'a homeland guaranteed in perpetuity for the Jews'. Now Rabbi Abraham Isaac Kook, the founder of the *Mizrahi* party, began promoting a new agenda, which could be summed up as 'the Land of Israel for the people of Israel in the name of the Torah'.

The first Jewish settlers in Israel received a moderate welcome. In 1891, however, the leaders of the Palestinian Arabs made a request to the Ottoman government that Jewish immigration and the acquisition of land by Jews should be controlled. In fact the Jewish influx into the Holy Land was based on a misunderstanding: the idea that the area could be considered as a 'land without people for a people without land'. The Palestinian people already lived there. And the Ottoman government and the Western powers were agreed that if the land were properly cultivated, it could support a much larger population than was there already.

The misunderstanding was fuelled by British diplomacy; there was a need to square the circle by putting together three irreconcilable objectives, and the British government succeeded. It incited the Arabs against the Turks with the promise of a great, united, independent Arab state; it distanced Zionist Jews, who were mainly German in origin and were thus closely connected with the German imperial cause, from the cause of the main protagonists in the First World War; and, with the aim of averting or modifying Zionist sympathy with Germany, it acceded to the demands of that part of the Zionist movement which could no longer be satisfied with the acquisition of any land for a landless people – it had to be that particular land, *Eretz Israel*, and Jerusalem.

On 2 November 1917 Lord Arthur James Balfour, the British foreign secretary, sent a letter to the financier Lionel Walter Rothschild, honorary president of the World Zionist Organization, in which he confirmed that the British government was in favour of the constitution of a Jewish national home in Palestine. His words then entered the official diplomatic canon: like the Sykes–Picot agreement, however, they were in direct contradiction to the promise of a 'great Arabian state' made to Sharif Hussein.

Thus when the Great War was over, the Jews and the Arabs found themselves in conflict with one another – something that was far from the intentions of either. In the late nineteenth and early twentieth centuries isolated bands of Arabs had mounted attacks on Jewish colonies, but these were attributed to endemic brigandage. In March 1919 Faisal extended a warm welcome to the Jews who were emigrating to Syria and

Palestine, and expressed himself convinced that the two communities could develop together in a spirit of harmony.

The tension that grew up between the Arabs and the Jews during the British mandate, the influx of Jews into Palestine immediately after the Shoah, the foundation of the State of Israel and the conflict that succeeded it contributed to the creation of the still unresolved Middle Eastern problem, one that remains apparently far from a final solution.

After the Arab–Israeli conflict in 1967, the entire city of Jerusalem, including the holy places and the entire historic and monumental centre of the city, was controlled by the State of Israel which, in spite of UN resolutions forbidding such an act, transferred its capital from Tel Aviv (the 'Hill of Spring', the Jewish city founded by early twentieth-century immigrants around the old Arab city of Haifa). Many solutions to the problem of Jerusalem have been put forward, from the Palestinian suggestion of a single city as the capital of two distinct states and governments, the Israeli and the Palestinian (the example of Rome and the Vatican city is quoted, divided by the agreement of 1929), to the Holy See's notion of a kind of international city (heavily disapproved of by Jews all over the world). Although apparently impossible to find, a solution is vital; as history has proven, what happens in Jerusalem affects the whole world.

The Arab–Israeli question, denographic changes and the global shift in productivity over the past two or three decades, followed since 1989 by the rise of a new global superpower, the United States of America, have profoundly affected and modified relations between Europe and Islam.

The defeat of the Arab world in the Arab–Israeli war of 1967 profoundly shook Muslim confidence in the West, and therefore affected their confidence in what has been improperly termed the 'secularization' (or 'modernization') of Islam.

Traditionalist and radical claims, no less improperly termed 'fundamentalist', first arose mainly in Egypt and Northwestern India in the 1920s and, until recently, had a very hard time surviving; supporters of such claims were divided into a welter of different schools and groups, forever on the run from modernizing, Westernizing, national progressive regimes which in general shared the government of a large area of the *dar al-Islam*. They began to grow in strength, however, until the watershed represented by the 'Islamic revolution' in Iran in 1979 revealed just how fragile were the foundations of the authoritarian and Westernizing regime imposed by the Shahs of the Pahlevi dynasty. The Kurdish problem was by now emerging ever more strongly. The victors of the war of 1914–18 traced the frontiers of the new Middle East but completely neglected Kurdistan, the mountainous area covering about half a million square kilometres between the Caucasus, the Gulf of

Alexandretta and half the length of the Euphrates, populated by nomadic Kurds speaking a Kurdish version of Persian. The area was divided between Turkey, Iran, Syria and Iraq; soon after its partition it became the focus of attention of international interests hoping to exploit its oil resources. The Kurds, divided by their new frontiers as well as by their own tribal structure, attempted in vain to interest the world in their cause. As long as they remained loyal to the authority of the sultan their voice went unheard. They were the victims of a policy of repression and extermination, and the terrorism practised by certain groups seemed the only weapon to counter such a policy; it was only in the last twenty years of the twentieth century that the Kurds managed to attract international attention.

Amongst the many Islamic states that have appeared or reappeared on the international stage during the latter half of the twentieth century, a particular role seems to have been played by Iran, which was transformed into an 'Islamic republic' in 1979, and by the countries of the former Soviet Union. These Islamic countries are predominantly Ural-Altaic (with large Indo-European majorities, however). Having previously belonged to the Confederation of Independent States with Russia, they were always influenced by a strong pan-Turanic feeling, which encouraged them to look favourably upon post-Kemalist Turkey and, in extremist areas, to dream of a 'great Turkish state', 'from the Bosphorus to the Pamirs'. The feeling was religious and was inspired by 'Islamism' (a preferable noun to 'fundamentalism'); their eagerness to return to the Arabic alphabet in preference to Latin or Cyrillic characters imposed by the Soviets is another indication of this feeling.

Today Europe no longer occupies political centre-stage. Although it is still financially and economically a great power, it no longer possesses institutions capable of handling international politics or diplomacy independent of its American ally. Europe's attitude to the governments and peoples of the *dar al-Islam* is indecisive and ambivalent, and its relationship with the United States appears to affect its independence of both action and judgement in confrontations with countries like Iran, Iraq or Libya. Public opinion in Europe is still very badly informed about most religious and cultural aspects of the Islamic world, and the adjectives 'secular' or 'integrist' (or other vague distinctions) seem totally inadequate. Scant information of mediocre quality, made to seem abundant by incessant mass media coverage, combines with lingering or grotesquely repeated prejudices to prevent the formation of any calm and tolerant view of Islam.

Europe is currently experiencing a fresh 'assault' by Islam, of a somewhat paradoxical nature. The Muslims who arrive in Europe, legally or illegally, usually in search of work and better conditions for themselves and their families, often have a very rudimentary religious background, yet their cultural background is the main key to their identity and their self-awareness. Muslims in early twenty-first-century Europe are in a position that is historically quite new. This is the first time that large, homogeneous groups of Muslims have lived outside the *dar al-Islam*, in lands where *shari'a* law does not apply. To the disadvantages inherent in belonging to a minority are added the tension caused by propaganda and, to some extent, by fundamentalist groups engaged in terrorist activities, and the problems caused by the growth of Muslim communities (due in part to the number of European converts), which are often large enough now to gain official recognition.

The 'third wave' of Islam has not therefore broadened the boundaries of the *dar al-Islam*, but it has had to come to terms with a Europe which is itself in a delicate state of redefinition, strong but uneven from an economic and social point of view, insecure from a political point of view, and uncertain of its own cultural identity. 'Islam will be what the Muslims make of it', in the words of the Egyptian Fouad Zakaria. Europe, too, will be what the Europeans make of it, a place in which the number of citizens and residents following the law of the Prophet is growing daily.

# Chronology

| | | |
|---|---|---|
| 622 | 15 June | 'Hegira' (flight) of the Prophet Mohammed from Mecca to Jathrib (later called Medina, 'the City'). |
| 632 | | Death of the Prophet Mohammed in Medina. |
| 638 | | Conquest of Jerusalem by Caliph Umar. |
| 639 | | Beginning of the Arab conquest of Egypt. |
| 641 | | The Arabs conquer Alexandria. |
| 647 | | Beginning of the Arab conquest of Ifriqiya (corresponding to the Roman province of Africa), completed by about 705. |
| 649 | | Muhawyya, governor of Syria, attacks the island of Cyprus. |
| 655 | | Important Muslim naval victory against the Byzantines at Phoenix. |
| 711 | | The Berber Arabs begin the conquest of the Iberian Peninsula. |
| 732 | 25 October | The battle of Poitiers (this is the most widely accepted date). |
| 750 | | Coup d'état and foundation of the Abbasid caliphate. |
| 756 | | The Umayyad Abd ar-Rahman founds the emirate of Córdoba. |
| 759 | | The Franks drive the Muslims out of Narbonne. |
| 762 | | Foundation of Baghdad, new capital of the Abbasid caliphate. |

| | |
|---|---|
| 797 | Establishment of diplomatic relations between Charlemagne and Harun ar-Rashid. |
| 801 | The Franks regain Barcelona. |
| 827 | Beginning of the Aghlabite conquest of Sicily (completed in 902). |
| 827–961 | Arab emirate in the island of Crete. |
| 833 | Palermo conquered by the Muslims. |
| 844 | The Normans attack Seville. |
| 846 | Arab incursions into Rome. |
| 847–71 | Arab emirate in Bari. |
| 849 | Battle of Ostia. |
| 859 | The Normans burn down the mosque in Algeciras. |
| 870 | Muslim occupation of the island of Malta. |
| 882–915 | Saracen occupation of Garigliano. |
| 890–972 | Saracen occupation of Fraxinetum (La Garde-Freinet). |
| 902 | Muslim conquest of the Balearic Islands. |
| 910 | Founding in Ifriqiya of the Shiite Fatimid caliphate. |
| 912 | Beginning of Muslim penetration of the Volga area. |
| 915 | Foundation of the Tunisian city of al-Mahdiyah. |
| 929 | Abd ar-Rahman III of Córdoba takes the title of caliph. |
| 960–1 | Byzantine reconquest of Crete. |
| 966 | The Danes under Harald Blatand ('Bluetooth') attack Lisbon. |
| 969 | Foundation of Cairo. |
| 982 | The Saracens defeat Otto II at Capo Colonna in Calabria. |
| 985–1003 | Repeated Saracen attacks against Barcelona. |
| 997 | Al-Mansur attacks and ransacks the city of Santiago de Compostela. |
| 1009 | Fatimid Caliph al-Hakim destroys the Church of the Holy Sepulchre in Jerusalem. |
| 1015–c.1021 | Pisan–Genoese war against Mujahid. |
| 1020 | Saracen attack on Narbonne. |
| 1031 | End of the Umayyad caliphate of Córdoba. |
| 1034 | Pisan expedition against Annaba. |

| | |
|---|---|
| 1062 | Foundation of Marrakesh. |
| 1063–4 | Barbastro's campaign in Aragon. |
| 1064 | The Castilians capture Coimbra. |
| 1085 6 May | Alfonso VI of Castile conquers Toledo. |
| 1086 | The Castilians are defeated by the Almoravids at Zallaqa. |
| 1087 | Expedition against al-Mahdiyah. |
| 1090 | Roger de Hauteville occupies Malta and Gozo. |
| 1094 15 June | El Cid conquers the city of Valencia. |
| 1095 18–27 November | The Council of Clermont, in the Auvergne. |
| 1095–9 | First crusade in Syria-Palestine. |
| 1099 10 June | El Cid Campeador dies in Valencia. |
| 15 June | Conquest of Jerusalem by the crusaders. |
| 1102 | The Almoravids occupy Valencia. |
| 1108 | Almoravid victory over the Castilians at Uclés. |
| 1113–15 | Pisan–Catalan expedition against the Balearic Islands. |
| 1118 19 December | The Aragonese occupy Valencia. |
| 1145 1 December–1 March 1146 | Pope Eugenius III publishes, in two different phases, his encyclical regulating the conduct of the crusades: *Quantum praedecessores*. |
| 1147 13 April | Papal encyclical *Divina dispensatione*. |
| July–August | German–Danish campaign against the Wends. |
| 17 October | The crusaders capture Almeria. |
| 24 October | The crusaders capture Lisbon. |
| 1147–8 | Second crusade in Syria-Palestine. |
| 1148 | The crusaders capture Tortosa. |
| 1149 | The Muslims evacuate the last strongholds in Catalonia. |
| 1157 | The Almohads reconquer Almeria. |
| 1187 | Saracen victory at the Horns of Hattin; Saladin conquers Jerusalem; the encyclical *Audita tremendi*. |
| 1187–92 | Third crusade. |
| 1195 19 July | The Almohads defeat the Castilians at Alarcos. |
| 1212 17 July | Battle of Las Navas de Tolosa. |
| 1217–21 | Fifth crusade; visit of Francis of Assisi to the Sultan of Egypt. |
| 1228–9 | Frederick II's crusade; Jerusalem recovered by a diplomatic agreement |

|           |                                                                                      |
|-----------|--------------------------------------------------------------------------------------|
|           | with the Sultan of Egypt, al-Malik al-Kamil.                                          |
| 1229–31   | Aragonese crusade against the Balearics.                                              |
| 1232–53   | Aragonese crusade against the kingdom of Valencia.                                    |
| 1236 29 June | Ferdinand III of Castile captures Córdoba.                                         |
| 1248 23 November | Ferdinand III of Castile conquers Seville.                                     |
| 1258      | The Mongols conquer Baghdad; end of the Abbasid caliphate.                            |
| 1267      | Christian conquest of Portugal completed.                                             |
| 1270 25 August | Death of Louis IX.                                                               |
| 1274      | Second Council of Lyon; *Constitutiones pro zelo fidei* is issued.                    |
| 1291      | Fall of Acre.                                                                         |
| 1340 30 October | Alfonso XI of Castile defeats the Merinids of Morocco at the battle of Rio Salado. |
| 1344–6    | 'Smyrna crusade'.                                                                     |
| 1355      | Genoese attack on Tripoli.                                                            |
| 1365 10–16 October | Pierre de Lusignan, King of Cyprus, besieges and sacks Alexandria.           |
| 1380      | Dmitri Donskoi, Grand Prince of Moscow, defeats the Tartars at Kulikovo.              |
| 1388      | The Genoese, Pisans and Sicilians occupy the island of Djerba.                        |
| 1389 15 June | Battle of Kosovo: Murad I annihilates the Serbians, but dies during the action.   |
| 1390      | Franco-Genoese crusade against al-Mahdiyah, led by Louis II, Duke of Bourbon.        |
| 1396 25 September | Battle of Nicopolis; crusaders defeated. The Portuguese conquer Ceuta.        |
| 1444 10 November | Battle of Varna; crusaders defeated.                                           |
| 1448 17–19 October | Murad II defeats the Hungarians at Kosovo.                                   |
| 1453 29 May | Ottoman Sultan Mohammed II takes Constantinople.                                   |
| 1456 6 August | Janos Hunyadi conquers Belgrade; the feast of the Transfiguration established in celebration. |
| 1463      | The Bosnians begin to embrace Islam, abandoning Greek Christianity and Bogomilism.    |
| 1470      | The Turks take Negroponte.                                                            |

| | |
|---|---|
| 1471 | The Portuguese conquer Tangiers. |
| 1475 6 June | The Turks take Kaffa. |
| 1480 | Exploiting divisions amongst Tartar leaders, Grand Prince Ivan III of Moscow supends payment of tribute. |
| August | The Turkish fleet attacks and conquers Otranto; establishment of the Spanish Inquisition. |
| 1481 3 May | Death of Mohammed II. |
| 1492 2 January | The Catholic Monarchs conquer Granada. |
| 1497–1510 | The conquest of various rocky outposts between Melilla and Tripoli by the Spaniards. |
| 1502 | The Tartar khanate of the Golden Horde separates into the three khanates of Khazan, Astrakhan and Crimea. |
| 1504 4 May | In Venice the Council of Ten discusses a proposal to cut off the Suez isthmus. |
| 1520–66 | Sultanate of Suleiman the Magnificent. |
| 1521 30 August | The Turks capture Belgrade. |
| 1522 | The Turks conquer the island of Rhodes and drive out the Knights of St John. |
| 1526 29–30 August | Turkish victory over the Móhacs. Treaty of Madrid between Charles V and Francis I on the subject of a 'general crusade'. |
| 1529 10 September | The Turks take Buda. |
| September–October | Turkish siege of Vienna. |
| 1530 | The Knights of St John establish themselves on the island of Malta and in Tripoli. |
| 1533 | Khair ad-Din is appointed head of the sultan's navy by Suleiman. |
| 1534 | Khair ad-Din ransacks the Italian coast and occupies Tunis, driving out the emir who is under Spanish protection. |
| 1535 June–July | Charles V's crusade against Tunis. |
| 1536 | Treaty between France and Turkey. |
| 1538 September | The fleet of the Papal-Imperial-Venetian League is defeated by Khair ad-Din at Prevesa, at the entrance to the Gulf of Arta. Suleiman conquers Aden to prevent Portuguese penetration into the Indian Ocean. |

| | |
|---|---|
| 1540 | Venice makes a separate peace with Suleiman and renounces her last foothold in the Peloponnese. |
| 1541 | Failed attempt by Charles V to attack Algiers. |
| 1543 | Publication in Basel of *Machumetis saracenorum principis vita ac doctrina omnis, quae et Ismahelitarum lex et Alchoranum dicitur* by Theodor Buchmann (Bibliander). The French and Turks besiege Nice. |
| 1544 | Convocation of the Council of Trent. Publication of *De orbis terrae concordia* by Guillaume Postel. |
| 1546 | Death of Khair ad-Din. |
| 1547 | First version of the Koran published in the Italian vernacular by Andrea Arrivabene in Venice. |
| 1550 June–September | Naval expedition against al-Mahdiyah, the base of the corsair Turghud Ali ('Dragut'), organized by Charles V. |
| 1551 14 August | The Hospitallers of Tripoli surrender to the Turks; the sultan appoints Turghud Ali governor of Tripoli. |
| 1552 | Russian conquest of Khazan. |
| 1556 | Russian conquest of Astrakhan. |
| 1560 March–July | The crusaders conquer the island of Djerba, but lose it again immediately. |
| 1562 March | The Holy Military Maritime Order of the Knights of St Stephen consecrated in the cathedral in Pisa. |
| 1565 | The Turks unsuccessfully besiege the island of Malta. The Barbary corsairs invade Andalusia with the support of the *morisco* population of the area. |
| 1566 | The Turks manage to capture the island of Chios and expel the Genoese. |
| 30 August | Death of Suleiman the Magnificent. |
| 1568 | Treaty of Adrianopolis between the Turks and the Holy Roman Empire. |
| 1568–70 | The revolt of the *moriscos* is crushed by the Spaniards. |
| 1569 | The Ottomans plan to build a canal between the Volga and the Don to link the Black Sea with the Caspian. |

| | |
|---|---|
| **1569–74** | Tunis reputedly lost and then recaptured by the Ottomans. |
| **1570–2** | War between the Turks and the Venetians in Cyprus. |
| **1571** 7 October | Battle of Lepanto. |
| **1578** | Battle of al-Qasr al-Kabir and death of Sebastian of Portugal. |
| **1583–7** | Beginning of diplomatic and trade relations between England and the Ottoman Empire. |
| **1593–1606** | War between Austria and Turkey ended by the treaty of Zsitva Török. |
| **1609** 9 December | *Moriscos* expelled definitively from Spain by royal edict. |
| **1622** | The English, with Persian assistance, expel the Portuguese from the Gulf of Hormuz. |
| **1627** | Incursions into Iceland by Barbary corsairs. |
| **1644–69** | War in Candia between the Turks and the Venetians. |
| **1664** 1 August | Field Marshal Montecuccoli defeats the Turks at St Gotthard an der Raab. |
| **1669** | Turkish embassy to Paris; Molière inspired for the investment scene in *Le Bourgeois gentilhomme*. |
| **1672–6** | War between Turkey and Poland. |
| **1677–81** | War between Russia and Turkey. |
| **1681–4** | War between France and the Bey of Algiers. |
| **1682–99** | War between Turkey, Austria and Poland. |
| **1683** 17 July–13 September | The Turks besiege Vienna. |
| **1684–99** | War in the Morea between the Turks and the Venetians. |
| **1686** 2 September | Charles of Lorraine conquers Buda. |
| **1687** 25–7 September | Venetian bombs fall on the Acropolis in Athens, damaging the Propylaeum and the Parthenon, used by the Turks as a magazine for gunpowder and weapons. |
| **1688** | Battle of Mohács. |
| **1691** | Defeat of the Turkish army at Slanhamen. |
| **1691–8** | Latin translation and commentaries on the Koran published by Father Ludovico Marracci. |

| | |
|---|---|
| 1696 28 July | The Russians take Azov. |
| 1697 11 September | Defeat of the Turks in the battle of Zenta. |
| 1697 | The *Bibliothèque orientale* by Barthélemy d'Herbelot de Molainville published posthumously in Paris. |
| 1699 26 January | Peace of Karlowitz. |
| 1711 21 July | Peace between Turkey and Russia: the tsar is forced to surrender the stronghold of Azov. |
| 1715–18 | War between the Turks and the Venetians, called the war of Corfu. |
| 1716 5 August | Victory of Eugène of Savoy at Petrovaradin. |
| 1718 21 July | Treaty of Passarowitz, written in Latin and Turkish. |
| 1722–7 | Russian and Turkish campaigns in the Caucasus. |
| 1729 | First book published in Turkish by a printing press in Istanbul (closed in 1742 but reopened in 1784). |
| 1736–9 | War between Austria, Russia and Turkey. |
| 1739 18 September | Peace of Belgrade. |
| 1742 9 August | First performance of Voltaire's *Mahomet ou le fanatisme*. |
| 1768–74 | War between Russia and Turkey. |
| 1774 21 July | Treaty of Kuchuk Kainarji between Russia and Turkey. |
| 1781 | Treaty between Austria and Russia for the division of the sultan's empire. |
| 1783–92 | War between Russia and Turkey over the Tartar territories between the Black Sea and the Caspian. |
| 1792 | Treaty of Jassy between Russia and Turkey. |
| 1798 | Bonaparte in Egypt. |
| 1801 | Russia annexes Georgia. |
| 1804 | While attacking Persia, Russia annexes Armenia and Azerbaijan. |
| 1816 9 April | In the French parliament, René de Chateaubriand tables a motion for a 'final crusade' against the Barbary Arabs. |
| 1821 | Insurrection in Greece and war between Greece and Turkey. |
| 1826 | The Sultan of Turkey, Mahmud II, abolishes the Janissaries. |
| 1830 | French occupation of Algiers. |

| | |
|---|---|
| 1839–61 | Sultan Andul-Megid I proclaims the 'useful ordinances' (*tanzimat*) under pressure from the European powers. |
| 1853–6 | Crimean war. |
| 1856 | Treaty of Paris and 'declaration of warranty': the ports of Turkey are opened to Paris. |
| 1859–69 | Construction of the Suez Canal. |
| 1864 | Turkestan annexed by Russia. |
| 1876 | Queen Victoria assumes the title of Empress of India. In Turkey, the 'Fundamental law of the State', the sultan's first constitution, abolished immediately by Abdul-Amid II. |
| 1878 | Congress of Berlin and 'organization' of the Balkans. |
| 1879–1901 | In Afghanistan, Abdur-Rahman grants rights of protection and control to Great Britain. |
| 1881 | French conquest of Tunisia. |
| 1881–99 | In Sudan, revolt against the Egyptians by the Mahdi, Mohammed Ahmed; the rebels are defeated and Sudan becomes an Anglo-Egyptian protectorate. |
| 1898 | Political and diplomatic trip made by Kaiser Wilhelm II to the Ottoman Empire; talks in Damascus and visit to Jerusalem. |
| 1903 | Construction of the Berlin to Baghdad railway. |
| 1905 | In India, formation of the province of Bengal with a Muslim majority. |
| 1906 | Algeciras Conference: the Germans recognize the French 'position of pre-eminence' in Morocco. |
| 1907 | Treaty of St Petersburg and division of Persia into areas of influence and interest, shared between England and Russia. |
| 1908 | Military revolt in Salonika led by Enver Pasha. Revolution by the Young Turks; Balkan crisis triggered by Austria's annexation of Bosnia-Herzegovina. |
| 1911–12 | War between Italy and Turkey over Tripolitania and Cyrenaica (Libya). |
| 1912–13 | Wars in the Balkans. |
| 1914–18 | First World War. |

| | |
|---|---|
| 1916 | Sykes–Picot agreement: division of the Ottoman Empire's Arab territories between France and England. |
| 1917 | Balfour Declaration, favouring the creation of a Jewish state in Palestine. |
| 1919 | Birth of the Turkish National Movement led by Mustapha Kemal. |
| 1920 | Constitution of the British mandate over Palestine. |
| 1920–2 | Greek–Turkish war. |
| 1920–6 | Anglo-American–French crisis over the petrol fields of Mosul, resolved by the Conference of San Remo (1920) and the treaty of Mosul (1926); shares in the Iraq Petroleum Company divided between countries, with a majority stake for the English. |
| 1921 | Emir Faisal proclaimed King of Iraq; his brother Abdullah made Emir of Transjordania. |
| 1922 1 November | In Turkey, the sultan is deposed. |
| 1923–38 | Nationalist, secular and progressive regime imposed on Turkey by Mustapha Kemal Atatürk. |
| 1924 | Abolition of the caliphate and dissolution of Islamic tribunals in Turkey. |
| 1925 | Iran proclaimed an empire under Reza Shah, whose regime is authoritarian and modernizing. |
| 1928 | In Egypt, Sheikh Hasan al-Banna founds the group of the 'Muslim Brotherhood'. |
| 1930 | In the United States, foundation of the Black Muslim movement. |
| 1932 | Union of Hejaz and Nagd in the kingdom of Saudi Arabia, under Abd al Aziz Ibn Saud. |
| 1948 | Proclamation of the State of Israel in Palestine, and first Arab–Israeli war. |
| 1954 | Pan-Arabic agreement between Egypt, Syria and Saudi Arabia. |
| 1954–62 | Algerian war of liberation. |
| 1956 | Suez crisis. In Pakistan, proclamation of the Islamic Republic of Pakistan, a member of the Commonwealth. |

| | |
|---|---|
| 1967 | Seven Day War: the Israelis capture the whole area of Jerusalem, including the holy places. |
| 1969 | India: clashes between Hindus and Muslims in Ahmedabad. |
| 1969 September | Islamic summit in Rabat. |
| 1971 3–17 December | Indo-Pakistan war: East Pakistan becomes independent under the name Bangladesh. |
| 1971–2 | Establishment of the Arab Emirates in the Persian Gulf. |
| 1973 May | In Libya, Ghaddafi declares Islam to be 'the road to social revolution'. |
| 1974 | Islamic summit in Lahore. |
| 1974–5 | Crisis between Turks and Cypriots in Cyprus. |
| 1975–6 | Civil war between Christians and Muslims in Lebanon. |
| 1979 March | Signing of the peace treaty between Egypt and Israel. |
| 1 April | Ayatollah Khomeini proclaims the Islamic Republic of Iran. |
| May | Conference of Islamic Republics suspends Egypt after the Camp David agreement. |
| 1979–80 | Soviet military intervention in Afghanistan. |
| 1980–8 | War between Iran and Iraq over control of the petrol outlets in the Persian Gulf. |
| 1980 | Abolition of slavery in Mauretania. The State of Israel declares the annexation of the eastern part of Jerusalem. |
| 1981 January | The Islamic summit condemns Soviet aggression against Afghanistan. The State of Israel declares that it has annexed the Golan Heights, in Syria, north-east of the Lake of Tiberias. |
| 1982 | In Lebanon, bombing of Palestinian civilians in the camps of Chatila and Sabra by the Lebanese Christian militias. In Syria, revolt of the 'Muslim Brotherhood' in the city of Hamas. |
| May | In Afghanistan, leading Islamic organizations form the 'Islamic Alliance of the *mujaheddin* of Afghanistan'. |

| | | |
|---|---|---|
| **1983** | April | In Lebanon, attack on the United States embassy by the Shiite group Islamic Jihad. |
| **1984** | | The conference of Muslim countries passes a majority vote (opposed only by Syria and Libya) to readmit Egypt. Clashes in Bombay between Hindu extremists and the Muslim minority. |
| **1985** | October | Israeli air-raids on the military base at Olp in Tunisia. |
| **1986** | | American sanctions against Libya; bombing of Libyan territory. |
| | 20 October | Constitution of the 'International Council of the Muslim *Dawa*' in Karachi, Pakistan. |
| **1988** | | In Lebanon, clashes between pro-Syrian Shiite groups ('Amal') and pro-Iranian groups ('Hezbollah'). In Israel, Palestinian revolt in the occupied territories ('Intifada'). |
| **1989** | | Soviet troops withdraw completely from Afghanistan. |
| | 4 June | Imam Rukhullah Khomeini dies. Egypt re-enters the Arab League. |
| **1990** | July | Beginning of the Gulf crisis between Iraq, Kuwait and the UN. |
| | August | Islamic summit in Cairo: the Iraqi invasion of Kuwait is condemned. |
| **1991–2** | | In Algeria, the Islamic Front for Salvation wins the election; military coup. |
| **1993** | 9–13 September | Reciprocal declaration of recognition between the State of Israel and the Palestine Liberation Organization; signing in Washington of the 'Declaration on the principles of independence of the occupied territories'. |
| **1994** | May | Accident in Mecca: about 800 pilgrims killed. |
| | 25 July | Jordan and Israel sign an agreement putting an end to the state of war that has existed between them since 1949. |
| **1996** | | In Afghanistan, the integralist movement known as the Taliban seizes power. |

# Bibliographical Note

The confrontation between Europe and Islam can be viewed from many angles. A limited list of published works on the subject might include: *L'Occidente di fronte all'Islam*, edited by S. Allievi (Rome, n.d.); F. Cardini, *Noi e l'Islam* (Rome-Bari, 1994); W. Montgomery Watt, *Muslim–Christian Encounters* (Routledge, 1991); B. Lewis, *Islam and the West* (New York and Oxford, 1993); E. Pace, *Islam e Occidente* (Rome, 1995). Many interesting ideas can be gleaned from P. Brown *The Rise of Western Christendom: Triumph and Diversity* (Oxford, 1996); J. Fontana, *The Distorted Past: A Reinterpretation of Europe* (Oxford, 1995); M. Mollat du Jourdin, *Europe and the Sea* (Oxford, 1993). See also M. Rodinson, *Entre Islam et Occident* (Paris, 1998).

Fundamental to the study of Europe and Islam in the Middle Ages are: A. Ducellier, *Chrétiens d'Orient et Islam au Moyen Age. VIIe–XVe siècles*, (Paris, 1996), and *Medieval Encounters: Jewish, Christian and Muslim Culture in Confluence and Dialogue*, 5 vols (Leyden, London and Boston, 1999). For the period preceding the general crusade, *L'Occidente e l'Islam nel'Alto Medioveo*, 'Study week of the Italian Centre for Studies in the Early Middle Ages', XII (Spoleto, 1965); M. Lombard, *L'Islam dans sa première grandeur* (Paris, 1971); R. Hodges and D. Whitehouse, *Mahomet, Charlemagne and the Origins of Europe* (London, 1983). On attitudes to Islam during the European Middle Ages, see W. Southern, *Western Views of Islam in the Middle Ages* (Cambridge, Mass., 1962); N. Daniel, *Islam and the West.: The Making of an Image* (Edinburgh, 1980). On Arab culture and its influence, see in particular J. Vernet, *Ce que la culture doit aux Arabes d'Espagne* (Paris, 1985); D. Jacquart and F. Micheau, *La médecine arabe et l'Occident médiéval* (Paris, 1990). On Muslim Spain, see P. Guichard, *Structures sociales 'orientales' et 'occidentales' dans l'Espagne musulmane* (Paris and The

Hague, 1977). On one particular aspect of the medieval 'prehistory' of Orientalism, see A. D'Ancona, *La leggenda di Maometto in Occidente*, new edition edited by A. Borruso (Rome, 1994).

On the role of Venice between the Middle Ages and the modern period, see *Venezia centro di mediazione tra Oriente e Occidente (secoli XV–XVI). Aspetti e problemi*, edited by H. G. Beck, M. Mamoussacas and A. Pertusi, 2 vols (Florence, 1977).

On Lepanto, there is a general picture in J. Beeching, *The Galleys at Lepanto* (London, 1982). On the Barbary corsairs, see J. E. Humbert and G. Vieusseux, *Les barbaresques et les chrétiens*, edited by L. Neppi Modona (Florence, 1983).

On the Ottomans and the relationship with the East, an excellent point of departure can be found in A. Pertusi, 'I primi studi in Occidente sull'origine e la potenza dei turchi', in *Studi veneziani*, XII (1970). See also the catalogue to the exhibition in Dresden, 1995, *Im Lichte des Albmonds. Das Abendland und der türkische Orient* (Dresden, 1995), which is also essential to an understanding of Orientalism/exoticism. On the relationship between the Ottoman Empire and Russia, see A. Ferrari, *La Russia tra Oriente e Occident* (Milan, 1994).

On the problem of the holy places, see N. Bux and F. Cardini, *L'anno prossimo a Gerusalemme* (Milan, 1997).

For relations between Islam and contemporary Europe, see *L'Islam in Europa*, edited by S. Ferrari (Bologna, 1996).

# Index